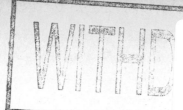

Written by:

Yvonne Sarch is an economist who v
hunter sixteen years ago. She studied at Trinity College, Dublin
and London. She has worked in the UK and USA and has
travelled extensively throughout Europe. Yvonne has specialised
in appointments in the Public and Voluntary Sectors and is well
known for her lateral thinking in making appointments successful.
She is still curious and is pleased to share her knowledge, concerns
and foibles with you.

Researched by:

Adam Sarch trained in architecture in London and then went to
Harvard to study computer landscape animation. He has brought
originality and insight to this book, enabling it to reflect the
emerging employment climate and conceptual world.

How to be
HEADHUNTED . . .
Again and Again

Yvonne Sarch

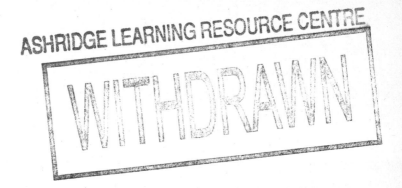
RANDOM HOUSE

BUSINESS BOOKS

First published in 1999 by Random House Business Books,
Random House, 20 Vauxhall Bridge Road, London SW1V 2SA

Ramdom House Australia (Pty) Limited
20 Alfred Street, Milsons Point
Sydney, New South Wales 2061, Australia

Random House New Zealand Limited
18 Poland Road, Glenfield
Auckland 10, New Zealand

Random House South Africa (Pty) Limited
Endulini, 5a Jubilee Road, Parktown 2193, South Africa

Random House UK Limited Reg. No. 954009

Papers used by Random House UK Limited are natural, recyclable products made from wood grown in sustainable forests. The manufacturing processes conform to the environmental regulations of the country of origin.

ISBN 0 7126 8076 4

Companies, institutions and other organizations wishing to make bulk purchases of books published by Random House should contact their local bookstore or Random House direct:
Special Sales Director
Random House, 20 Vauxhall Bridge Road, London SW1V 2SA

Tel 0171 840 8470   Fax 0171 828 6681

www.randomhouse.co.uk
businessbooks@randomhouse.co.uk
Printed and bound in Great Britain by
Creative Print and Design (Wales), Ebbw Vale.

Contents

How to be

HEADHUNTED . . .

Again and Again

Welcome

How to be Headhunted . . . Again and Again is written to satisfy your curiosity about what happens when you are headhunted.

It is a guide book for the rest of your life.

You will be fascinated by the ways to position yourself in and out of the workplace. It will give you confidence to see into the methods and thinking of the headhunter and to look ahead and visualise life at the top.

Yvonne Sarch explores the current thinking of the management gurus and other sources to provide you with an insight into what is happening across the world of work. She values and enjoys the input of the next generation – the researcher is Adam Sarch, who has added his knowledge and lively intellect to bring vigour and analysis to the newest ideas and dimensions which would otherwise be 'beyond her ken'.

She writes in 'plain speak' that is based on wide research and is pragmatic, even dogmatic, in her approach. She bases her thinking on her observations and knowledge both as a trained economist and as a successful headhunter with a reputation for 'getting things done' and getting them done well. Yvonne Sarch is determined that you will be involved in successful appointments, whether you are an employer or a candidate.

The book is focused on how to position yourself on both micro and macro levels. Analysis of management thinking, corporate pressures and public service ethos are all included. There is no longer a guarantee of long term employment so the issues around short term contracts, project management and isolation in the work place are recurring themes. You will see how others have succeeded in the case studies and you will be led through some complex 'knowledge' areas.

No matter how old or young you are, what you have done already or if you are at the end of the line, Yvonne Sarch believes in your potential. She talks about how you can take responsibility for your own working life and maximise your values and time whatever is happening around you. She encourages you at all stages.

Her own life experience includes time spent in both east coast and west coast business scenes in the USA. She later joined her husband in high level political spheres in the UK and in continental Europe. She has had to learn how to balance family and professional commitments; be part of the growing 'womeneconomics' and to satisfy her own curiosity about the world at large. This adds flavour and fervour to her work.

Her previous books include 'How to be Headhunted' 1990 Business Books, and 'How to be Headhunted across Europe' 1993 Macmillan.

Two frogs fell into a can of cream, or so it has been told.
The sides of the can were shiny and steep, the cream was deep and cold.
'Oh, what's the use,' said number one, 'It's plain no help's around.
Good-bye, my friend, good-bye sad world' and weeping still he drowned.

But number two, of sterner stuff, dog paddled in surprise.
The while he licked his creamy lips and blinked his creamy eyes.
'I'll swim at least a while,' he thought, or so it has been said.
It really wouldn't help the world if one more frog was dead
An hour or more he kicked and swam, not once he stopped to mutter.
Then hopped out off the island he had made of fresh well churned butter.

Author unknown

· 1 ·

Positioning: Yourself

The generation in power has the luxury to ignore the debt they're imposing on us. They'll be gone when the bills come due. We won't.
                                          Student, Yale University

THE GENERATION GAME

The New Agenda

Work itself is no longer a place. It is seen as an activity, much of which you can do anywhere. Organisational change is here to stay, and the speed of change is accelerating. This is probably the most difficult aspect of work for you to manage.

Institutions are reinventing themselves continually. Long gone is the predominance of manufacturing companies, steel mills and coal mines. The concept of the fifteen-year-old entering the factory gates and remaining within until retirement has shifted to the belief that most people will be on short-term contracts from now on. Companies are relying more on information, knowledge and creativity regardless of whether they are producing goods or are in service industries. Media, telecommunications, software and entertainment companies make up some of the newest industries. They need help from headhunters to find the technically qualified and imaginative people who can adjust to having to get and exchange information, and who can understand cultural issues such as control versus autonomy, and cope with thinking about time, dress, courtesy, money and language.

You are living in the creative economy and the information age so you have to keep up with the constant transformation both of yourself and of what you are doing. With the current tidal wave of mergers of organisations there is a paradox in the need for the visionary alongside operational to keep the whole workplace efficient and profitable. Success commercially comes in many new forms, so school-leavers today have many different choices. Few of these include full-time work, but this is not necessarily a dis-advantage. You will have noticed the short-term possibilities for work no matter what age or stage you are. Headhunters are involved in finding potentially keen people for clients who are always looking for ideas and people to carry them out, whether they are full-time or interim employees.

Manufacturing in 1998 accounts for about one fifth of the British economy. It is a 'swing' sector and is an indicator of overall growth or recession, depending on how it is performing. At the end of the twentieth century, this sector is swinging downwards with orders, investment, expectations and employment plans all declining sharply and predictions for further job losses rising. This should alert you to prepare to take care of your own job prospects. Some parts of manufacturing, such as food production, look reasonably secure, but the likelihood is that a 7% cut in numbers will occur. This means 290,000 jobs may go in the near future. Once these jobs have gone, they tend not to come back, and the current main concern is the low level of productivity in British business. You may prefer working for large organisations rather than taking entrepreneurial risks, so you may have to change your mindset as well as your role if you are made redundant.

A London School of Economics survey in 1998 of 200 leading entrepreneurs/outsiders (aged forty-nine upwards), shows that 85% had left school by the age of sixteen. By contrast the next generations of the knowledge era will be mainly graduates with professional qualifications and constantly updated technical skills. It takes a long time to acquire the fundamental education and training for employment. Lifelong learning is the name of the game for the future. Currently government task forces are looking at education standards, and the emphasis is now on finding and training teachers to be the guides for the future. They are going to have to be explorers leading the way into the world of information – both for the young and the older. Parents are concerned and are more involved than ever: for example, 2% of children of school age in the USA are being 'homeschooled'. Education is now seen as an industry in its own right. 'So uncertain is the future that I have a sneaking suspicion that the jobs that my grandchildren will do have not yet been invented', says Lord Puttnam in the report 'Redefining Work' (RSA, 1998). Education and training to equip you for the knowledge society of the twenty-first century will be your keys to success.

With an increasing percentage of the population becoming old, the growth area of business will be the provision of healthcare and pensions. The National Health Service is the biggest employer in the UK, with approximately sixty million people on its payroll. Headhunting is now acceptable in both the public and private healthcare industries, and in education, because recruitment has become fair and open when finding people from across sectors to fill staff and professional jobs. You will see advertisements in the national and specialised press describing a wide range of roles in all sectors.

The approach to work is also changing. You are responsible for your whole working life, and you will need to be astute and make financial preparations in this ever older and growing population with reducing State benefits. Unemployment is a real possibility at some stage in your career. Already a quarter of people working are doing so on a part-time basis, with another fifth on short-term contracts or self-employed. The balance is changing between those in full-time work and those otherwise engaged. Training in skills and personal development and the purchase of pensions and insurance are the necessary adjuncts to work for current and future generations. Your empathy, creativity, communication, ingenuity and humour will take you through difficult times in earning your living and achieving your dreams.

Politics, business, markets and life all work in cycles. Some are long-term and measured in decades – even centuries – while others span only a few years or months. The post-industrial 'revolution' is predicted to render most large organisations obsolete, but presently we are seeing the largest consolidated drive to create global organisations. There is no sign of it ending yet; if anything, the Asian and Russian collapse have accelerated the trend. At present there is a rash of mergers and privatisations, so the next stage will probably be their deconstruction. Stephen Covey in *The Seven Habits of Highly Effective People* describes the paradigm shift in perception and the new focus on personal values. Others argue that debt deflation, the growth of new industries (biogenetics, cold fusion), independently run communities and small owner-managers, combined with increasing numbers of self-employed, will enable rapid gains in productivity from simple tasks rather than from complicated operations. Locally produced food will be at a premium and the increase in infectious diseases will lead to highly protected environments. People living under these evolving conditions will have to be confident of their own values and goals and will be more concerned with emotional and spiritual wealth than the material. Peter Drucker in *Post-Capitalist Society* shows educated people as the elite because they encourage flexibility, integrity and interdependence. Edward de Bono uses lateral thinking to achieve novel solutions and demonstrates its importance in coping with the changes facing current generations.

The processes of re-engineering, de-layering, downsizing, outsourcing and requiring employees to be flexible, multiskilled and innovative can leave people feeling insecure or challenged, depending on how they regard change. Job satisfaction has come top of the lists of recent employee concerns. Some managers are still focused on updating technology or putting in quality systems, even when they know that they should be concentrating on their people. The Swiss say they have the highest level of happiness in their work, followed in second and third place by the Danish and the Norwegians, according to the International Survey Research (ISR) survey of 1997/8. The UK, which used to be bottom in Europe, is now replaced by Hungary, but still remains second bottom in the list.

Another study by the Institute of Management has correlated the profitability of companies with the satisfaction quotient of employees. It demonstrates that job security and knowledge of what is going on in the organisation lead to higher levels of personal contribution and greater profits. The experience of the 100 companies taking part in the analysis was that good people management is not simply about traditional recruitment, appraisal and training, but about the development of whole communities, in which people feel socially included rather than alienated by their work. Organisations achieve this by having concern for welfare, good communication, high-quality training, broad autonomy and mutual respect. Economic stability and growth are helped by management's ability to deal with diversity and the unpredictability of the aspirations of each employee. Given that employment forecasts in the next decade range from catastrophe to a mini global recession, it is especially important to find out about an organisation's culture and record for looking after its people when you are considering working there.

Responsible organisations get the most out of all their assets, especially from people and are preparing for the downturn in their markets. Of 1000 workers surveyed by Investors in People (1998), over a quarter felt that they were underused often or all the time. The resulting demotivated workforce is debilitated by frustration and boredom. Effective organisations are skilled at achieving their business and organisational aims by harnessing their strengths – either their own or those borrowed from elsewhere. Ineffective organisations allow their management to undermine individual and group performance by failing to take advantage of the available strengths – a phenomenon known as skilled incompetence. This includes a deficiency in managing their people.

You should be aware of the type of climate within which you work best. Full-time jobs will soon be replaced by a series of tasks. You will have to adjust to the market's needs and identify what you have to offer. 'What can you sell and who will buy it?' is how Tom Peters describes this in his 'Wow Seminar'. The young are at an advantage because they do not depend on the 'job for life' syndrome. Some even feel that the possibility of employment is eluding them. However, they are equally determined to only get out of bed for a reason. Qualifications, education and experience are necessary but not the only attributes which employers are now seeking. Tenacity is the key.

The combination of living in the information age and the

jobshift culture means that you have to be more entrepreneurial than managerial and be aware of opportunities. You are shaped by the time in history in which you live and by the culture around you. Cultures are populations of individuals with relatively similar mindsets and world views. You may be aware of particular information at a particular time, and when it grows, changes and evolves, so will you. The accumulation of cultural information will play a vital part in forming the ideology of an organisation. The varied beliefs and viewpoints shared by people in groups of all sizes all contribute to the group's uniqueness.

Winston Churchill once said that 'the empires of the future are empires of the mind'. Alvin Toffler, in *Powershift*, has written about the degree to which raw, elemental power – at the level of private life as well as at the level of empire – will be transformed in the decades ahead by the new role of 'mind'.

Organisations have been perfecting their techniques for recruiting talented and ambitious people. The problem arises when these people do not want to stay or get headhunted elsewhere. The present economic turmoil is making the young, gifted and fast-track employee negotiate an options package with a future, but the promises made to attract bright people can be a trap for the employers later because of unfulfilled conditions and market changes. The increase in bulk recruitment and the rise in the number of headhunters seeking talented people in a limited pool has caused the costs of recruitment to rise, so the need to retain people once they are hired and established is recognised. For the employer, the big problem is to retain bright people; for you it is to have choices in how and where you work.

Who Are You?

There are five generations in each century, calculated on the basis of twenty years for each. Overlapping generations also show the effects of external forces on their actions and reactions.

The Silent Generation (Born in 1925–45)
Those who grew up during the Great Depression and in the 1930s were influenced by their parents' hardships and learned to value

job security. 'Organisation Man' and 'Corporate Man' were invented to describe them. They reflect their background, the war, the education of their parents and the experience of post-war employment markets. The introduction of free education, health and other state benefits went some way to compensate for the sacrifices made during their early years.

Baby Boomers (Born in 1945–65)
The Baby Boomers grew into the Yuppies of the eighties. Their rebellious attitudes were influenced in America by the Vietnam War and Watergate, which taught them to distrust authority. They began an assault on status. They grew up with the safety net of State provision but are now concerned for its continued existence. They are the first generation to deal with the impact on the environment of business and technology.

Generation X
People born between 1964 and 1977 have a different attitude to careers from previous generations. Douglas Coupland's oft-quoted *Generation X* (1991) described many X-ers now occupying management positions. *Managing Generation X*, written by Bruce Tulgan in 1996, asserted that X-ers expect to depend on natural entrepreneurship to attain security in an uncertain world. The challenge to employers is how to create a new psychological contract to meet the needs of the X-ers. Tulgan offers a new career manifesto for the post-job era. The 'five essential ingredients of the reinvented career' are:

- Learn voraciously
- Be balanced
- Take it one year at a time
- Concentrate on relationships
- Add value continuously

The X-ers are also different in their attitudes to management. This is partly because they are the offspring of dual-career families, growing up in an era of record divorce rates. Better educated than their predecessors, like the Baby Boomers, they are not impressed with the trappings of authority. They distrust hierarchy and they prefer to be judged, and to judge, on merit rather than status. They are far less loyal to their employers than their predecessors because the employers are far less loyal to them. They like money. They like to enjoy life. Because of their upbringing, they work to live rather than live to work.

The career aspirations of X-ers are based on the non-expectation of lifetime work. They insist that organisations find more flexible ways to integrate time for families and private life into their working life. They expect sabbaticals and other sorts of career breaks and look for flexibility and opportunities when accepting jobs. They will not stay with employers who are rigid in their thinking and objectives for employees. Computer employees in Silicon Valley are typical of this group, moving on to the next big project, time and time again. The outcome is the development of the 'campus' culture. The best way of encouraging X-ers is to harness their knowledge, not to restrain it.

'Out of the Mouth of Babes: Generation X Speaks for Itself' is a report published in 1998 by Thoughts for the Millennium Think Tank. James Wright set up a group to look at problems from new angles and to turn traditional solutions upside down. He sent unpaid volunteers to nine cities to distribute questionnaires to randomly selected respondents from wide-ranging backgrounds. The average age was 19.7 and the results are culled from the eighty-five completed documents. Generation X has been branded as lazy, unambitious and unopinionated. This report shows that instead there is a strong entrepreneurial culture with one fifth aiming to be wealthy by the age of forty. This generation is more ambitious and determined than any before. As Coupland says, 'The world is going to have to make room for Generation X.'

X-ers have seen more booms and busts than most previous generations and at an earlier stage in their lives. This has given them a certain cynicism about adopting or signing up to corporate dogma. The pain of the negative equity suffered by their parents and the downsizing of companies has bred a new attitude of resistance to setbacks and willingness to attack new opportunities by trying anything to progress their careers. They want to change the world by running it – owning their own businesses and focusing on hard work, decent education, determination and natural talent. The motto is: 'It is not who you know, but how hard you try.' Many are mapping out their future before leaving college. According to the Think Tank report, they have career preferences:

- 66% want their own business
- 20% media, public relations and advertising
- 11% traditional professions
- 3% politics

They are uninterested in politics and see the current system as redundant. They have other ideas. They reject the nanny state and they want the government to have fewer responsibilities. They want to look after themselves, as is evidenced by their wish to:

- Own their own houses (95%)
- Have private healthcare arrangements (75%)
- Send children to independent schools (27%)

How do younger managers organise their personal lives? Of those asked in a WFD/*Management Today* survey (*Work Life Issues*, 1998), most said that shopping was mainly their responsibility, housework was usually done by their partners, day-to-day decisions were shared equally, and family finance and house maintenance were mainly their province, based on the traditional male/female and attached/single ratios. Recent graduates are still maintaining that they do not want to give up their private lives for work, yet they are already working extended hours and will continue to work longer hours than their predecessors did. The new attitudes to work have not really impacted on companies yet. Once people are involved in their jobs, they get sucked into the organisational culture and the prevailing work ethic.

Generation Y
Born 1977– (Generation 13 in the USA, based on the number of generations since the War of Independence), or the Now Generation/the Millennial Generation/Generation Y as it is

referred to in the rest of the world. The members of this generation intend to take control of their own destinies and are traumatised by the me-first ethics of their parents. They share a single ambition – to get married, have children and live happily ever after. They know it means putting their children first, sticking with their spouses even if they fall out of love and protecting their families from the evils of infidelity and a materialistic culture. Most of them are the products of broken homes. Now they are fighting their way back to the family values that were rejected by their parents. Right across Europe these aspirations are being articulated. In the USA, this generation is identified as the first generation that will not 'do better' than their parents financially. They have given up trying to get the attention of their very busy parents but are determined to be different with their own children. There is a passionate reaction against the modern corporate culture which extracts maximum work from employees whilst disclaiming responsibility for their families and communities. They intend to be self-employed and take control of their own destinies. They are drawn to professions with human interaction. Their non-traditional backgrounds have made them much more self-reliant, self-confident and outward looking. 'What about us?' is their cry.

Growing up has not been hard for the children who will come of age around the millennium. They are the designer generation and set store by wearing the 'right' labels. Their favourite recreation is clubbing and they drink alcopops and designer beers, while smoking is usual. They retain traditional moral attitudes despite their hedonistic lifestyle. Most see themselves aiming to be millionaires, yet at the same time they want to marry and have children. They pride themselves on their determination and have more respect for those in authority than did their predecessors, the X-ers. Only 1% see any sense in public service, and the Civil Service is not a career which attracts them. Generation X wanted to work in the media; Generation Y has realised the difficulties of the short-term contract climate there, and so is looking forward to being employed in business, industry, banking and accountancy in so far as they will still exist. This is a major change from the seventies, when more young people wanted a career in public administration than anything else.

Generation Y is not afraid of taking risks. They are not expecting anything for nothing. They want to run their own businesses and they distrust politics and want the law to stay out of their lives. All in all they have a down-to-earth approach to the realities of life both at work and with relationships. They believe that each person is entitled to make their own choices and are optimistic that they can cope, not least because of the level of security they had while they were growing up.

Through the Generations

The debate about nature versus nurture came to a head in the sixties and has been going on ever since. What you are born with is one aspect, but what happens to you and how you react to your environment are also relevant. The tools of understanding enable you to grapple with your world, to interact with others and to express and articulate your values. These tools are being used when you modify and re-fuse the old to create the new and add to your experience. By communicating and adding to your social learning you are acquiring the ability to critically appraise your surroundings.

In your twenties there is the exhausting scramble to get qualifications and find the entry into the corporate pyramid. All those 'mind-numbing nights out trying to up your cool factor, increase your social circle and determine whose gene pool you want to dip into', as described by Tina Gaudoin, editor of *Frank* magazine. The yearning and the striving for a vision of the future all suddenly turn into reality when you hit your thirties.

Never before have thirtysomethings had so much clout. Television is obsessed with you, you dominate the bestseller lists and you are setting precedents in politics. This is the defining decade for many people, when they find they have limited time and energy and are facing some fundamental life choices. Your thirties seem to be about consolidating your position, about coming clean about becoming comfortable. Someone put it succinctly when they said, 'Your thirties are about how great life can really be before you hit forty and realise that your job sucks, your marriage is a nightmare, your kids are dysfunctional and you are going to die.'

The other side is the joy of being 'grown-up', being independent, money-earning and still able to sow oats whilst forming
opinions and making mistakes. This is the stage where you start to
want to just veg out at home on Saturday nights, and don't feel like
a loser doing it. Branding has become paramount in this market
place. It is the time when you buy a new car, or a very expensive
jacket, and regard both as investments.

The fourth decade is 'make your mind up' time. For the female
the biological clock is running out and for the male, the current
concern is about the sperm count. The idea that Generation X had
the advantage of being born into a foolproof contraceptive world,
so long as you actually took the pill, is dynamic. It has given the
choice whether and when to have children as never before. The
increased awareness of healthcare, going to the gym and dieting is
prolonging the good life for many people well into their fifties,
sixties and seventies and beyond.

The story of English Lakes Hotels illustrates the passing on from
generation to generation in a family. The great-uncle gave up
being finance director of an engineering firm and bought his first
hotel in 1952. In 1972 his nephew took over the original plus two
other hotels. Now Simon, the great-nephew, has just stepped into
his father's shoes as managing director, and the group owns four
hotels in the Lake District plus another at Lancaster University,
where Simon was marketing director. Now he lives on the shores
of Windermere and enjoys water-skiing, windsurfing, mountain
biking and squash. He has reaped the benefits of his father's risk-
taking when he turned the first hotel into a 99-bedroom, year-
round business complete with conference centre and leisure club.
The Wild Boar at Crook is in the country house style, the Royal is
a budget hotel and the Waterhead provides family accommodation. Simon trained as a chef and worked at Claridges and
Berkeley Hotels in London. His brother has also joined in the
family business, and between them they have three sons and three
daughters, so there should be lots of competition for who runs the
hotels in the future. The third generation is predicted to be less
entrepreneurial and achieving than their parents and grand-
parents. Time will tell.

Worldwide Generations

For the global marketplace, languages are useful. Formerly the world need was for French, German and Spanish; now there is an unmet demand for Westerners who communicate in Mandarin, Japanese and Portuguese, although English and Spanish are the most used languages.

There have been significant changes in access to further education. In 1980 14% of all eighteen-year-old males went to university, compared with 11% of females. By 1997 not only was a greater percentage of all eighteen-year-olds going to university (34%), but 37% of women possessed a degree, compared with only 32% of men. In 1996, 53% of graduates were female. The employment situation has changed, too: 1996 was the first year in the UK where more women than men had jobs. Male graduates are in danger of being unemployed. The balance of the workforce is changing as more women work through the system, and the dominance of men at senior levels is forecast to be diluted.

Corporations are communities wherever they are located. Defining your territory within these structures is paramount so that you can find out if you are a nomad or an operative within the institution. Work experience is popular, and many take low-paid internships to find out what goes on in the jobs which they think they might like. It is a way of becoming noticed in a competitive or unfamiliar market.

The Pension Link

The whole idea of the mobile pension is interesting. Having to be responsible for providing for your old age and contributing for the benefit of other generations continues throughout your working life. It does not matter whether you will be working for an institution or for yourself, you will have to be looking ahead. The millennium generation are already thinking about old age. Yet the reality for many job-hopping young people is that they can reach the age of thirty either without any provision or else a ragbag of pension schemes with charges biting deeply into their funds. Should the young ditch their time in nightclubs to prepare for their old age? The evidence is clear that starting early pays off. Pension payments become a priority after you have found your first home. Join a company scheme where it is offered, provided it is portable.

Check the surrender values, capital units, annual management fees, past performance, policy fees and waiver of premium. The key is to have as flexible a pension as possible. Consider the effects of job changes, mortgage, marriage, divorce and unemployment possibilities in an ever changing market. A plan with high early surrender values could be useful if crises occur. You should avoid 'capital units', which is a device used by the pension companies to load the charges over the early years rather than later. A young purchaser may want to buy out or freeze a pension after only a few years and would find that capital units could have taken up as much as the first year's premium. One way to keep costs and charges down is to opt for a recurring single-premium pension rather than an annual premium, as your advisers will explain. Avoiding plans with high annual management charges is fundamental, and they vary greatly. The insurance market is still loath to provide clear comparisons, even after all the recent enquiries.

Beware of situations where you pay in full but the insurer still levies annual charges. This can be as bad as creating a zero value at the end of the day. Past performance shows how the pension money has been managed on the stock or other markets. Future returns are never guaranteed and you pay for what you get, but success usually breeds success. Waiver of an insured premium can be taken out at very little cost and this enables the premiums to be paid even if there is illness or unemployment for six months. Planning ahead is all part of taking responsibility for you and yours, vital in the present economic and social climate.

PERSONAL EVALUATION

Motivation

All institutions are beginning to realise that motivation is the key for success. The more you have analysed what you want to do and what motivates you to do it, the more you are likely to find it. You won't be able to do the high-quality work the employer expects unless you're doing what you really want to be doing. Your abilities, temperament and assets, including a talent for working together with others and achieving a common vision, are highly sought after. Add to that some language fluency and then you can go global.

Personal and professional factors come into play in motivating people and their performance, both at work and play. Needs, drives and goals will influence the quality of work and its rewards. By finding out what is propelling them forward, most people will gain a richer insight into the most effective ways of motivating others as well. In this way, self-awareness can transfer directly into effective management and motivating skills.

It used to be considered necessary to supervise people constantly because it was assumed that people are intrinsically lazy and are only motivated by rewards and money. Nowadays, the more usual assumption is that people are self-motivated and that they are looking for more than the pay cheque at the end of the month to achieve satisfaction. Motivation is greatly aided by the recognising and setting of meaningful targets. Choices can then be made in how to gain the goals – and by repeating the processes, eventually it is established which ways of doing things are the most effective. Nowadays the seductive models of the movers and shakers in business and politics are having a ripple effect on management and leadership.

In 1954, Dr Abraham Maslow theorised on the motivation of the individual. For example, he postulated that personal needs are the primary focus. When these needs are satisfied, behaviour is influenced and work becomes less challenging. Basic needs have a hierarchy, rising from food and shelter to fulfilling the ego and achieving goals. When survival needs are satisfied, such as having food and a roof over your head, then primary needs move on to another level such as needing a mode of transport, more home comforts and so on. Eventually the need is to find tasks, the successful accomplishment of which is satisfying in itself. The hierarchy of needs according to Maslow is:

1. Physiological
2. Safety and security

3. Social and belonging
4. Ego, status and self-esteem
5. Self-actualisation

Each of these five levels can be used when identifying what motivates you, your colleagues or staff. Following on from this, in 1959 Frederick Herzberg proposed a two-factor theory, which has since been widely used in management thinking. He surveyed 200 accountants and engineers and discovered that when they felt they were doing good work and accomplishing something which involved challenge they felt good. Meagre rewards, low recognition and poor working conditions are demotivating. In 1972, Alderfer sought to establish 'human needs in organisational settings' and condensed Maslow's needs into existence, relatedness and growth.

Expectations affect management style and increase or decrease motivation, so managers need to be aware of effort-performance-reward relationships. When comparing individual input or outcome with others, or in comparing one person with another, then assessment has to be fair, clear and communicated well to be useful and effective. If there is doubt about the performance or other measurements, then there will be dissatisfaction. Power to reward or punish, which is recognised even at school, is one of the primary mechanisms of authority for a manager. When praise or criticism is offered, or when there is a good chance of promotion based on managerial assessment, there will be related motivation to perform well depending on how fair the senior management is seen to be in their judgement. This is passed on down the reporting line so that even the most junior member of staff will reflect back the effect of the process.

Whether goals are set individually or collectively, these mechanisms of motivation come into play. In simple terms, easy goals increase performance, harder goals result in higher performance.

Persistence

The most useful attribute you possess.

Drive

In order to get ahead, start a quality improvement focus at work. It can become both a consuming passion and a competitive weapon. A good time to begin is when there is a change of circumstances, for example, when there is a new boss or a new location. As far as customers/clients are concerned, objectives for fulfilling their needs and expectations have to be identified, then met by performance through a careful, detailed process. For example, in an executive search, all candidate papers have to be prepared and circulated well in advance of the client short-listing meeting so that the interviewing can be based on thorough briefing.

Researching at Harvard in the 1960s, David McClelland studied competencies and identified the following personality drives:

- Achievement – the need to do things well and, as much as possible, by oneself from beginning to end.
- Affiliation – the need to maintain close interpersonal relationships, even if this means compromising the objective requirements of the tasks.
- Power – the need to feel strong or to justify oneself by exercising influence or making impact on others. There is also the power of facilitating.

McClelland went on to sub-divide these personality types into a detailed set of needs and attitudes.

The need for Achievement is defined as:
- Growth – self-imposed standards, mastery of the difficult, willingness to change, desire to learn, use of experts, processing failure, personal or product improvements, unique accomplishment
- Endurance – internal control, persevering effort, risk calculation, reliable follow-through, overcoming of obstacles, concentration on technique, hardiness under stress

The need for Affiliation is defined as:

- Relations – maintaining friendly contacts, involvement in long-term relationships, insisting on inclusion, exchanging personal anecdotes, manoeuvring for acceptance, concern for popularity, commiseration with others
- Nurturance – capacity for empathy, compassion for sympathetic persons, ministering consolation, comfort, or service to others, sensitivity to body language, non-threatening communication, coaching skills, supportive relationships
- Deference – self-abasement, resignation, ingratiation of authority, conformance to peer pressure, passive, deflecting, avoiding, smoothing or compromising conflict management style

The need for Power is defined as:
- Dominance – assuming leadership, commanding others, insisting on disciplines, exercising control, shaping others, negotiating/persuading, forceful or opinionated actions
- Exhibition – image projection, impression management, behavioural rehearsal and role play, clever or witty statements, exuberant/intemperate social behaviour, monitoring of audience response
- Recognition – concern for reputation or professional prestige, desirous of credit, striving for status position, decision-making authority or winning awards, maintenance of visible or instrumental associations

The breakdown of these three characteristics into needs, attitudes and drives is key to assessing your personal motivation and performance. They are also useful for recruiting employers, who can profile the individual and the job in order to match one with the other.

Determination

Once you have the habit of visualising yourself in any situation or job, you are halfway to doing it – and doing it well. When interviewing candidates, after matching their experience to the criteria of the position and the briefing on the organisational structure, the headhunter needs to detect whether they are visualising themselves in the job and their future there. Some manage this easily, others understand the situation and may even want the job but have not actually visualised themselves in the position and so do not see themselves doing it. Strong candidates demonstrate this ability and imagination, whether or not they have actually got the relevant track record. In the experience of this ancient headhunter, it is this visualisation which marks out the successful candidates. Determination to fulfil the role comes from that.

A way to heighten awareness and enable you to perform better is to use a very simple four-step cross-referenced decision-making process:

1. Think of an idea
2. Imagine it happening
3. Talk about it
4. Do it

Living in the present, with your awareness fine-tuned, makes it possible for you to spot details, pick up information and research concepts further, all of which help you to stay ahead of the game. Your abilities to analyse and act positively will be augmented by increased concentration. The more you concentrate, the more you are absorbed in what you are doing, and so the more you live in the present and the more you will be able to achieve. The past creates experience and the future lies untouched, but what is done in the present is the key to your destiny.

By being diligent you can reduce anxiety. Carelessness is avoidance of detail or lack of concentration, but instead of worrying, you can take considered action. Practice does help – and a problem will only remain a problem as long as it is regarded as such. The stronger the determination, the less the anxiety, and so problem-solving is increased. Make extraordinary demands on yourself. Organisations are often managed by example. In every structure there is one element which bears the load. This is the human face of an institution.

Energy

Fatigue only becomes chronic if it is not dealt with. Energy needs to be restocked. Being tired is just part of life, but if real rest and change are not in your routine as a positive part of the day, then something needs to be looked at, and quickly. Some people have more energy than others. Evaluate the situation and make a decision about the reputation you are looking for and how much energy is going to be needed. Generally there is a choice available as to how to ration time and efforts, so the sooner you make a decision about personal priorities the sooner the effects will be noticeable. This assessment should be related to your abilities, goals and ambitions, and the rewards you are seeking. It has little to do with the number of hours you spend working, a great deal to do with your use of time.

Energy levels can be measured by considering waking hours versus sleeping hours, physical versus mental occupation, stress versus calm. In other words, balancing life to include those things which enhance your energy rather than drain it.

There is a difference between being a hyperactive workaholic and being energetic. Stamina is the key to managing energy. It is not simply a case of having a healthy body, or even of having a well-balanced life; it is having the staying power. Business is relentless, clients are demanding, production schedules do not wait, and family crisis do occur, so being prepared is essential. Stamina is the ability to always be alert, ready to grasp an opportunity on the one hand and to withstand trauma (disasters, disapproval and upheavals) on the other. It is good to keep in top form to meet challenges which usually arise when they are least expected and just when the television or tennis court beckons. Survival depends on stamina. Jobs, projects and careers establish who you are professionally. It is essential to sustain your position and have the stamina to progress onwards and upwards.

Energy can run out. Some potential high-flyers plateau in their thirties, city high performers burn out, some fade out on managerial promotion and others are content to stay at their familiar tasks. Energy means effort – an extra mile when tired, another file dealt with, dry-cleaning collected on the way home, another e-mail sent. Whatever the cause, the effect of low energy levels is to stunt activity, so it is imperative that you learn to store energy. Executive fitness helps you to perform better. Here are the basic, practical guidelines:

1. Hard work, long hours. Hard work never hurt anyone and contrary to some fashionable thinking, it is pressure that makes a person alert and healthy. Getting up early and going to bed at a regular time is a helpful routine, but it depends who else is there . . .
2. Make time to exercise. The gym, the sports field, swimming or walking are all there for regular use. The minimum is half an hour a day, done briskly. It can also be a form of social interaction.
3. Healthy eating is eating what you need and balancing your intake for energy. No drinking (alcohol) after dinner.
4. Use a reliable set of scales. Weight is an indicator of health. Keep to the recommended range.
5. Avoid business breakfasts and dinners. Talking and eating under pressure is not enjoyable, nor is it necessarily effective. Headhunters often have to use these occasions as neutral talking shops for the mutual benefit of the participants.
6. Take a daily power-nap. Get a recliner or use the floor, take off your jacket and shoes and have up to forty-five mins after lunch each day as a regular habit (if possible!). You will benefit from the rest and refreshment. Open offices are a problem, however.
7. Never talk business during meals at home – relax with friends and family instead.
8. Be sure to have a small, well-equipped office at home. Use it for the work you have not done in working hours *but* discipline yourself there as well – and see whether the joy of having a clear desk on a Monday morning is worth the sacrifice of playtime at home.
9. Time management is a specific management tool. How to prioritise, use gaps and generally be more focused and productive is basic (see *How to be Headhunted*, 1990). Managing your time, energy and focus will help you to achieve, wherever you are.

Curiosity

This is a characteristic of the successful from all generations. Without curiosity you are not alive, alert or active.

Satisfaction

Life is what you make it – so find out what you want and go for it. Take others with you.

The reason for discussing the generation game in the opening chapter is to depict relevant aspects of the landscape in which we all live and breathe. It is to give you the opportunity to find yourself. Positioning yourself for work is defined not only by who you are but where you are and where you've been, as well as what you've done to date. What you are capable of and what you wish to do is another matter. Be aware that you are conditioned to expect to be busy all the time. For example, the CV is only one way of accounting for your past.

Positioning yourself and exposing dynamics in relationships at work, in the community, in the family and life in general, while maintaining your clarity of perspective, will mean that you will soon know what is really your own particular agenda. This is your way forward.

· 2 ·

Positioning: Within the Institution

Find out what you like doing best and get someone to pay you for it.
Katharine Whitehorn

People are the Best Assets

The more you know about your possible employer, the organisation or client firms, the better you will perform. Research, networking, and professional connections are all ways you can help yourself to be aware of current market requirements. Headhunters and recruiters will expect you to understand your particular value for their clients. In return, you should ask the headhunter to give you full briefings on both the organisation and the role so that there will be a limit to the 'surprises' awaiting you if you decide to accept their offer.

Corporate Profiling

Many companies have remained successful because of the quality of their senior people. Newspapers recently listed the most influential people in the country and they included many chief executives and chairmen. Other companies, such as those in Silicon Valley, are very dependent on the creativity of their employees. How do you know which organisation to join and to which institution you will want to give commitment? Getting to know what is going on within the firm is essential if you are going to make an informed decision to work for them. You need to find out what is expected of employees and consultants and how they interact with suppliers and customers. Financial data is available in the press, and your stockbroker, accountant and other financial advisers can supply reports and analyses of performance and predictions.

Executives often spend more time on internal politics than on production, marketing and customers. Those who overcome this preoccupation and the need for political control will succeed in managing their people better. Leading an organisation includes managing both process and people. Co-operation with colleagues and staff, combined with the senior manager's determination to achieve, will help the 'boss' to be respected. Conversely, the 'bosses' must facilitate others so that they can work well too. Peter Senge, MIT, writes about 'the learning culture', which is encouraged from the top down, but he emphasises that it does not happen in a vacuum. All employees need to be included. Noel Tichy, in *The Leadership Engine*, espouses the theory that most successful organisations create a climate in which managers can achieve and always encourage their staff.

Professor Jerry Porras, an expert in organisational change who is based at Stanford in the USA, has undertaken a study of eighteen European companies across a range of sectors and countries. He chose Glaxo Wellcome, Marks & Spencer in the UK, Royal Dutch Shell and Unilever. Other leading names selected include Deutsche Bank, Daimler-Benz, Ericsson, Fiat, Philips and Siemens. Porras asked the chief executives of these companies to nominate companies that they thought were 'visionary'. He found significant differences between the management styles of the institutions that relied on visionary consensus and had a stated ideology and the management styles of the other companies. The visionary founders operated in the belief that if great companies are built they will inevitably produce great products and services. In contrast, company leaders who focused on products and services only allowed their companies to develop round them in a haphazard manner and were not so successful.

People, structures, systems and processes have to be developed so that when the original leader dies or leaves, the institution still flourishes. Visionary companies have much more chance of progressing than other companies. The ideology which has more than five or six values stated is not strong or limited enough. Strategies come and go to meet the market demands, but the core values last for ever. Once the core ideology is clear, then everything else can be fluid while the core remains solid.

How does this all apply inside the institution? It is important to inaugurate and share core ideology at team or project level. The older and larger the company the more entrenched will be the habits. Philip Morris did not become a visionary company until it was 100 years old. Inspirational founders of companies do eventually go, and the current trend of business organisations is towards flat and geographically disparate structures filled with knowledge workers, so the core ideology will become even more important in keeping them together.

Three examples of core ideologies:

Boeing
Being on the leading edge of aeronautics: being pioneers
Tackling huge challenges and risks
Product safety and quality
Integrity and ethical business
To 'eat, breathe and sleep the world of aeronautics'
General Electric
Improving the quality of life through technology and innovation
Interdependent balance between responsibility to customers, employees, society and shareholders (no hierarchy)
Individual responsibility and opportunity
Honesty and integrity
Hewlett-Packard
Technical contribution to fields in which it operates
Respect and opportunity for HP people
Responsibility to communities in which it operates
Affordable quality for HP customers
Profit and growth merely as a means to other ends

Virgin employs 15,000 people, producing a turnover of £2.4 billion a year from operations in 24 countries. The corporate giant is not run from a skyscraper but from a house in residential West London. A raft of sober-suited, high-calibre executives supply the ballast to Branson's casual air. These are the people who work in the house-cum-office and who manage the day-to-day operations of Virgin. They enable him to be a venture capitalist, to be part of the company PR machine, and to ride in his balloon or do whatever currently intrigues him. They work well with someone with a butterfly mind who likes to delegate as much as possible. Virgin companies are of two kinds: a wholly owned subsidiary or one in which Virgin is a partner. The first includes the airline and megastores, the second includes the insurance and drinks businesses. He makes sure that each part of the operation is run by people he knows and trusts. Employees rarely meet Branson or the senior executives.

They are in a spoke and wheel organisation and are only told about what is going on in their part of it. Employees have to read the papers to find out what the latest Virgin moves have been. There is small sense of unity as individual businesses use their independence and report to HQ only when asked or it is essential. The senior team have been trying to change the culture and to bind people together more. Yet Branson remains king with an inner circle of courtiers ruling over the successful empire. The image of Camelot or Star Wars is easily applicable here.

In other sectors, privatisation has had a marked effect on corporate identity. Privatisation has taken place in BT and British Gas and other utilities in the last decade. Since the process started, in the early eighties, the Treasury has taken seven billion pounds. Between 1971 and 1997, council houses and flats have been transferred into private ownership (which includes homeowners, building societies and banks), to a total of 25 billion pounds. Housing Societies now account for 2.2 billion pounds as well. Under Private Finance Initiative (PFI) thinking, the financing, management and risks of capital projects are transferred to private companies, and mortgages on these are then paid out of fees or taxes. The PFI reduces government spending. The effect of this on employment has been to change the ethos of long-term public service jobs to business-based roles. The reduction in the number of people needed has led to many redundancies.

Another form of PFI is outsourcing. This means that a council or department buys a service from a private company, estimating that it will be more efficient than the in-house team. Research shows that this is creating a saving of 20% but causing discontent among existing employees. Privatisation in all its forms has created a large potential market for lawyers, management consultants, financiers and the relatively new industry of managed services.

The Corporate Individual

How do you react and behave within the constant shifts in corporate culture? Organisations change and the individual has to 'go with the flow' unless you are prepared to stand out and lead the thinking. Progressive managers achieve change by avoiding the 'dead hero' trap, which is the outcome of forcing through change without understanding and co-operation. The 'with it' manager may be flamboyant in style, but to deliver a manager has to use a more controlled, professional manner. He has to be a professional radical. Professional radicals know that lasting change takes time, because you have to persuade people and have to overcome resistance to the new. Jon Leach, of *Management Today*, has written about the dos and don'ts of being radical. His checklist includes the following:

- Know when change is not wanted
- Be patient
- Respect age
- Acquire humility
- Be selective in what you change
- Work with others who are of similar mind
- Know your own weaknesses
- Know when to do nothing
- Make allies at the top
- Do it

Do you recognise the signs that your people are looking for a radical professional, or are they satisfied with a 'safe pair of hands'?

Few people get ahead just by being smooth and playing politics. The 15% who are regarded as star performers by their bosses and colleagues have a 10:1 ratio of productivity. You can learn to increase your productivity. However, you can also enhance your personal position in the group, bearing in mind that bosses and colleagues see you from different viewpoints. You can do this by showing:

- Evidence of initiative, taking responsibility beyond the job description
- Good networking – especially for acquiring information
- Self-motivation and management
- Teamwork
- Leadership
- Perspective (seeing other people's points of view)
- Independent thinking while supporting the corporate thinking
- Organisational savvy
- Presenting the right information at the right time to the right people

In the early nineties fast-track management schemes were slashed, but now they are beginning to make a comeback. Linda Holbeche of Roffey Park Management Institute headed a recent survey of 200 organisations and found that 'Delayering has taken place and employees are being told to manage their own careers and be prepared to move sideways. But then some organisations introduce schemes that look elitist.' The people who have been looking after themselves feel as if they have been conned, and those who are not chosen are upset. These schemes can be divisive. When there is a culture that accepts that you should not be competitive, that to have winners and losers is unacceptable, then you will be demotivated. Yes, each person's talents and skills should be recognised, but it should be done in a way that is motivating.

Balancing of specialist and general skills and knowledge is being prioritised by more people. The most noticeable disadvantage of selection schemes is what to do with those who do not match up to the expectations of their superiors or who have not earned the respect of their subordinates. Outside objective advice on your progress is preferable to assessment by those who may have a vested interest, but you do not always have the choice. The institution which recognises these facts is well on the way to having fulfilled employees, and you will be able to perform better there.

Family/Work Values

The WFD/*Management Today* 1998 survey highlights that four fifths of managers have complaints about the hours that they work and the level of stress this causes. They admit to the toll that their work life is taking on their domestic and social lives. They go on to lament that in making sacrifices for their careers they have missed out on their children growing up. Managers are taking work pressures home and home pressures to work. They feel they are losing control. In the survey, 84% felt that they had made important sacrifices for their careers and that things are not getting better. Are you in this category?

The under 35s have identified their particular personal sacrifices:

• Work put before family
• Missing children growing up
• Missing leisure/hobby time
• Moved home for employer
• Divorce/strain on relationship
• Away from home (short-term)
• Putting off having children
• Time spent on training
• Away from home (long-term)
• Unable to form relationships

Conversely they have a wish list to:

• Work fewer hours
• Change company culture
• Work flexible hours
• Reduce/avoid commuting
• Work from home

- Change/relocate jobs
- Earn more
- Increase number of staff
- Reduce stress
- Retire

The Government White Paper, 'Fairness at Work' (1998), includes a section on family-friendly policies, one of which promises employees three months' unpaid leave when their child is born. This reflects the desire shown across Continental Europe for more recognition of parental responsibilities. Wider family responsibilities also need to be addressed, in particular the needs of those caring for elderly relatives. Some firms are setting up centres where staff can leave dependent elderly relatives to be cared for during the day. The 'granny' crèches have restaurants, hair stylists, art classes, bingo sessions and indoor bowling. In the management struggles to hold on to valued staff, this pensioner care is being seen as a vital service to keep workers happy and to stem resignations of highly trained personnel. Research by Help the Aged has shown that up to a third of the current workforce has the responsibility of an aged relative. The first granny crèche has been opened by Peugeot cars in Coventry and many are planned to follow this example. These services are being funded by a daily charge on the basis of mutual benefit for the firm and the employee.

Even as unemployment is climbing steadily in Germany and France, their trades unions are demanding an ever shorter week. The nirvana thinking of the sixties was that of full employment and longer playtime. It was an illusion. In the USA there is near full employment at the time of writing, with strong measures to maintain this rather than increasing time out of the workplace as a right for the employee. Even before the financial crisis in the Far East, it was noted that if workers in Europe were to compete with the low costs and the very long hours of the workers there, no amount of mechanisation and upgrading of production would be enough.

In the UK it used to be accepted that manual workers had long hours and that professional and management people had support.

For example, until World War II, it was commonplace for there to be servants, often living in, in many homes. Wives, whether in the Diplomatic Service or married to the local doctor, were expected to hostess dinner parties, cook for guests, manage the surgery and so on as a matter of course. This has changed as more and more women and partners are fully occupied with their own careers and holding on to their jobs, whether part-time or full-time – as well as looking after their children.

From 1947, professionals such as lawyers, academics, doctors and teachers were people with some leisure. Until the Big Bang in 1987, those who 'did something in the City' had an apparently light load. City lunches were notoriously lengthy affairs, and many City gents saw no reason to return to the office after them. Gentlemen's Clubs were well used and life was pursued by many at a leisurely pace. This has changed. The need to be competitive as individuals and corporately in order to survive is now the norm. Extra financial demands rising from political change (such as children's university fees no longer being fully paid by the State) have added to the burden for everyone. The expression 'hard work never harmed anyone' seems to be literally true. The richest or top people who are most active have a good health and longevity record too. Ambitious people often thrive on stress and achieve more. This contrasts with the situation in Japan. Until the eighties, the Japanese had a paternal State which looked after all its citizens' needs, but then the culture started to change. The 'salary man' was devastated when he was made redundant. Holidays have had to be imposed on the hard-working population.

The other side to these observations is that many people enjoy their work and find such fulfilment there that the hours they put in are not important. Rewards are immense in many instances. Others have the ability to escape the humdrum level of work and appreciate the need to balance work and play.

Alternative Work Environments

Mary Ann is thirty and is married with one daughter aged two. She used to work full-time as a manager of a team in a City financial services firm, but the birth of her daughter caused her to re-evaluate her job and she presented her boss with a proposal on the best use of her time. Eventually, after much negotiation, she was able to achieve the reduction in hours but she had to accept the promotion of one of her staff into her job while she went on to the three-day week. She is doing virtually the same amount of work as the full-timers by having short lunches, being more focused and being flexible when necessary. She has adjusted to the drop in income (£20,000) by making less go farther. She resents the view of part-timers as workers with less commitment and responsibility, the perception of the casual, laid-back person as opposed to the sharp professional. Her advice is to be clear and definite when negotiating for part-time hours, to be good at the job, and to demonstrate that flexibility works both ways. Flexibility can help the employer too, especially when there has been an investment in training and corporate understanding.

Another example is Fiona, who was a newly divorced mother of two young children in 1966 when she decided to leave her successful career at an advertising agency to find another way of working. Fiona is an entrepreneur and has a stubborn streak. Starting with a phone, fax and computer in her back bedroom, she set up a Human Resources consultancy which would help companies to recruit, assess and develop their staff. She got through the lonely and desperation stages and launched into serving some existing clients from her workplace who wished to retain her personal expertise. Two years later she employs seven full-time consultants and thirty associates. She is still in that back room and has no intention of going to the expense of a central office. Communication is on a daily basis by phone and e-mail. Her clients include blue-chip companies and her turnover is now over £1 million. She is proud of the speed of her success.

Anyone contemplating going on their own has to have contacts in place, the ability to build on their specialist knowledge and expertise, plus stamina and determination. Analyse what potential clients want. If you decide that you do not want to work on your own, as soon as the volume grows, find the key people you need to expand. Teamwork is the best part of company life – someone to bounce ideas off, to encourage when things go wrong and to cheer when things go right. Work hard at building relationships, both with your clients and with fellow workers. Support networks help you maintain your nerve on the slow days.

Families resent the time and space occupied by work. You must insist on the value of your work and the necessity for commitment if you are going to be able to balance everything. An academic said that his family thought he was having fun and playing games when working on his systems. Freedom, flexibility, independence, reducing travel time and being at home are perceived by the inexperienced as the bonus factors of the arrangement. Better income is the real goal. The experienced and fortunate home-based businessman or -woman probably achieves this eventually, but the lack of boundaries both in time and space do continue to be problematical. The example of the customer requiring answers at midnight is not unusual. It boils down to having the ability to work under clearly defined conditions, being firm in following up and networking, and, of course, having a service or product of value to the purchaser. The Home Business Alliance was set up to help people who work away in their attic or garden shed, etc., and to keep them in touch with the marketplace.

More than 150,000 people set up in business from home this year in the UK, yet only two in five take any steps to ensure their safety when they have people visiting them. Barclays Bank have researched the situation, and though incidents are rare, the risks are increasing as work patterns change. Most home workers are on their own when they are working and so are vulnerable. It is sensible to make first meetings with either suppliers or clients in a public place. Another practical idea is to have a 'buddy system' whereby you fax a daily itinerary at a regular time to a person who can check that all is well from time to time. Another tip is to make a phone call after the visitor has arrived within their earshot, promising to call back at a particular time after the visitor has left. This can act both as an information call and as a deterrent.

Womenconomics

Looking at some of the 1997/8 statistics from around the world, it seems that 'womenconomics' has arrived. From Silicon Valley to Siberia there is evidence of women running businesses – often their own. In Europe there are 110 women with degrees for every 100 men. In France there are new laws requiring at least 50% of all government members to be female. In the UK it is expected that 1 million of the 1.4 million jobs created in the next twenty years will be occupied by women. However, of the top 1000 rich people in the UK, 936 are men. Optimistic forecasts about increasing numbers of women succeeding in business are unlikely to be fulfilled. There are fundamental reasons for this:

1. Economic competition is becoming more and more ruthless. From finance to football the top players are demanding – and getting – unimaginably high incomes compared even with a few years ago. The lust for power does corrupt males and females alike, but more men are successful in getting to the position to exploit this.

2. Occupations that become dominated by women, for example, secretarial work, or in the well-documented case of the public service in Finland, get devalued. There are now more women in the House of Commons, but the power base has moved to Downing Street and the EU. Is this because social change is allowing women a glimmer of political equality, or are the power-hungry men looking for it elsewhere? In the last twenty years men have been inventing, developing and dominating the technology relating to communications and computing, creating gigantic corporations in the process. Women are being left behind again.

3. Financial incentives are not enough for women. Men get more 'toys' the more powerful they are. They acquire gorgeous companions and create more 'fun' for themselves while senior women look for satisfaction in their work. Moreover, women often tend to like men who are stronger than they are and to whom they can look up, whereas men are threatened by a powerful woman. So the higher a woman rises, the fewer potential partners are available and the less she is needed to help the partner to be successful. This is a major disincentive. Besides, it is perceived that women do not need to create their own success as much as men do.

4. Women have alternatives. They can marry the rich and famous and bask in the glory, even if they have to suffer for it, whereas a man who marries a rich and powerful woman is looked down upon as a gigolo or toyboy. There have been many

handsome divorce settlements and inheritances which have enabled women to avoid the stresses of top job achievement. Many women exchange high-status careers for high-satisfaction lifestyles.

5. Women spend more time on childcare. In theory having children should make no difference to the opportunities available to the working woman. At present 70% of mothers are working, and the Blairites want to increase that to 100%. The problem is that most women have a constant nagging urge to look after their children pulling against the satisfaction they get from their work and their earning capacity. Many compromise by doing part-time work. Fathers feel that it is their duty to earn the money for the family. He is more likely to gain promotion and earn more, so that makes some sense.

6. Risk-taking. Women have more self-preservation techniques than men – they are less likely to have a road accident, to go bankrupt or to drink themselves to death. They have a strong mothering instinct, whereas the male's predominant instinct is to fight to win. Even though these traits are changing marginally, the need to take risks is inherent in the attainment of success.

7. Competitiveness. Women are just not as interested in competition as men are, even though they can compete and do well. What's more, the brains of the male and female act differently under this type of stress. He gets high – she gets anxious.

8. It appears that women do not seek the external trappings of power to the same extent as men. They are said to have the power of beauty, sexuality and reproduction. Men have to assert themselves in order to prove their existence, starting by pulling away from their mother and other females who may wish to restrain them.

9. Women are thought to be not so extreme as men. There are always the exceptions which prove the rule, for example, female terrorists.

10. Women rule the men who rule the world. More women work nowadays in the UK than ever before. They work either to supplement their husband's income or they have the responsibility of being a single parent. However, despite the increase in both full-time and part-time working amongst mothers, some women

still choose to stay at home with their children. That is their prerogative. The majority of mothers make the obvious compromise – they work part-time. But they may pay a price.

Part-timers tend to have fewer benefits, less job security and lower status than full-timers. For many professionals, going part-time means working at a lower level than before. The person who left as managing director may return part-time to do market research or to work freelance or as a consultant for the same organisation. As far as the employers are concerned, they are off the career ladder. The assumption is that anyone who wants to reduce hours has relinquished ambition. Part-timers all regret the loss of identity and many recall the imprint of their working years.

Job sharing can create an office identity crisis for you, but it also frees time for raising a family or pursuing more than one career path at the same time. Employers are very wary of such arrangements and need to be persuaded to consider them. The obstacles to the share are more psychological than practical in reality. Good communication between the job sharers is the key, plus the ability to make colleagues and clients understand that this is one job being done by two people. For holidays and time off, it is simpler for the organisation if both people go at the same time. It is easier to start at the workplace at the beginning of the week rather than in mid-week, but practice makes perfect.

Job shares are not limited to women. There is a movement towards professional roles which can be matched to be shared by both men and women. Trusting each other completely and accepting that the job still goes on in the absence of one or other is imperative: there is always someone who knows all the ins and outs of the job and what is actually being done and planned. Unfortunately job shares are still unusual. Fewer than 4% of part-time roles are filled this way. There are costs incurred for both the employers and the employees. The hangover time and catch-up allocation cause extra costs; and each individual will earn less even though the employer is paying more overall for the position. However, the compensation is enormous, as two challenging careers are created and the employer gains an extra input into the job.

'Ending the Mother War', a report by Jayne Buxton of the

University of London is all about supermother having to learn to say 'enough!' and forgo some of the potential of her career success. Jayne has analysed that this is the realistic situation with the current work place attitudes. She sees flexibility and support systems as the main ways of making a good job work better. Susan Williams and Sue Osborn share the role of CEO at Barking and Havering health authority, and they claim that letting go of established notions of power and success is essential to being comfortable with job sharing: 'You've got to share power to do this, and you can't worry about accreditation or individual recognition.' Emma Mathews is a job-sharing appeals lawyer in the Lord Chancellor's Office. She finds she is motivated by the opportunity to keep in touch with the real world, having an income to call her own and the self-esteem which comes from making an impact in a case. Job-sharing enables people to keep a toe on the ladder and keep future choices at a reasonable level open. Corporate life has encompassed technological, economic, environmental and social changes – so why not changes relating to work/life issues?

Partnerships for Success

Alliances between companies, groups, organisations or bodies which share a common purpose will speed up progress and development for all. The methodology which has been tried and proved includes:

- Identifying the issues and any barriers, both visible and invisible
- Creating a shared vision, giving ownership to all the alliance partners
- Plotting action plans incorporating the best use of the strengths of the shared partnerships
- Developing a strategic plan
- Including all agencies and external bodies to increase effectiveness
- Inaugurating joint corporate communications for internal and external profiling
- Working with the community and voluntary groups for mutual

support
- Linking the weak and strong areas of activity so that the balance will be of wide benefit
- Using change to create change: using events to induce changes in behaviour
- Planning on a project basis rather than the usual territory basis
- Checking and updating operating conditions

Priorities:
- Raise the joint corporate profile
- Create a positive working culture
- Instigate a number of sustainable partnership at all levels which involve the key players, both organisational and individual
- Develop broader and deeper training and education programmes to improve transport and distribution systems
- Produce an integrated regeneration framework in those parts of the group which require it
- Use dynamic leaders to maintain the determination and persistence necessary for successful outcomes
- Remain open to new ideas from anywhere, anytime
- Be inclusive
- Be alert to values and ethics at all times

Leaders create change; managers manage it. They need to:
- Find the mutual benefit approach
- Facilitate rather than lead or co-ordinate
- Encourage a two-way learning ethos
- Emphasise quick wins and successes
- Continually look at the best use of people and resources
- Show commitment to 'onwards and upwards'
- Eliminate the gap between strategic formulation and implementation

The outcomes will include:
- Optimising the use of all resources
- Managing the multi-faceted, multi-sized and multi-task projects
- Anticipating and satisfying all the stakeholders
- Releasing the potential of all the individuals involved

- Changing the culture by changing perception, attitudes, philosophy, values and purpose of all the partners

Action:
- Spin-off satellite programmes, products and projects should be self-sustaining
- Maintain your reputation for quality, independence of thinking and corporate success

Corporate Governance

It has been recognised that there is a need for guidelines and regulations for the top-level management of organisations. Annual reports are being checked by the press, shareholders and interested parties for the existence of non-executive directors, remuneration and audit committees and effective boardroom practice. The chief executive has the extra burden of fulfilling the governance requirements on top of running the business. The investor has to accept the reports as stated. In early 1998 ICI was criticised for giving too much information to the analysts who were interested in their trading. On the other hand, Abbott Mead Vickers was exposed for not having an audit or remuneration committee and for having only one non-executive on the board.

Shortly before ICI was criticised, its chairman, Ronnie Hampel, had chaired the committee on corporate governance, so it was assumed that they 'should know better'. The Stock Exchange rules say that no investor should be given price-sensitive information before it is generally public, so the opinions expressed by the analysts after their conversations with ICI, which led to a fall in shares, are being questioned. ICI is clear that it gives the same information to all, so if a small investor wants to call them like the analyst then this is what will happen. SME companies maintain the stance that they will only discuss information which is already in the public domain.

The AMV situation was brought about by a politically correct agency manifesto which deals with corporate voting. The Chairman had stuck to his guns that he is responsible to his share-holders, corporate advisers and employees and does not need a raft of non-executive directors. Lean and mean, AMV has a fine record. Non-executives and committees can serve a valuable function. If you are considering being a non-executive director, there are many aspects of corporate governance which need your attention. Candidates are very senior people, usually aged between fifty and sixty, with previous main board or senior executive experience. They all must show success in their career to date and have an enviable reputation for making things happen. Many do it for fun, to 'give something back', or to satisfy their curiosity. Networking at the highest levels brings lucrative opportunities. Expert advisers with many positions can add up this income quickly and reach the stars.

Advisory boards are common in the USA and are increasing in the UK. Bob Horton is the chairman of Horton International, an American search firm which is setting up a European Advisory Board and has found a wide range of people to choose from. They will be paid a small annual fee, but the attraction is the possibility of joining the main board and the understanding of the developing markets which they will be targeting. Everyone will gain from the increased network while the company grows.

Members of the advisory board help managers to assess the marketplace, gauge future trends, develop strategy and draw in new business. They are non-executive directors without legal responsibilities. Advisory boards can be general in scope, or specialised in issues relating to the market or industry concerned. Knowledge about new technologies, predictions on competitors' actions, advice on political, legislative and regulatory changes which will affect the company can all be covered by the members of the board. It is attractive for expanding companies to accelerate growth by using the expertise and experience of people working alongside them. They will have backgrounds which complement the interests of the company without giving rise to conflicts of interest. Headhunters reckon that high achievers with potential are the best people to fill the seats. They have to be accustomed to analysing business issues and be used to diversification. In the present European economic climate there is a wide range of people who could make themselves available and thus expand their working remit. An interesting development in America is the all-women boards which a New York firm, PartnerCom, have found for AT&T, Swissotel and Avis Rent-a-Car. This is the outcome of discussions about who makes the decisions on the products and services they provide. For example, women are the fastest growing users of business travel.

Advisory boards are no longer informal or luncheon clubs. They are active forums for developing business in new territories. Haruko Faruda has been promoting Nikko's interests throughout the world. She represents the group at conferences and in governmental and other global conferences. Her background with the World Bank and the Overseas Development Institute has proved invaluable.

In the 1980s a study of 325 large UK industrial companies found that family controlled businesses out performed their non-family counterparts in five key areas: higher valuation ratios, greater profit margins, higher returns on shareholders' capital, higher growth rates of sales and higher rates of net assets. *Forbes* magazine found that when a member of the family was the chief executive then these companies were 15% more profitable and 14% faster-growing than their industry average. The Family Business Network was founded in Lasagne in 1990.

The study of family businesses is relatively new. The writers Fred Neubauer and Alden G. Lank have analysed the governance of family concerns in their book *The Family Business* (Macmillan, 1998). They define the family business as one where the family has voting control and where they have the final say in the strategic direction of the firm, especially in the appointment of the chief executive. The family members do not have to be involved on a day-to-day operational basis. The strengths of the family business range from first-class management development systems and training of family members in stewardship to realising that the good name of the firm depends on the value and quality of the product or service. They work to maximise the shareholder wealth even a generation later. Conversely, these companies can be fragile and are prone to the effects of strong personality conflicts. Also, they have the problem of raising outside capital while keeping the family holdings intact. They may or may not be fortunate in the calibre of the family succession, as only 15% make it to the third generation.

The composition of the board is different for the family firm in terms of the control they have over who they invite to join. This brings with it the problem of close friends who may expect the positions. Advisory boards are particularly useful to the family firm as a way of bringing to it bigger scale, wider experience and other specialisms, without giving away the family's power and influence.

Nothing is too exotic when it comes to equipping modern directors for their solemn tasks. On away-days, they may experience rock-climbing, white water rafting, fire-walking, playing Lego or even going on retreat to a monastery. They have been required to read Machiavelli's *The Prince* and Sun Tzu's *Art of War* – after they have finished the writings of Jacques Derrida. As Christian Tyler put it (*Financial Times*, June 1998): 'Caught between the demands of industrial efficiency and human decency, they are searching at the same time for sure-fire success and for moral guidance in a world of shifting values.'

Philosophical thinking has entered the training and language of professional facilitators. They are there to help people think their problems through. They look at a person's conceptual history rather than just their professional and emotional history, and examine how that person's thinking may have got stuck. At first sight, Socrates looks absolutely the wrong model for managers, executives and non-executives, but the new Socratics say that the point is for managers and directors to learn what they really believe, not by shouting or pulling rank, but by slowly and rigorously arguing the thing through. Only in this way can they reach a durable agreement. The supervised brainstorming this entails (which usually takes place round a table, sharing a meal) makes the business of thinking more enjoyable. The standard justification for employing management consultants is that it is easier for the informed outsider to see what needs doing than it is for the insider, so the socratic thinking equips the insider to be more objective.

Ethics

Adam Smith, the eighteenth-century moral philosopher, pointed out that the butcher, the baker and the brewer do not supply their goods for your sake alone; they have an interest in earning something from the transaction. The hope for a better life is a driving force in itself: 'Money makes the world go round.' Before Adam Smith the elite kept the privilege of feathering their nests for themselves, now the requirement to succeed is more like a moral duty, and any failure to do so is regarded as a sin. Job-seeking is part of keeping up with the expectations of society. The ethics involved go beyond 'doing an honest day's work for an honest day's pay'. Yet the first generation that will not do better than its parents is now entering the workplace.

Moralists have always had a problem with money, but it is useful for looking after yourself. The big issues, such as debt paying, either on one's own behalf or on behalf of others, are complex. Should the World Bank bail out Indonesia? Who should help out the small supplier who has to wait too long for the big customer to pay its bills? The ethical system applies to the individual and the organisation alike. The central dogma at present is that they should strive to be better off and not just better.

The need to protect the environment is moving up the corporate agenda, according to a 1998 survey sponsored by AEA Technology and supported by Business in the Environment (BiE) and Business in the Community, who wanted to encourage Britain's companies to bolster their environmental performance. It aimed the questions to measure the environmental engagement of Britain's largest companies at board level. The seventy-four FTSE companies that participated demonstrated an improvement in their activities since the last check in 1996. The top ten performers were BAT, British Gas, BP, BT, Enterprise Oil, ICI, Marks & Spencer, National Power, NatWest and Rio Tinto, and most of these had appointed a board member with environmental monitoring responsibility.

The environment is considered to be a strategic business issue with long-term implications. The Co-operative Bank was one of the first institutions to have a stated policy on investments only in environmentally acceptable businesses, and it has been proved a success. The ethical approach extends to social as well as environmental issues. Peter Hughes of NatWest Group says, 'Taking an ethical line has to make good business sense. When banks are making complex decisions they need a framework to help them balance the conflicting demands, so we have a code of conduct that helps workers taking such decisions to look at long-term viability rather than just economic performance.' Their code includes advice on good banking practice and customer service, with guidelines on ethical issues. David Matthew, director of the New Academy of Business, sees no conflict between profitability and social concern. His organisation advises companies about the benefits of taking an ethical approach. The Institute of Directors has supported the Hub Initiative, headed by Oonagh Mary Harpur, to add love and integrity to the workplace.

Competitive intelligence offers all sorts of opportunities, but it is not always clear what is legal, let alone ethical. It is a pervasive process, ranging from the person collecting literature from competitors' stands at trade fairs to the highly sophisticated bugging methods that are used when mergers and similar are being undertaken. Corporate snooping goes on all the time, and most of it is legitimate and in the public arena. The problem lies in negotiating through the grey areas where the legal and ethical signposts are unclear. How far is the company or the employee prepared to go to find out economic information? Many competitive intelligence professionals do not consider that dirty tricks or skulduggery are necessary to achieve results. They believe that clandestine activity is a waste of time and that deception is merely an admission that there is not an adequate internal system for collecting legitimate intelligence *in situ*.

Many managers go to great lengths to find out what is going on both in their own organisation and in competitors' or buyers' outfits. The two main benefits come from cutting costs and boosting sales. Knowing about wrong routes taken in research, or about the imminent launch of a new product, aids their expenditure and planning. Some frequently used methods of getting information about rival organisations are described in reports and literature about ethics in the workplace, and headhunters find out a great deal when interviewing candidates. Yet many large companies spend and report on competitive intelligence gathering without giving a full explanation, and few can point to the real pay-off. There is an ongoing debate about what is right and wrong when seeking information. For example:

- Asking a new employee about work in progress in their previous employer's firm (illegal and unethical)
- Conducting a market research exercise which finds out what customers think about rivals (legal and ethical)
- Placing an employee/detective in a rival office to discover their secrets (illegal and unethical)
- Contacting a firm as a student requiring information for research and passing on the information (possibly illegal and positively unethical)
- Wining and dining staff, directors and customers in order to glean economic data, etc. (legal and ethical)
- Using surveillance workers to check refuse and personnel activities in order to evaluate a rival company's products, etc. (legal but doubtful ethically)
- Bugging in general and electronically in particular on IT and other systems
- Listening to conversations in public places, for example, on mobile phones in trains, restaurants and airports, using the information this supplies (legal and ethical)
- Advertising senior jobs in order to interview key people from competitors' companies and pick their brains (legal but unethical)
- Analysing products and using the scientific or other information for gain (legal and ethical)
- Including environmental and political bias/influence in products and services

The real heart of ethical competitive intelligence is the situation internally. Most information is already there in the heads of employees. Internal and often unaccessed information accounts for 70% of the data the firm really needs. The key to discovering and using internal information lies in motivating people and in structuring groups appropriately. Employees should be able to see the relevance of what they know in conjunction with the needs of the employer. The importance of recording information and making it fit into the regular working day is fundamental. For example, the recording of telephone conversations in city offices about sensitive areas of transactions is generally accepted.

Processes are needed to ensure that information flows freely round the organisation, and the use of 'shareware' to achieve this is now widespread. Information needs to be analysed and edited for accuracy and reliability as well as relevance. In large organisations this requires a full-time dedicated staff, while in a small company it can be part of the marketing/research role. The more that is known, the more likely it is that future planning and predictions will be helpful and sound.

A survey of the chief executives of the Top 1000 companies conducted in 1998 by PA Consulting showed that 96% thought they were delivering value to shareholders, and this was their main goal. Many experts, including the five big accountancy firms, are preaching the virtues of value based management. This means looking at how much each part of a company costs and how much income it can generate. Any organisation will have a cost of money, the cost of equity and of debt. In the UK this overall cost is about 11%, and once that hurdle is cleared, value is created. It enables finance departments to look forward when making financial assessments. The usual way of looking at share price is by looking at its history. Michael Maskell, a partner with PricewaterhouseCoopers, believes that value management should include seven operational drives, all of which help to rank projects. The key driver is the computer which has cut down the time taken to make complex calculations.

Different firms use different nomenclature. VBM (value based management), SVA (shareholder value added), MDP (managing drivers of performance) and EVA (economic value added) are all terms in common use. The trend for value based management is gathering momentum particularly since it has been adopted by firms like Coca-Cola, AT&T, Wal-Mart and Quaker Oats in the

USA, and by Lloyds TSB in Britain. Budgeting to increase value enables the allocation of resources to the right places. Management reporting gives the right information to the board and helps them to focus on value at all times.

Employees/Employers: Synergy

Working together basically means two or more outfits generating greater value working together than they can by working separately. There are recognisable formats:

- Sharing know-how: Improving results by pooling insights into a particular process, function or geographic area. Value can be created by exposing one set of people to another who have a different way of getting things done, and often this happens informally.
- Co-ordinated strategies: Aligning strategies within a group reduces inter-unit competition. Sharing marketing thinking, corporate logos and the like is cost-effective, and co-ordinating responses to shared customers and competitors can be a powerful and effective way to counter competitive threats. Balancing intervention and autonomy takes sophisticated management.
- Shared tangible resources: This is a way of saving money. For example, using a shared manufacturing facility can achieve economies of scale and avoid duplication.
- Vertical integration: Co-ordinating the flow of products or services from one unit to another can reduce inventory costs, speed up product development, increase capacity utilisation and improve market access.
- Pooled negotiating power: Leverage with suppliers, reducing costs and improving the qualities of the goods purchased. Companies can negotiate, jointly and severally, with other stakeholders and the gains can be dramatic.
- Combined business creation: Corporate regeneration and growth benefits from this synergy.

Planning Ahead

It is widely recognised that security in retirement for employees depends on a combination of the basic state pension and a good secondary pension, preferably an occupational pension. However, occupational pensions cover only 50% of the workforce. Many people use personal pensions instead, but they give poor returns to the ever increasing number of people with work breaks and job changes. The stakeholder pension is a way of including employees who are outside other types of retirement schemes. This sort of pension should be simple, secure, flexible and offer value for money. Collective, multi-member schemes are possible and could cover those who work for more than one employer. A trustee board would represent the interests of all the stakeholders, both employers and employees. These schemes could include the self-employed, freelancers, and people who work on short-term contracts or through employment agencies. There should be sufficient flexibility to accommodate people who change employers or jobs, or who wish to transfer between schemes, or to suspend payments when they take a career break. The traditional employee with confidence in the organisation, annual increments and a growing pension is extinct. Employees now prefer their senior management to be seen to be strong and progressive, giving protection from insecurity both inside and outside the workplace.

Smart thinking about the effects of the decrease of jobs in a corporate framework is necessary. The corporate individual who holds a long-term job in the same organisation is a fading phenomenon. Trust between employers and employees is being stretched. The increase in global hiring, in transparency of pay and remuneration packages and in skills shortages are all giving the individual more choices as well as headaches. Good quality candidates, especially those with IT, a sales and marketing background and certain specialist knowledge, have the prospect of being approached for their talent and having to respond rapidly to close the deal. You should check your skills, target the organisations, read the advertisements, talk to the headhunters and act quickly when there is a response.

· 3 ·

Positioning: You

The person who wakes up and finds they are a success . . . has not been asleep.

Anon

Egonomics

This means self-definition: telling your own story, being heard, having people pay attention to you. In this way you become more self-aware and increase your self-worth. The idea is that in a fast-changing world, you have to take responsibility for you and yours, so you need to be equipped.

Be Your Own Headhunter

If you need a job, want to change your job or just want to test the employment market, you might consider contacting a headhunter to help you. Inside, outside, or in the job you should always be testing. Making yourself stand out from the crowd will make this possible. The reason this is essential is because headhunters work for the paying client organisation, not for individuals, so you will have to take responsibility for finding or winning your new role yourself. A career counsellor will help for a fee, but they do not have the skills, insight and motivation of a headhunter (not to mention the contacts). A headhunter might identify you, but their allegiance at all times is to their corporate clients. Headhunters thrive on repeat business, and they will find you if you are a match for any of their client searches. Letting a named headhunter have your details will give you exposure, but no guarantee of placement, except on the offchance that they are looking for someone like you at the right psychological moment. Your best bet is to depend on your own cunning to create your destiny – but use the model of the headhunter's techniques to help yourself.

Do your research, target the organisations where you would like to be (or set up your own firm), and network yourself into the circumstances where you can be hired. If a headhunter does call you, you must be ready. Even if the job is one you want, you will still be competing with other candidates. All candidates will be prepared for meetings with potential employers by the head-hunter, and you will have to market yourself as the best candidate for the job. Your mission is to find your own job, do it quickly and intelligently, and make it into the 'right' job. Follow the head-hunter's example:

- Go after jobs that you know you could do and would be a good match for you. Tailor your paperwork to the exact role after you have researched the employer and the institution. Highlight your unique selling points in your covering letter which you send to a named person.
- Watch out for the emotional roller coaster which happens whether you receive no replies or if you are invited for interview. Immediate offers give an ego boost but may be a long-term regret if you do not take care in checking the chemistry and the details.
- Make sure that the jobs advertised or talked about are real. Treat the initial information as a lead, and be aware that you may be in a numbers game where you will be screened out. There is always a possibility that the job is on someone's hidden agenda or empire-building exercise.
- Research the industry, the company, the department, the location, the team and the interviewer as well as the job. Find out who is the boss's boss. Get to know the secretary, other employees, some customers and some competitors, and only go to the interview if you know that your chances of winning an offer have been maximised ahead of time.

- Check out how you will impress the selection panel/director/ manager/personnel person best.
- Do the job in the interview. This you can do by visualising yourself there in your mind beforehand. Make sure that the employer is convinced that you can do the job you are both discussing.
- Ask for feedback after the interview or the selection process is completed, whether you are successful or not, so that you will have learnt more about yourself and your performance. When there is a headhunter involved make sure that they give you a debriefing.
- Be enthusiastic and quietly confident so that the employer is aware that you really want the job.
- Close the deal. When you are offered the job, most employers want to know if you will take it. It will also be subject to references, and often to the outcome of a medical. Thank them for the offer and say that you are looking forward to receiving it in writing – along with the employment contract, the job description and the start date. You then promise to respond within a given time. Think about any reservations you may have and check them out. Have your employment lawyer check the terms and review the situation carefully. This is a commitment you wish to be able to fulfil. Does anything need to be negotiated? This is another area where you can emulate the headhunter.

    When the offer arrives, contact the employer. They may be surprised how long it has taken to reach you, but at least they now know that you are about to respond. If it is for you, proceed. If it is not for you, thank them and say no quickly.

Understanding the etiquette of presenting yourself is a confidence booster. Persistence will win.

Visualisation

Start well. Go to the best organisation you can find that will provide what you have decided you want and is of the professional calibre appropriate for your aims. It is no longer possible to visualise your working life within just one company, so moving sideways, upwards or outside of the corporate structure may be your choice.

Nobody has an easy time getting to the top. In fact nobody actually admits that is where they are aiming until they are nearly there. Be sure that you are prepared for the struggles at the critical points in your working life, which will surely happen. As a future mover and shaker, a senior executive or even running your own company, are you prepared to be mobile, flexible, innovative and up to date with your communications skills? The smart person is keenly aware of opportunities and has antennae out all the time. Otherwise you never know when the next step is in front of you. There will be key points in your life that may or may not be matched by the stages in the responsibilities you are given. The impetus to buy a house, start a family or take the risk of patenting your latest invention may be curtailed by your cashflow at that time. How are you going to cope?

There will be other times when you have to manoeuvre yourself into position to be recognised, to be in the right place at the right time and to take advantage of the project or promotion that will move you on. Those who stumble at these points are often just as bright and hardworking as those who succeed, but they may have not been sufficiently astute politically or may not have made as much of their assets as they could. Being a hard worker, a keen team player and actively loyal to the group is assumed. Be persistent. Dust yourself down and keep going. It is not the state of the economy that will trip you up – it is yourself. Get help from a mentor, a relevant friend or whoever you can find and share your concerns before they spin out of control. You will get good jobs when you are the best candidate for the role: make sure you are targeting well and equipping yourself sensibly.

Working out your ultimate goal is time well spent – even when it takes several years. Practise looking up from your little patch and get a global view. This is sometimes called the helicopter approach. Learn to see as much as possible of the big picture that is your life in order to recognise the pieces and how they will fit into your blueprint. Women are particularly prone to being task-oriented – keeping involved with the immediate rather than the overall or long-term implications. This bigger view will help increase your independence, because by stopping, thinking and planning you will gain control over your situation rather than simply reacting constantly to urgent requirements. A cautionary note: you must accept, even at an early stage, that it is impossible to separate your work from the rest of your life. You will be affected in one sphere by what is happening in another.

If you want instant acclaim, you will be attracted to jobs where money is related to performance, and where you can show off your success in having the fastest car, travel, night-life and so on. This is different from positioning yourself but may be part of the methods you need to use. High-profile people do get noticed. The disadvantage for the highly public life is that you can rise and fall publicly. Or you may be the sort of person who thrives on reward for effort, in which case, make sure that you find a culture to work in where this is built in. If you do better with long-term security, then find a firm with a brilliant pension plan and package at the end of your time there. You will find that recognition goals recede in importance in times of family or other crisis. Then the comfort goals are paramount. Even a high achiever needs to know that their daily needs can be met when there is illness or a disabled child to be cared for. Your desire for status and applause needs to be strong enough for you to continue when such responsibilities come to the fore. There are times when really difficult choices have to be made, and it is made more complex when others are involved. So your determination to succeed has to be strong and continuous.

Self-confidence

Prepare for the interface with work:

1. Set aside half an hour each day for worrying. So if something goes wrong or a problem arises, plan to think about it in the worry time tomorrow. This frees the brain for clear thinking about the tasks in hand.
2. Learn to confide in people slowly. Start by telling the small, insignificant things and build up to the greater and more

important aspects later. This is the way to accept emotional support and to build confidential relationships for the future.

3. When things go wrong the trick is to consider how much worse they could be at that moment.

4. Learn to express your emotions by writing them down first: what is upsetting, what is pleasing and so on. Practice makes it easier to communicate verbally. There is scientific evidence to show that it is therapeutic to write down problems.

5. Self-esteem is bolstered by thinking beyond the job and the career part of life to include activities and involvement outside the work situation. Work addicts as role models do not have the width of experience to be helpful for confidence.

Fear is the cause of hesitation to speak out about the stresses of managing work and family. Many are in insecure and low-paying, albeit convenient, jobs. They dare not reveal the difficulties, let alone request the changes in working conditions that would alleviate them. Struggles to cope remain hidden, except when worries are shared with a trusted colleague. A female cashier in a supermarket was heard asking her assistant if she thought she might be sacked for taking three days off to look after her sick child.

It is fear of a different kind that keeps professional and management level people silent. Macho cultures that deem long hours to be essential for success and penalise any who challenge the rules, are as powerful a deterrent to the expression of truth as is the fear of losing the job. Many pretend that working fifty hours and more a week in challenging jobs and then raising children in the time that is left over is OK. The arguments as to whether mothers should or should not work rages on. Often fear is at the bottom of the belief that if a female manager gives a hint of uncertainty the 'opposition' will use the opportunity to enforce the argument that she should be at home. This intellectual battle is just below the surface in most organisations. It is not helped by the drip drip of the media, which blames parents for all the wrongdoings of children in school, on the streets or on drugs. There is another hostility to contend with as well. Those parents who are not in work often resent those who are.

Balancing Your Whole Life

Some institutions are better at making it possible for you to balance life at home, work and play successfully. Support systems such as crèches, employee assistance programmes, internal restaurants, dry cleaners and transport systems are often acknowledged to be mutually helpful. When Penny Hughes resigned from her post as President of Coca-Cola UK to be a full-time mother, she was met by a barrage of criticism. She wanted new ways to blend family and working life, believing that life should not be rigidly departmentalised. Four years later, she has created a portfolio career which gives her an income of over £100,000 for ten days' work per month. She is a non-executive director of Next, Beresford, Body Shop and the Mirror Group. She lectures on global branding and cutting-edge management to other top 1000 companies. She is astonished by the variety and quality of the life she is now leading, which is completed by her working husband, two young sons and nanny. She believes in flexibility in work, including the best use of people and the best allocation of time. The energy, time and passion she had put into management, she now gives to the children. She recommends this style of life to those who can arrange portfolio work, but she recognises the necessity for efficient core operating in corporate life too.

The resignation of another high-ranking female executive who wants to spend time with her family has sent a shudder through feminist ranks and reopened the painful debate about pressures on women who attempt to balance motherhood with high-flying careers. Diana Baker earned £553,000 in 1997/8 in salary and bonuses as chief financial officer of the *New York Times* media conglomerate. The shares dropped when her resignation was announced. Brenda Barnes, president of PepsiCo North America, walked away from a £1.24 million salary and was accused of giving companies the perfect excuse not to appoint women to top jobs. Only seven of the top 1000 companies in the USA are run by women anyway. Avon Products Inc. were open to criticism when they recently appointed a male CEO when there was an even better qualified female available. However, the debate was cooled when Lieutenant-Colonel Eileen Collins was appointed the first female commander of an American Space Flight. The next generation should concentrate on believing *There's nothing I can't do*. This is not just a gender issue. Many senior people find it hard to commit to both work and family at the same time, and struggle accordingly. Younger generations are becoming more demanding of their employers to make it all easier. You will have to look at institutional practices and how people cope, and work out if this is applicable to you too.

Organising, delegating, juggling, balancing and making trade-offs are crucial for managing family and work lives successfully. Few of you dare to talk about the feelings of longing, sadness and regret that can characterise your daily experience of trying to balance your lives. Why do you do it? Barbara Cassini, head of the new British Airways cut-price airline, said that she was completely comfortable with her choices. She is unfazed by the daily routine that involves leaving before the children are awake and returning most often just in time to read them a bedtime story. Nicola Horlick wrote her book, *Can You Have It All?*, yet it seems she has failed to grapple with the true emotional and psychological costs of the attempt. Is Kate Figgis right when she writes in her book, *Life After Birth*, that women are economical with the truth about all aspects of motherhood and work-family dilemmas, and cover up to keep their peace of mind? Many are loath to challenge the feminist message that it is possible to have everything.

Working mothers can be cowed by the condemnation of other women. There are myriad examples of women sending faxes within hours of giving birth, referring to their children as their hobby, as one did in an article in the *Guardian* on powerful women, or fathers who join in the conspiracy and deny that life is complicated. Many women really want to be with their children but need to work and are torn apart by their conflicting wishes and aims for fulfilment. Ruby Wax, the comedienne and talk-show presenter, admitted that her life is a mess when it comes to the balance of work and family. She is a brave and outspoken rarity. There is a growing question about the need to work in a male-defined culture which fails to recognise the realities of family life. However, job sharing and the like is helping a little. Some firms are showing an enlightened attitude to the family background of their employees. Asda has introduced term-time-only contracts and shift-swap schemes. Lloyds, TSB and Xerox are experimenting with rearranging work processes to render them more family friendly. Being judged on output rather than the number of hours worked would be helpful.

Leading companies share their best ideas on career management in the belief that they can gain more by divulging their secrets than by keeping them. The notion of 'twinning' came out of discussions on cost-effective development at a meeting in 1997 of the Careers Research Forum. This is a group of senior managers from fifty companies who select topics for research, and then business schools undertake the work. This way they can find out what other organisations have done and whether they have experienced success or failure. Knowing what has worked best curtails duplication and failure elsewhere. Organisations have a number of issues which are common, whether they be strategic, global or local, relate to people or to products, and this network of professionals with similar concerns has proved useful and profitable.

Your Curriculum Vitae

The CV, curriculum vitae, or résumé as it is known in the USA, is an outline of your personal details, qualifications and experience. CVs prepared for headhunters are not necessarily the same as those favoured by potential employers. We look for very brief outlines of careers in clear chronological order, not thematic appraisals without precise facts. Busy people like you will have an up-to-date CV at hand at all times, of course. You never know when it will be useful. So what constitutes a useful CV?

CVs for search firms should always include salary details, age and marital status, because we are not allowed to ask you and our clients really, really want to know. You will help us, so we are more likely to help you. Each CV should be individually prepared using the standard document with core information as a starting and not a finishing point. The document should be an original and not photocopied or printed off a computer on copy paper, and it should be accompanied by a short covering letter highlighting your unique selling points which are relevant to the sector, role or job that you are writing about. Make sure you sign it.

All CVs must be addressed to a named person. Otherwise it will go in the pile for the junior researcher to make a decision as to who to give it to in the firm, or whether to simply put it in the waste bin. Do not be disheartened if you do not hear immediately. 'Switch off' letters, acknowledging your approach, probably mean that you are not what they are looking for at the moment. Try and ask an influential friend who has been headhunted who head-hunted them and ask for an introduction, especially if you are of the same high calibre.

The format of CV that pleases headhunters is one where all the dates of job changes are clearly stated. For senior executives who have not moved for a long time, there may be a problem of breaking down their moves internally in one organisation. Conscientious and professional headhunters will not take the details at face value, but will check their authenticity, and factual data such as educational and professional qualifications are checked automatically.

Using firms or individuals to help make your CV look and sound wonderful is dangerous. First of all, we recognise the format that certain outplacement and career advisers recommend all the time, so it is an indicator that you needed their help. They encourage you to give general statements as opposed to firm track record details with evidence of financial, people and other responsibilities analysed and listed.

If you are offered the job your level of commitment will be discussed, so make it clear why you are interested in moving. Each of your roles to date should have a description of how and why you left.

The headhunter will be alert to your attitude to the salary/package. We will expect you to ask about benefits and stock options, bonuses and perks such as company cars, education and health provision, and offers of travel and low-interest loans. It will be helpful to have a breakdown of your present situation listed on the CV.

The first page will lay out your database type details:
Correct contact telephone numbers and e-mail address
Name and address
Educational qualifications
Professional qualifications
(These will have dates, names of institutions and levels and subjects)
The next two pages will show:
Track Record in current job
description of employer/client organisation
Role
Responsibilities
Any statistical information that is publicly available

References (only after interviews are arranged and you are asked
    for them)
Interests
IT capabilities
Travel, etc.
Community activities

No matter how important and high profile you are, it is not acceptable to send a photocopy of your entry in *Who's Who* or *People of Today*. Always have an up-to-date version of your CV prepared, so that you can tailor it to the profile of the next recipient.

Command and Control

The architect principle is implemented when senior management shapes a firm's structures through the design and redesign of infrastructures necessary for the operation of self-designed teams. Are you a specialist who excels in the efficient scheduling of human, capital and information resources as well as the setting up of incentives for the resources command themselves? Or maybe you are on the control side of the organisation, minimising costs by making information more accessible, monitoring processes, and making the decision makers accountable for the outcomes of their thinking. These activities were all limited in the industrial economy, but now information systems provide immediate feedback which is transforming organisations. You have to be up to date on management information systems, but that does not replace production or service processes. Prioritising is the name of the game.

The more effective an organisation is, the more important the part played by you, the individual. The reverse is true as well. Good people make good teams. When an organisation is ineffective it is likely to be peopled by impotent teams and dysfunctional individuals. You need peripheral vision to work well in today's globe-spanning horizontal organisations. The worldwide climate of recession makes heavy demands on personal performance as well as on corporate strategic thinking for survival. You need technical skills, acceptance of the scope for achievement and resourcefulness to cope with constant challenges. The most important ingredient of the emerging global business network is the participation of all those with drive, imagination, experience and insight who make up the network of professionals. You are not allowed to be passive. Global prospects are great, but the cost of failure is high.

As a potential innovative manager, you have to have your finger on the pulse of operations and listen to what customers say. You have to conceive, suggest and set in motion new ideas that not all of the senior managers will have thought of yet. So just how innovative are you? Find out by checking to see if:

- You are comfortable with change and confident that uncertainties will be clarified. You are the sort of person who has the foresight to see difficulties as opportunities.
- You select projects carefully and use a long-term viewpoint to minimise setbacks on the way to achieving goals.
- You prepare well for meetings and are professional in presentation. You have acquired and use strong political skills.
- You actively encourage subordinates to participate and be part of the hard-working team, as well as providing them with rewards they appreciate and promises which you deliver.
- You are persuasive, persistent and discreet.

There is a strong association between carrying out an innovative idea and using a strong collaborative leadership style. Innovation works best when everyone is invited to contribute. Bill Morton of Morton Associates cites Williams Grand Prix as a classic example. They have one aim: to make their cars go faster. Most innovative companies are privately owned and in growth. James Dyson of the cyclone bag-free vacuum cleaner is the most quoted innovator. Since its launch in 1992, he has achieved 25% of the market. Apart from his determination, the invention of a good product and constant research, he worked hard to find good investment and is now continuing his quest for products designed to make life easier for customers.

New Horizons

The full impact of electronic communications has to be understood. Older people who grew up before these communications options existed may be reluctant to change their familiar patterns, but new generations are bringing new perspectives. Get to know these empowering new technologies as best you can. The more you know about the personal computer, the Internet, e-mail, video-conferencing, virtual banking and shopping and desk-top publishing (to name a few aspects), the less disconcerting and more helpful they will be for you. Technology's role is to provide flexibility and efficiency, and your goal should be to take advantage of it.

No corporation can promise lifetime employment, and no employee is expecting it any more. Headhunters are the new 'princes of industry', with their scope increasing as employee loyalty decreases. Stephen Rowlinson of Merton Associates/ Bartlett Recruitment Advertising believes that corporate loyalty is dead and is leading his group forward to making recruitment more effective at all levels and across all sectors. Clients use headhunters to find upper management people who are qualified for the emerging competitive world. Staff and middle managers apply to the advertisements and manage themselves better in a shrinking market. You will have to deal with an increasing amount of insecurity, and this will make you pursue your own goals no matter who or where your employer is at any time.

Anthony Sampson, in *Company Man*, sees exciting visions for a new era. He quotes Charles Handy from *The Age of Unreason* (1994) as looking forward to a 'post-heroic manager' whose job would be to develop others' capacity like a good teacher, and predicting that the word manager would disappear in the new un-stratified society. Handy saw company jobs developing in the wider context of life patterns, leisure and fulfilment, and pre-dicted that organisational life would be a small part of people's working life. Sampson goes on to show that liberation from bureaucratic employers frees you up to make many other choices. Short-term contracts and project management are now common working methods. The young are not expecting to work any other way.

How are you thriving in this marketplace? It is a more demand-ing master than any single boss, while customers are becoming more unreasonable, demanding instant availability and flexibility. Computerised controls, requiring instant reactions and decisions, impose their unseen discipline so that you have to combine your search for inner harmony with real commercial and competitive actions. The lone operator, the hired gun or the mercenary is the new model. You have to be flexible and mobile, joining and leaving short-term assignments and teams, or forming and reforming small companies like the entrepreneurs in Silicon Valley. You will have to transform yourself to survive and prosper. Take heart, take risks and take action.

· 4 ·

Positioning: To Be Headhunted

Seek and ye shall find . . .

Who Does What

Headhunters, or executive search consultants, as we like to be
known, have been roaming the USA since the 1930s and have
existed in the UK since the 1950s, when Peter Brook set up the
first office, which has expanded into the major group called
Spencer Stuart. There are now estimated to be over 700
recruitment companies and more than 7000 consultants operating
in the UK, with a growing number expanding across Europe and
the rest of the world. There is some confusion about the levels of
recruitment methods outside organisations, but basically there are
three types:

1. An agency (handling mainly vacancies with salaries between
£10,000 and £40,000) will use databases of clients and applicants
to provide a brokerage service by matching career details to
organisational needs. They are successful for junior managers,
especially within accountancy, computer and information technology, and administration.
2. Search and selection consultancies (dealing with salaries of
£20,000 upwards) conduct assignments through advertising, by
search or a combination of search and selection. They are widely

used by the public and voluntary sectors, which concentrate more on equal opportunities and fair and open competition. Selection covers mainly operational vacancies and middle management, notably marketing, sales, production, systems, engineering, finance, general management and specific functions.

3. The executive search consultancies (dealing with salaries over £40,000) usually look for the appropriate candidates through research (sometimes with advertising), and with much consultation with the client, with sources and with targeting people. They look for the best people for the best jobs, no matter where in the world they may be working at that time. They provide selection advice, candidate counselling, remuneration and other negotiation, alongside the search process. Chief executives, non-executive directors and most senior positions are filled by headhunters.

When an organisation has a senior position to be filled they will either have someone in mind for promotion or they will have to find a suitable person elsewhere. Search is an extremely successful method of finding the best person for the post and is being used more and more for senior and reporting roles. This assumes a high level of professionalism and confidentiality.

The old-boy network is no longer reliable, but it was the starting point for headhunting. When senior people were discharged from the services after the war and hit the outside world, they needed guidance to find a new role. This came from a network of post-war officers who talked to each other about who could do certain jobs. That network has now evolved to a process-driven, lateral thinking, thoroughly researched consultancy-based industry. Up until ten years ago the message was 'Find them a job' when an old school contact or colleague introduced a friend or relation to the recruiter or organisation. Now it is realised that talent and ability probably matter more than where you come from, though 'nods and winks' still work sometimes. Life may still be helped by 'who you know', but it is becoming more difficult in this rapidly changing world of work.

The System

Headhunters are looking for active, successful people at all times. The mysterious and secretive world of the search professional is dependent on the client requiring senior people to fill specified roles and on building a relationship with that client. Search is monitoring what senior executives are doing at all times and deciding when is the right time to approach them. This is the scenario, whether it is City high-fliers or core professionals within global companies or bright young creative people who are wanted.

People are sometimes tracked for many years, possibly without ever being contacted or aware of the process. Often, when a headhunter calls you to ask 'if you know someone' who would fit a role, they are testing you as well as tapping your knowledge of your colleagues and your network. It is the business of the headhunter to know who is doing what where, why and how. They are constantly gathering information, and the clients are the beneficiaries. Attention to detail does not fit the common perception of a glamorous, dining-at-the-Ritz lifestyle, but it is a crucial aspect of the headhunter's work.

The latest senior appointments in the City, big business, government agencies and elsewhere have been the outcome of search and selection systems and discussions rather than just internal promotions. It is estimated that 98% of the City's corporate players and institutions now use outside help to make these key appointments. Headhunters are taken on exclusively by the client to find a particular person for a particular job. In order to be taken seriously by their clients, headhunters have to have been successful in their own careers before joining the headhunting fraternity. Miles Broadbent was high up in IBM and Grand Met before becoming the confidant of the captains of industry and finding people such as Sir Richard Sykes of Glaxo Wellcome and Sir Clive Thompson of Rentokil. David Kimbell of Spencer Stuart used to be in the motor industry; Yve Newbold of Heidrick and Struggles came from being Company Secretary at Hansons; Christopher Sykes is a Mandarin speaker from the Hong Kong Police; while Rae Sedel of Russell Reynolds has used her background in telecoms to make 'lots of money'. Recruitment agencies find jobs for people; headhunters find people for jobs.

The more senior the job, the more specific the details and the deeper the relationship with the client need to be. The search and selection industry has ballooned in the last decade. Being head-hunted has become progressively more precise and scientific. The days when headhunters used their social contacts, had long lunches in their clubs and had a notebook of appointees have gone. Now the headhunter relies on a database, researchers and access to worldwide information to gain a greater knowledge and understanding of client needs and to be able to respond quickly and effectively. Prospective candidates have to be creative as well as professional, just like the headhunters.

It is a lucrative business because the unit price is high. The Internet is a serious threat to the growth of the existing consultancies because it allows direct access to candidates. Head-hunters typically charge a high minimum fee, and they relate the fee to the remuneration package of the job, often agreeing a percentage of around 30%. The big firms also have a minimum charge for expenses, based on 15–20% of the fee. However, negotiation on a fixed fee basis is becoming more common. The terms of business of most headhunters give the client the opportunity to cancel at certain stages, but the usual practice is to be paid whether the job is filled or not.

Ultimately the decision about who is appointed is up to the company or organisation itself, but the headhunter is expected to present a strong short list from which to choose. There is currently a shortage of high-calibre middle-management people with certain experience and qualifications, which has led to an increase in the number of search projects being done lower down the salary levels. Up until recently, jobs paying under £40,000 were under-taken by recruiters and selection processes, but with the increasing scarcity of skills and knowledge, search is now relevant there too.

Howgate Sable, search and selection, which is based in Manchester, Leeds, Newcastle and London, found that it en-hanced its credibility nationally by having an association with an American firm with a network of offices there. They also have their own website on the Top Jobs part of the Internet. In the London office, Paul Carvosso and Ian Robertson say that their global clients expect headhunters to be able to meet requirements regardless of location, and they are satisfied that Howgate Sable can deliver. Headhunters are proud of their records of successful appointments.

The Search Process

Assignment Management is dependent on agreed dates for each stage. The average timescale from commencement to completion is twelve weeks.

Stage 1: Specification, Research and Report to Client
The headhunter might be approached by an existing client, or by a new client who has responded to a recommendation or the reputation of the headhunter for specialist knowledge. The assignment might even come from winning a contest with other headhunters after a presentation formula.

Step One: Two-way briefings with the client

Detailed discussion with the client leads to:
- Full understanding of the institution and its objectives
- Agreement in writing of the brief and the 'ideal' candidate specification
- Listing of key target industries/organisations

Step Two: Briefing the researchers

- Research of targets to identify potential candidates
- Computer file search for candidates and sources
- Use of external business information services as necessary
- Informal references, recommendations, personal contacts, published material

Step Three: Progress report to client
This should be a systematic and thorough review of target organisations and relevant people working there. It starts with a

quick analysis of the existing database, checking off-limit clients, alerting outside database providers with specifications and descriptions of the client requirements and arranging the team for specific responsibilities. The research manager will be the person who has the deepest experience of the sector, the function and previous searches. The contact researcher will be the person with the most relevant language, telephone and Internet experience; the assignment researcher will work closely with the headhunter to meet deadlines and client specifics. Sometimes these aspects are all covered by one researcher. Regular reports will be produced and checking carried out on qualifications and key CV information of identified candidates. The client is encouraged to look at the reports, which include personal details, candidate track record and appraisals, and add to the information flow at any time.

Stage 2: Attracting potential candidates
This involves:

- Making it happen
- Arranging for the headhunter to meet the potential candidates
- Evaluating the candidates against the 'ideal' specification
- Counselling the client and each candidate throughout the selection process
- Close involvement with preferred candidatures to resolve doubts, reservations and outstanding issues so as to ensure complete commitment
- Acting as intermediary in negotiation for all terms prior to the written offer, followed by reference checks
- Follow-up contacts with client and candidate at appropriate intervals after the starting date (these become long-term sources and potential purchasers)

Step Four: Contacting candidates
Identified potential candidates are contacted, either by the researcher or by the headhunter, to discuss their possible interest and suitability for the job. Then the headhunter will arrange a meeting, either in or out of the office as appropriate, to take matters further. Candidates will have been sent the job/person

specification and required profile as well as organisational information. Where it is a sensitive appointment this will only be available at the actual meeting. The candidate should always try to find out exactly who the client is and what precisely the job is all about. When the headhunter is cagey, I advise candidates to refuse to continue, because I believe that it is a two-way situation where there must be mutual trust. Candidates must expect to be probed, analysed and scrutinised about their CV and then answer open-ended questions about team play, dealing with difficult people, flexibility, innovation and success to date.

Step Five: Long- and short-listing stages
The headhunter will do a candidate report on the long-listed candidates and show it to the client. Other candidates who know they are in the frame need to be 'switched off'. Short-listed candidates will have another meeting to prepare them for the agreed selection process, which can range from a short head-to-head meeting with the client to months of meeting key directors and managers in varied locations. In sectors other than the private, it is possible that you could be called before panels of up to thirty people at any one time. It is helpful to have the head-hunter in attendance at the time of the final/appointment interviews to manage the situation so that everyone involved is aware of what needs to be decided.

Step Six: Testing and use of other management tools
Step Seven: Interviewing
Step Eight: The offer/references/medical check

Stage 3: Securing a successful appointment
Step Nine: Contract negotiation and introduction to the employer group
Short-term contracts need to be dealt with by an employment lawyer just as much as detailed employment contracts do. In the euphoria of the appointment it is easy for the appointee to overlook the importance of the written agreement, and the headhunter has to encourage them to arrange everything before joining. It is essential to making relationships flourish and the job

work – and having damage limitation covered if there does end up being a problem.

Step Ten: Feedback and follow-up
Whether you are a successful or unsuccessful candidate, the professional headhunter will take time to debrief with you. This encourages you to learn from every experience and leaves you with a better impression of the potential employer than if you are left up in the air with no information.

Headhunters are the best informed people you will ever meet. We hear details of the internal workings of organisations all day. This comes from clients, interviewing candidates and applicants, talking to sources and listening everywhere we go. Beware of how much detail you go into at interview . . . However, these flows of knowledge work in everyone's interest because of the levels of confidentiality and the way it all helps the matchmaking process.

Employment Climate

When there is a flourishing economy and low unemployment, confidence rises, and this makes it difficult for some businesses to find the 'ideal' candidate for key posts. In a candidate-driven market it is sensible to use as many ways of finding people as possible.

Networking is an effective way of talking about the job with people who understand the role and might even know some candidates who would be good for the company. It has the advantage of starting the selection process with candidates who are already known to people for whom the potential employer has regard. Even during a global recession, headhunters will be used to find the core people. The more formal route is to appoint an agency or to place an advertisement and process the replies internally. When times are tough, as they have been for the last decade in the construction industry, which was first into the last recession and the last out of it, all routes to finding candidates have to be explored. Traditionally the construction industry has always depended on subcontracting and casual labour, so labouring staff are used to being hired and fired as the work flows and disappears.

Such flexibility is not so readily practised at management and executive level. This is a model for the general workplace in the next decade.

Retaining staff between projects is a problem. People have to take any opportunity that arises, so corporate loyalty drops down the list of their priorities. Many high-calibre people have moved into other industries and geographical areas when approached. Those who have stayed within the industry are now getting some payback and see themselves as valuable commodities. Training and personnel development drop down the spending budgets when a company is under pressure, and this affects the skill base of the firm. This leads in turn to a high demand for people who have specialised experience and expertise.

The shift in the balance of power between employer and potential management employee is often ignored, but employers are finding out that they have to become smarter at recruiting and retaining the people they really need. Candidates who are in a strong position can negotiate well for the packages that will suit them best. For example, key technical staff in all sectors are at a premium. Recruiters have to be able to identify and persuade these people into appointments – at times this will necessitate massaging egos. As new markets open up and overlap or replace the traditional employers, candidates and applicants need to be alert about where to focus their efforts. For example, for contractors and consulting engineers there are opportunities in the emerging markets of the railway and the private finance initiative projects.

Recruitment decisions are often based on sideways moves, which means offering a job to someone who has carried out a similar job in the recent past. It is more exciting for the headhunter to take a risk and identify you when it is the next logical step in your career and where your potential is obvious. You will be more motivated by meeting the challenges rather than having to do more of the same and ending up going round and round the same mulberry bush. Upward progression helps your medium- and long-term personal development and provides a strong base for your work, ensuring satisfaction and an inclination to remain with the employer who gives you the broadest experience. The secret of successful recruitment is to identify the people with potential and confidence who are progressing with their lives rather than 'cruising on the flat road of trouble-free mediocrity'. Strong candidates look for innovation and the potential for progression in their jobs as they recognise the motivating forces that work well for them. Search and selection is based on 90% research/applications/targeted candidates and 10% inspiration.

Clients

Employers are using headhunters and recruitment agencies more and more to find star players for senior roles, especially since they have cut back on their personnel departments. Sectors such as healthcare and retailing have joined the business purchasers of these services. There has been a massive increase in the last two years in the number of appointments filled with outside professional help. Charities and the voluntary sector have now accepted that it is OK to use fund-raised money for professional services, including headhunting.

Headhunters are accustomed to the matchmaker role they often play and emphasise their usefulness as negotiators between the employer and the employee. There is a growing practice of tailoring the package to the individual rather than just costing the job, and this takes time and trouble to achieve the best results for all involved. When you are directly approached (as opposed to when you reply to an advert), you are in a strong position for negotiating. You will also get an ego boost that you have been sought, identified and found. You have the impression that the headhunter, unlike the recruiter, is working for you and not just filling a space. For various reasons, the sectors desperate for strong candidates at present are construction, engineering, IT and technical services. Anyone working in these areas with good qualifications, accumulated experience, strong communication skills, numeracy and developed literacy will soon find themselves in the headhunter's net.

Organisations must develop the skills of those who are already there and promote them if they want them to stay. But with constant change, there is always the need for new blood, both as staff and as leaders. All the ideas of mental and physical flexibility, job sharing, portfolio life, home-based work, lifelong learning and talented cultures, necessary for the nineties and through the millennium, are more in the gurus' minds than on the shop-floor and in the office in the UK at the moment. For example, British workers have the longest working hours in the West and have an idiosyncratic view of the current practice of open-plan work spaces – they hate it.

Making Appointments Work

Employers make bad purchases from time to time. Over a third of managers are in jobs that do not work out as well as expected. The average cost of a graduate appointment which is short-term is about £70,000, so more senior placements and training cost even more. 'Surviving the Honeymoon', a report published by Sanders and Sidney (the outplacement firm) which was based on interviews with 100 employers and 217 employees, indicated that everyone involved may learn something from the experience, but the company has to bear costs which are on average spread over eleven months. The boss was cited as the main reason for the manager not fitting well into the job. Clearly it is essential to meet and evaluate a potential new boss before agreeing to a job; better still, discuss the role with future colleagues before accepting.

Sometimes there is the temptation to appoint from the 'best at the time' rather than continuing the search. Mutual expectations of both employer and employee need to be explored and checked for reality. The headhunter can be useful in making sure that they really know what each is offering the other before acceptance. You will not automatically be told about the organisational objectives or receive a full and clearly stated job description, so you should ask and make sure you get the information before you commence. Once you arrive in the new position, find out what resources and support are there for you to be able to perform well. Conversely, an employer can avoid the massive expense and disruption caused by an unsuccessful appointment by supporting the new recruit in developing themselves within the group through internal and external training, and by the provision of a mentor/coach as available.

Graduate Recruitment

The *Sunday Times* Survey of Graduate Careers in 1998 charted the progress of one in five final year students at the universities most favoured by recruiters. In March, 32% of the 10,102 students had accepted offers and a further 17% had applied and were waiting to hear. Of the remainder, 19% were planning post-graduate studies, 8% were doing independent work, 16% were going travelling and only 8% had no ideas. Management consultancy is the most popular job at present, followed by marketing, accountancy and engineering.

Employing new graduates means that a process to meet objectives in the organisation's strategic plan is in place. Usually the focus is on hiring the best possible candidates in order to train them up to be tomorrow's business leaders. Despite the huge success of non-technical people in the business of computing and the vast salaries they earn, today's students are still wearing blinkers when it comes to considering IT as a career. The latest research by Apex Computer Recruitment confirms that students think the subject is too technical and complicated, and the kiss of death on their social lives. Those who have studied IT lack vital business and social skills, and this holds them back more than an absence of good exam results. Seven out of ten companies will not recruit new graduates because they have not acquired the necessary combination of technical skills and business acumen. Recruitment professionals, internally or externally, will understand ways to attract, retain and advance the candidates with potential. Consequently, the continuous development of leading-edge, practical and appropriate initiatives is of paramount importance. Furthermore, the recruiter, acting on behalf of the employer, has to have a passionate belief in the contribution that motivated, aligned and empowered graduates can make to a constantly changing core business. All headhunters and recruiters have to have lateral thinking, vision, imagination, energy and flair – just like the eventual short-listed candidates whom they identify.

Searching for Work

You will suffer from frustration at some stage when you are busy looking for work. One common experience is being invited for a meeting with consultants who do not have a particular role in mind and who do not pay travel expenses. Often this is due to your style and career not matching up to the paperwork which had encouraged the person to call you in the first place. As for getting your expenses – did you ask? It is rare for a consultant to pay something towards your expenses, unless you ask for it. You may find these suggestions helpful:

1. Sending your CV into the ozone is a complete waste of time. This is especially true of the headhunting offices. The CVs that are sent on spec to such agencies/consultancies (on average, 200 per day) are dealt with by the most junior researcher because they are regarded as a paper-flow dilemma and of little value to the headhunter. It is now too expensive to reply to unsolicited post. Most CVs end up in the bin. Find someone who has been headhunted recently and get the name of the headhunter concerned from them so that you can introduce yourself and send your CV to a named person who is likely to be interested in what you have to offer.
2. Beware of head-shunting. If you are in a dead-end job and a headhunter suddenly calls you with an amazing possible job offer, take a deep breath and listen carefully. Some companies have started to use headhunters to get rid of people they no longer want. This reduces the amount they have to pay out and the possibility of an industrial tribunal or similar. This is head-hunting in reverse.
3. Database agencies are to be avoided. These add CVs to their database and send them on a scatter-gun basis to any company they come across in the hope that their suggestions will be used. You will never know where your paperwork has gone or who has considered you and for what purpose. You run the risk of your own employer being alerted to the fact that you are looking elsewhere.
4. Advertisements should be read regularly so that you become

familiar with house styles, corporate image and the frequency of inserts. Jobs are rarely completely fictitious, so take care with your replies: tailor your CV to the stated requirements and use a brief covering letter to highlight your unique and positive points. Try to ensure that you are a 90%-plus fit before wasting your time and creating more frustration. Watch the *Sunday Times*, the *Financial Times* and the *Economist*, as well as specialist columns in professional journals. You should also check other newspapers on special days when they cover your area of interest – for example, the *Guardian* used to have the most adverts for jobs in the public sector and in charities, particularly at the middle and lower levels. When answering an advertisement you need to be alert to the effect your application will have.

Studying regular recruitment advertising and information packs is the most successful way for the young to find out about the employment market. Employers may state that there are long hours or user unfriendly locations, and this will help to save time and numerous useless applications. Conversely, candidates are getting more skilled in matching their CVs to corporate descriptions and needs. Scatter-gun approaches and job-hunting on a generalised basis do not work: the more specific the targeting is both ways, the more the employers and potential employees can agree. The very best graduates are looking for challenge and want to be stretched within the role, so the recruiting companies should focus on the levels really required.

For the global marketplace, languages are essential. Formerly the world need was for French, German and Spanish, the latter being the most widely spoken language in the Western world. Now there is a scarcity of Westerners who communicate in Mandarin, Japanese and Portuguese, though English is still the most used internationally.

Personnel departments give applications and approaches the most demoralising responses. The 'people who like to work with people' are often the ones who demonstrate the least understanding. Sometimes the department seems to be a competitor to the parent company, determined to make sure that no appointments are made. Profiles seem to be set by clerks who have no knowledge of the role and are too self-protective to check with anyone who does. This happens in organisations like the National Health Service and other large public bodies too. Spec letters are rarely read by the decision-maker in the receiver organisation. So make sure that it is addressed to a named person whom you have identified in the company, employer office or consultancy who will be pleased to hear from you because they deal with the roles you are seeking.

Communicating

1. Using the Internet

Recruitment agencies are seeking an increase in the volume of both clients and applicants. There are more graduates in the marketplace, with many of them prepared to take short-term employment, and the Internet is proving to be very useful for them. The Federation of Recruitment and Employment Services (FRES), has launched a finder service on the Internet. This offers candidates and would-be employers the chance to find the most relevant agency by surfing their list and sifting through the details of the association's 4700 members. The site is divided into geographical regions, sectors and functions. Many of the agencies have their own specific sites as well. With no office, no interviewing rooms and no bulletin boards full of 'situation vacant' cards, a new virtual jobs agency is up and running.

The Internet recruitment agencies are burgeoning. For example, Chris Pawsey has already been successful with his agency, Yelcom. He gives the example of a Moscow-based Russian who signed on seeking work anywhere as a technical copywriter. This bilingual candidate can work from home and have work sent over the Internet, and is being kept busy. Pawsey has nine years' experience in IT and global services, so he had the experience to set up the database of teleworkers, the web site and the Windows-style icon facility for CVs. He intends that access will be simple for employers and candidates alike. By actively going out to build a global skills base, Pawsey has extended the traditional ways of recruiting to a speedy and ongoing communications network. The

Internet is regarded as the latest technical development, but it is actually a very different animal from the telephone or fax, and none of us really understands its implications. For recruitment purposes, there are some caveats:

- It is a very public form of communication. Every time you visit a site or give someone your e-mail address you are leaving a footprint and giving the unscrupulous clues about yourself. It also gives headhunters access to a whole organisation, like an internal directory, and there are few regulations about the use of your information. Other recruiters have 'advice' web sites, and if you respond you are automatically transferred on to their database.
- When recruiting, the most important stage of the matchmaking between the employer and candidates is the face to face meetings. You can have the best possible paperwork and telecommunications skills, but the minute you walk through the door other messages are given immediately. This can never be superseded by the Internet.
- Unless the headhunter is prepared to invest in new software all the time, finding people online will lose its effectiveness.
- The increased functionality of each person in a team on a creative and changing role basis means that what works today will be different tomorrow, so assessing your potential is more useful than just the track record, which is all the Internet and any other database can provide.
- The expectations of the employer, applicants and candidates are raised as they send information down the line and wait for a positive response.
- Interviews can be done on screen. Is this a real substitute for the personal meeting? It is useful for first discussions and saves air fares but eventually people have to talk to each other in the same place.

2. The telephone

The telephone is still the most important form of communication for the headhunter. This is how we keep in touch with sources, and how we make the first contact with you when you are a potential candidate. Typically the headhunter rings round the contacts when the next assignment is beginning. When the same name comes up over and over again, and it is reiterated by the researchers, then the headhunter gets on the phone. When you get the call, take control. If it does not suit you to talk at that moment, say so. Arrange to call back at a set time. This is the same way you should deal with any approaches from the media too. It saves hasty statements or giveaways which happen when you are caught off guard.

3. Interviews

Professional interviewing and use of the formal interview are the most used selection techniques. If they are properly focused and analysed, interviews are very effective. An experienced interviewer is aware of the need for:

• Planning and preparation, which are the key components of good interviewing technique
• Provision of private, comfortable surroundings with refreshment, heat control and good tables and seating for the interviewer and the candidates
• Panel or individual – the number of interviewers is immaterial but they should all be introduced
• Previous instructions – structuring the session with clear guidelines about what is going to happen
• Process – job specification, person profile, company history available
• Practical work tests geared to the role

Body language is potent in the interview situation. It works both ways, so just as the interviewer will be reading the signs in the candidate, so you can read their signals too. The total impact of a message is generally accepted as 7% verbal (words only), 38% vocal (tone, inflection and other sounds), and 55% non-verbal (Institute of Personnel Development). Dress well and then forget about your clothing so that you can concentrate on communicating well on other levels.

After the initial discussions of your track record to date, the enlightened interviewer will want to know more about you as a 'whole person'. When they ask you apparently simple questions such as 'What do you like doing in your spare time?' it is your opportunity to sell your wares all over again. What about the community, playing sport with others, family, eccentric interests, technical prowess, creative writing and so on? You are making statements about your personality and about your level of comfort in different social circles. Interestingly, the most often stated hobby in the eighties was fell-walking – a curious reflection of the 'loner' in the yuppie world.

There are some interviewers who take the opportunity to goad you into debate or discuss controversial issues. Provided you do not try to dominate the conversation, this is a chance to demonstrate your level of articulacy, analytical skills and quickness of thinking. Always let the interviewer think they have 'won' the point at the end. Clients like to know that they are recruiting people who can stand their corner. Avoid riding your hobby horses and try to think comparatively. It helps if you understand why certain questions are being asked. For example, when you are questioned or given the opportunity to talk about your spare time activities, it is more to see if you are a team player than just to know whether you like sports. The interviewer is keen to find out whether you like to take responsibility, whether you are creative, and how outgoing you are.

Your qualifications may show your academic ability and opportunism but that is also the case for anyone with a recognisable CV. What is being looked for is what makes you distinctive – what differentiates you from the competition. Past achievements are an indicator. The employer is keen to assess your future potential. Are you a risk taker? Are you an initiator/finisher?

Why do the same questions get asked in various ways? There are subtle emphases which you need to listen for carefully. For example – 'How comfortable would you be in moving offices annually?' and 'Do you want to change your scene regularly?' One is testing your wishes and the other is checking your tolerance. Putting open questions and listening to the answers is a sign of a good interviewer. The guiding principle for the interviewer is not to make snap judgements, but to collate as much information and to check details as carefully as possible, before comparing the candidates and creating the short list.

The experienced interviewer will not ask questions which have gender, ethnic, religious or sexual implications. The routine interviewer will record the interview and probably have a check list of questions as well as giving a briefing on the job to the candidate. This enables the candidate to respond well and to ask questions which are relevant and show an intelligent insight into the situation. Employers are looking for easy, reliable and effective ways of sifting applicants and identifying candidates who will succeed after appointment.

4. Psychometric testing

Psychometric testing and interactive interviews conducted via video tape/computer are used increasingly often. Methods are becoming less interviewee-friendly and more standardised. The use of interactive testing using the Internet is now used as a matter of course, especially where a large number of people are being recruited at the same time. Computers are regarded as more objective, and make good use of everyone's time. The drawback is that you could be asked to fill in the same questionnaires each time you are in the frame for a job.

The traditional view of selection testing is to assess the suitability of candidates given the stated attributes of the job and to make necessary decisions. Selection is also a way for job seekers to judge their level of credibility with potential employers. According to Dr. Robert McHenry, chairman of Oxford Psychologists Press, future assessment methods will place emphasis on doing as opposed to knowing, and will be more creative, practical and fun. He wants selection tests to relate to the intended work environment and to the things which the candidate will be doing on a daily basis. They should also measure how people learn rather than what they already know and understand. This change has not happened yet. Large companies have set up internal assessment centres as well as using outside consultants. They use them as objective, systematic and helpful ways of finding out and checking what candidates have to offer and their potential. This is valid especially in the cases of those who have not yet achieved a track record of work.

Candidates can and should prepare for assessment. Being able to walk into an interview with confidence and looking good is now assumed. Selection techniques can require simulation exercises, individual and group exercises, role play, personality tests, aptitude tests, group and one-to-one discussions and presentations. Preparation is difficult but essential. Buying typical test books from the local bookstore is now possible. Familiarity with the language and layout of written and multiple choice tests is helpful. This will not necessarily increase scores but it minimises the shock factor. Candidates are compared with each other at the time and with the preordained sample group of the expected standards. It is not a competition and should not be entered into in such a way. The candidate scores brownie points by demonstrating team-work rather than bullying tactics. Assessors collate useful information from the group and individual behaviours. Answering personality and similar tests quickly and honestly is the best bet. The questions have been carefully structured to balance any manipulation which candidates may try to invent. Preparation by practising role play and other things with friends is useful too. Increasing fluency of thought and speech before going to a new situation releases energy for thinking on the spot.

The whole question of testing as part of the interview process is a vexed one. For example, why ask a mathematician to take numerical tests? The answer is that the application of numbers in the business situation is another set of skills compared with academic ability. Also it is to give straight comparisons with other candidates. Where questionnaires are used either before or during the interview take the view that you are being given a chance to display your knowledge and abilities. They are carefully weighted and checked so do not try to 'double guess' them. The objective assessment of candidates is a serious tool to aid the employer in coming to a successful appointment. Pay attention and treat them with respect. The need for more accurate methods of testing is always under discussion both by the practitioners and the purchasers. The psychometrics industry is an oligopoly of a small number of companies that have little competition and face little economic pressure to change. Clients are still accepting information and answers based on very old data and expectations. Technology needs to be continuously developed and needs to progress within the testing and interactive formats.

Conventional ability tests measure a narrow range of skills, where employers are looking for more creative talents and practical skills. The candidates can have their recruitment possibilities dogged by the results of inappropriate testing. It has been acknowledged that personality tests have gaps in the areas of gender and ethnicity. So what is being done? A new range of tests, 'aptitude for business learning exercises' (ABLE is one of the ways which is being offered). The testers provide all the information necessary for the candidate to perform well rather than checking up on knowledge and experience already gained. The emphasis is on assessing how well people learn and their ability to adapt what they learn and apply it. For example, on testing aptitude for financial applications, the candidates are shown how to use ratios to assess the viability of projects and tested on how they apply them. The aim is to have fairness in the testing. Women do less well with numeracy than men, and this has been balanced. Other subtle advantages are shown by Dr. Steve Blinkhorn, director of Psychometric Research and Development, linked with Robert McHenry and the Oxford Psychologists Press, based on motivation. They are still working on senior testing and are aiming to demonstrate strategic thinking and decision analysis. It is a slow march towards change. It seems to take fifteen to twenty years for new tests to appear in a refined form.

The dilemma for global testing of existing and potential employees by applying tests built under one set of cultural traditions to people from other cultures still needs to be solved. Cross-border testing is a universal problem. Language translations, local performance indicators, individualistic behaviour patterns, hard skills and communications/soft skills all have to be taken into account when applying a battery of tests for any appointment. In the UK, SHL is the leading testing firm, using their own professionals to administer and advise on the tests which are relevant according to their knowledge of the client and their analysis of the job. The Occupational Personality Questionnaire (OPQ) test is the most used by SHL as it is based on the soft skills analysis which is the most easily transferable test. The OPQ instrument has been developed to provide more dimensions and a more subtle profile than other available tests. Multinationals are looking for a standardised set of tests which they can use world wide but the psychologists are resisting providing quick model-built solutions. The development of Extranets, allowing access to a web site by password only, offers new scope for testing on an interactive basis.

References

Don't let your former employer throw a spanner in the works before you even start your new job. After you have had a successful job search, or been headhunted, and the appointment is to be confirmed subject to references, have you made the preparations for a smooth finish?

Your CV was impressive, your presentation before the selection panel worked well, the letter of offer has arrived and all that remains is the references. It is sensible to alert referees at the stage when you think a job offer may be forthcoming. Personal referees are easier than employers because it does not put your existing job in jeopardy. Make sure that they are prepared for the phone call from the new organisation, that they have a copy of the job specification and person profile for information and checking. They should also have a copy of the CV which you have used for this particular job.

Then at the latest possible moment, but not the last moment, decide who you need to inform at your existing employment and brief them. An employer is under no obligation to give a reference, but much can be read into the situation if they don't. This means that it is worth your while to be diplomatic, grovelling or do whatever is necessary to get what you really, really want. References have to be produced giving due care to the accuracy of the statements. Legal action can be taken if the referee is overly favourable or defamatory, neither of which is helpful for the new employer, or indeed for the employee. It is common practice for new employers to have an informal chat with people they know in your old firm. You have got to make it clear when you are going through the recruitment process that you do not want anyone contacted until an appointment is on offer because you are happy in your job, do not want to upset the applecart and the move is not necessarily known to your boss. These are sensitive situations and you must think, plan and talk to the recruiter, headhunter or company representative carefully.

Giving away trade secrets or carrying information across to a competitor is the usual reason for disagreements at the time of exiting from one job and entering another. The more senior the role, the more essential it is to have the advice of an employment lawyer and the reference stage is when this relationship often begins. Where there is a good work record, the transition can be managed and kept simple. If there has been a bad situation, work criticism or a falling out, then things get very tetchy and the withholding of references is often used as a weapon by the more senior person. Again, there are legal implications here.

A reference may not be worth the paper it is written on, but the fact that it exists is the comfort factor which the new employer needs. It is a source of checking the CV, at the level of dates, responsibilities, achievements and contributions to company life. Usually there are standard statements and in some trades and professions there is an unacknowledged code for good, bad and indifferent performers; reliable or unreliable, and so on. If you need a reference, always get the consent of the person before you name them. Do not attach written references to CVs or list the names of referees as a matter of course. You need to tailor each list to the situation. One of my favourite habits when checking out people on behalf of their potential employer, was to ask for a boss, a friend and a person who worked for them. Guess who gave the most interesting information? If you are unable to give your last employer's name, ask someone in the company (director, supervisor or manager) to referee for you. Otherwise ask an outside source or even a previous employer.

Anyone who has been dismissed needs to negotiate a reference as part of their settlement terms. If you are asked to give a reference for an employee, confine your comments to checkable information, i.e. to the relevant parts of their employment with you – do not give a personal comment on their capabilities for the new position. When you take up references, make sure you have the permission of the candidate/applicant. If you are rejected after your references have been given, the employer is not obliged to give you a detailed explanation, just that 'the references are unsatisfactory'. They are not legally required to tell you the contents.

Being the Best

Each time you reach for a more responsible position, the selection process gets tougher. The new surroundings, teams and colleagues mean that your abilities, personality traits, your life-style, values and aspirations will all be vigorously scrutinised by your colleagues and also your bosses. Do you know how to handle yourself when you are under the microscope? If you are to realise your ambitions, now is the time to learn how to do justice to yourself and prepare for formal selection processes.

Learn about the different ways you can access the way into a different institution, gain a more sophisticated understanding of how headhunters work and learn to position yourself to be found easily. Taking advantage of any situation to maximise your visibility is very useful. Even when you are not offered a particular job for which you have been considered, do leave an impression which will remain in the mind of the headhunter for other possibilities.

You owe it to yourself to have positioned yourself and performed to such an extent throughout the selection that you are satisfied that the decision has been made with the greatest amount of up-to-date and accurate information about your capabilities and unique selling points. Do you know what they are and do you have some stories prepared which will illustrate them well?

· 5 ·

Positioning: Dealing With Information

Mastering an area of change and innovation is about using change to create change.
        Michael Frye, Chairman of Business Links, London

What Is It?

Each generation is working faster. You are feeling the impact of the information age, which is manifesting itself everywhere. Levels of data, the amount of records and details, global access and technological know-how have all been accelerating at a confusing rate. Whether you are producing a line of goods or switching on the washing machine, you are activating the microchips embedded in their works. Since the introduction of the Intel processor in 1971 there has been an upsurge of available hardware and software in the open market. The huge mainframe computers have been superseded by the personal computer. Networks such as the National Grid for Schools are in use. You have to join in or be left behind, which means that you have to get over your fear of the unknown and learn to participate. The generation game comes into play again, because the younger you are, the less confused you will be by the Internet and other technology.

The knowledge economy rests on three pillars: the growing role of knowledge in transactions, the rise in importance of knowledge assets, and knowledge management. The worldwide web via Alta-Vista reveals 26,586 matches for knowledge management, and involves every big consulting firm and hundreds of software providers. The speed of growth is something that will impinge on your life wherever you are.

The Potency of Intellectual Capital

In organisational terms, a big part of intellectual capital is the knowledge each employee has about the company's business, its products, services, customers and suppliers. This includes both business data and anecdotal personal experience, plus all your own creative thinking. The high value of intellectual capital leaving an institution each day is staggering. Look at the escalator or the lift and see the employees going out of the door with all that knowledge and know-how and hope that they return next day. Intellectual/process investment, like other forms of capital invest-ment, is investment in the future. It is people dependent. The economic value it generates can be immediate, but it usually takes time. Any significant modification of an organisation calls for planning and co-ordination of teams and complex processes. Crash programmes or crisis management are characterised by stress and uncertainty and are not necessarily the best way to engender companywide trust and co-operation. The pace of business demands agility and responsiveness, but long-term goals and anticipation are often better than quick cures. Short-term gain is rarely worth long-term risks. The impact of technology means that power within the company can be at the top and the bottom simultaneously. Middle managers have been replaced by project managers in many organisations, and personal interface is the current way of making your mark.

Technology drives many of the pressures for change. Firms are struggling to harness the new technology to support business processes, including innovation and creativity. Innovation is needed continuously in all aspects of products, services, processes and structures, while the firm has to find the creativity in order to do this. Education, gender, age and experience all affect you and are the major influences on creativity. The creative environment has both physical and psychological aspects which will be affected by long-term planning and the ease of internal communication. In trying to understand the potential for changing the way business is done, each person is seen by the firm as having a part to play. Knowledge management is now a key strategic issue. The challenge is for organisations to develop employees and processes equally effectively.

Useful information is harvested continually from systems through keyboards, microphones, video cameras, surveillance satellites, point-of-sale terminals and desktop document scanners, and then stored in databases like wheat in silos. There are innumerable small operations and a few massive extraction and refining enterprises, such as the conversion of large libraries and image collections into digital form which is then put on-line. Raw information is transformed into products and distributed to customers. Software is in command, with a role similar to machinery in the old industrial factories. Then there is cyberspace, where information retailers, brokers, agents and middlemen earn a living. Just as publishers evaluate and select books for publication, so when gatherings of people shift from bars to bulletin boards, someone has to sift and edit. As retailing and banking go on-line, sales jobs will move to cyberspace. Networks and cyberspace communities connect players in different sectors. There is booming activity at all levels on the worldwide web and in the commercial on-line services.

Intellectual property and capital requires further development and monitoring. Lawyers are busy helping institutions to protect their knowledge, creativity and information flows. Cyberspace activity is being regulated by copyright and patent law, modified and extended to take account of the novel characteristics of digital media and distribution systems. Digital artefacts – such as application software files, text files, digital movies and audio files – differ from tangible property like land, buildings and cars in crucial ways. They are reproduced indefinitely at trivial cost, and through telecommunications networks they can be distributed almost instantaneously throughout the world. They take up little space, and can be moved around without detection. It is also quick and easy to transform existing digital information to produce completely different new works. One person can use a resource without interfering with any others, either on a network or separately. The owning institution is unable to keep up with the daily activities of the systems without trust and reasonable mutual responsibility. Insurance companies are hearing alarm bells as they look into cover requirements within cyberspace and hear their clients' concerns about risks in the intangible world of intellectual capital.

The combination of numerous corporate mergers and the worldwide recession is leading to stronger legislation and controls of intellectual property while intellectual capital (mainly people) is at a premium. Infobahn-orientated strategies are emerging. This is the outcome of the need to design charges for the downloading of information and the time this takes, for editing of available information, for initiating new searches, for subscriptions for consumer use of movies, et cetera. Invention of mechanisms like these is helping towards the construction of a workable framework for cyberspace business. William J. Mitchell is concerned and argues in his book, *City of Bits*, that there is 'the emergence of a broadly shared sense of morality in these matters. Whatever technical and legal controls are implemented will succeed only to the extent that they have community acceptance; unresolved moral disputes will create conflict among the members of the cyberspace communities as surely as they do in other contexts.' The inverted economic effect, combined with communications which are faster, smaller and cheaper, is having a huge impact on working life everywhere. Each additional user on the Internet, e-mail and so on, makes it more valuable for the owners and licensees.

You too are benefiting from being able to access an ever increasing amount of information. It is what you do next that will give you further choices. Advances in electronics, computing and telecommunications have come about because of research and design departments of large companies and governments backed by commitment and investment. You will probably be attached to your personal/networked computers for at least another decade. Lose your fear of the machines and make friends of support people who take the angst out of crashes and other frustrations, and then you are free to explore the possibilities of the technology age.

Information is only part of knowledge. Knowledge uses the accumulation of information, and it takes time to acquire and assess what is relevant and reliable. You combine experience with intellectual understanding so that you can consider and apply what you know. You will be integrating what you understand with other congruent knowledge to help your professional development. Dealing with information is all about setting up sources and doing research, constantly updating and managing pay-offs with colleagues, bosses and future partners, as well as with virtual contacts.

Increasingly, the wealth of organisations is their intellectual capital, and much of that – from the secret ingredient in the textile finish to their customer's favourite garments – lies between the ears of the workers. Organisations have had to think of ways to glean this wealth, especially when there is movement in and out of the organisation by employees, and they have managed to do so by using exit interviews and other incentives. The longer a person can stay within the organisation, the more the details of their triumphs, failures and understanding get knitted into the fabric of the company. Ironically, the more essential this is, the shorter the term of employment for most people. The usual example of the call for an investigation is heard when a computer disappears from an office, but when a highly paid executive moves on or gets poached by another firm, they leave with all their client relationships, et cetera, and little can be done. Gardening leave is a small sop for the boss. In their massive study, *The War for Talent*, McKinsey and Co. find that very few employers keep precise data on 'the attrition of a wide swath of medieval managers and that just 40% of HR executives keep tabs on the so-called high performers'.

Tower of Babel

Until the last five years, unless you were a techie, you did not need to know about the flows of information. Now you do. Babel comes from the idea of language. It is no longer just the traditional concept of the spoken language. Now there are computer and technical communicating languages as well as French, English and Chinese. The age of 'babble' includes such technical language as e-mail and the Internet. It enables communication globally and beyond the spoken frameworks. It is not universal, but is as good as the existing networks. The boundaries are set by the level of technology available. Limitations exist which are both geo-graphical and due to the need for training. With multilingual, continuously updated amounts of data, you need discernment and the capacity to edit down the sheer amount of babble for your own purposes. The existence of chatrooms and the networking of industrial and all sorts of other units provides more people for you to talk to. There is an argument that all new technology and software are designed to be confusing, so that you have to find help. The computer supplier and support groups have an integral part to play in an organisation, even though they are independent and external. Even if this is the case, there are ways of learning to help yourself as an employee or a supplier. Being trained and able to fit into the new scenarios and trade both learning and expertise is all part of the new economy.

Need to Know

The new economy is about duplication too. Following the principles of software, everyone benefits from the replication and cloning of processes and the repeated output of information, for example using smartcards instead of chequebooks. New rules are in their infancy as the regulators try to find out how to manage the globalisation of the Internet, the numbers of people and activities which are now enabled to participate in it, and the growth of techniques. The headhunter becomes an interpreter or translator in these circumstances. Not only are negotiations between employer and the employee important, but discussions about roles become complex in the new economy where new technology/systems/information and expectations are involved. You have to be active and effective where communications are paramount. You must equip yourself to join in. Headhunters understand that their clients expect everyone to have keyboard skills, personal computer experience and be familiar with corporate networking processes which use the latest innovations. It is no longer enough to have a good personal assistant who does it all for you. Secretaries have been superseded in many cases by the new technology. You need to know how to do presentations on-screen, how to use your lap-top to communicate with both board members and staff without too much confusion. You cannot be expert in everything, so the secret of dealing with information is to manage the people around you and on-line to your advantage.

Knowledge management is a buzz concept of the 1990s, but it has recently come under much criticism for being nothing but a money-spinner for management consultants and the IT industry. The main problem is that knowledge is inherently intangible. It is hard to identify exactly what a company's intellectual capital is and how it can be captured. There are few companies that manage knowledge well, but it is essential that they all learn to. Nokia, Skandia and Microsoft have already set up specific programmes to enhance their creative viability. Intellectual capital in the organisation is made up of the ability of each employee, their know-how and technical expertise, as well as the overall building of relationships with customers. With constant restructuring, delayering and redundancies, corporate knowledge is being eroded and re-formed at an alarming rate. Some way of retaining core knowledge must be found to prevent seepage as employees go out of the door at the end of each working period. Management of intellectual capital is probably essential to success in the new economy. An open, participative culture which values the skills, abilities and contributions of employees is crucial to the free flow of information. Samuel Johnson said, 'Knowledge is of two kinds. We know a subject ourselves, or we know where we can find information about it.' Knowing 'the man who can' is imperative.

Progress within astute organisations is the acknowledgment that managing knowledge will formulate future business practice. Brainpower is most significant as the millennium looms. It is invisible, difficult to measure accurately and hard to value. But it contributes more to earnings, growth and competitive advantage in manufacturing than raw materials, buildings, muscle and finance. Intellectual capital is the ability to translate thinking into money. At this stage in technological developments, too few managers realise that the wealth of manufacturing is being created increasingly by ideas and brainpower – logistics, design, marketing and sales and information systems. Traditionally these have been viewed as services and add-ons. Now they are the core activities. Value and worth are attached to the firm by best use of its intellectual property – which means the constant updating of the combination of ideas and brain power with industrial/other processes. Having an awareness of your competitors' movements helps too. There is a gap between what companies show on their balance sheet and the intrinsic worth of the organisation. This is reflected in the market view and share price. It is said that about forty per cent of the true value is often missing from the given figures. Glaxo Wellcome or Microsoft, obvious examples of knowledge-intensive companies, have more hidden than shown assets. History shows that this can cause other, less knowledge-intensive companies to lose their position as market leader. For example, IBM was overtaken by Microsoft and Xerox by Canon.

Managing the present by predicting the future based on people, processes, customers, structures and innovation is very enlightening. Skandia, a Swedish global insurance company, is one of the first to measure and report its hidden intellectual assets. This is done by publishing a complementary report with the financial one. Intellectual capital is based on the people, customer relations, internal and external processes and the company's ability to renew itself. Now, instead of a high percentage of assets going home at night, the company has designed templates, put computer networks in place and has a twenty-four-hour grasp of everything at any time. Once on the Skandia intranet (its internal computer system), the intellectual capital is available in thousands of places simultaneously and can be used over and over again, which improves rather than wastes the assets. This increases the potential to contribute to earnings, growth and competitive advantage.

Information is an easily available and cheap commodity with a very short value span, whereas intellectual capital is more long-term. However, information can be valuable after the application of editing and interpretation, which require time, experience and mental effort. The organisation that goes beyond the assembling of raw materials to create a series of transformations relevant to the market will increase its chances of profitability and longevity. Bill Gates of Microsoft predicts that machines will soon learn from us. He sees wristwatch computers, computerised wallets and computerised cars as soon being commonplace. He is investing more than 16% of revenue on research and development. What is really holding back Microsoft is not the money but finding the right people. The cost of installation, evolution and maintenance of systems and intelligence is integral to the organisation that is keeping ahead of markets.

Steve Jobs has revived Apple, his first and still greatest creation, and heads up Pixar Animation Studios, where Silicon Valley is blended with the imagination and creativity of the movie business. He sees himself as 'a consumer technology impresario, an adroit Chief Executive and a cultural revolutionary'. He reiterates that most good products are the extensions of previous products and emphasises the difficulties in spotting new products based on entirely new ideas. Like Bill Gates and others, he maintains that computers are still awful and don't do all the things you really want them to do. They are too complicated and will take a long time to be refined. Cars are still being developed, so the assumption that technologically designed products should be immaculate from day one is obviously mistaken. They are in their primitive stages and are very young products. Consumers believe they are getting very sophisticated outcomes, and so the dichotomy continues.

A report on knowledge exchange has been issued by the Centre for Research in Employment and Technology in Europe (Create) to highlight corporate culture in 1998, starting from the premise that to beat the competition, companies must manage the knowledge of their workers. Senior staff should play a part in this, acting as knowledge champions and putting the collective wisdom to good use for the organisation. Interviews were carried out with 150 employers in Europe and America, many of them in the finance sector. The report divides knowledge into explicit – that which you are conscious of having learnt – and tacit – that which is subconscious and more difficult to analyse and communicate. Management of knowledge to turn tacit into explicit is fundamental to corporate culture. IT is very useful in the exercise. In the rapidly expanding marketplace, mental capital has to be harnessed to develop new products and services. For example, in 1979 there were seven main financial products being produced by the City of London in lending and insurance. Now there are over 1200 identifiable products, most of which are derivatives of the seven. The increase will probably be one hundredfold in the next five years. You will see changes in technological advances which are faster than government, legislative and global actions and thinking. The job shifts in such circumstances are painful for those who are not employable.

Since pension products were first launched in the 1960s, the underlying thinking for recruitment and development of fund managers and other staff has been to manage what they need to know of the company and then to distil what they learn for the benefit of the firm. New recruits are made aware that they have to acquire, analyse and communicate information from day one. Then they join teams that meet with senior managers of clients. Ideas flow from all those involved, regardless of age, length of employment or whatever. Companies that work globally and have offices scattered throughout the world have to have systems so that they can all talk to each other. Some of the people are skilled techies, some know the history of the company, some know about the clients, and it all needs to be accessible and melded into the general framework. It is impossible to be able to buttonhole the person you need when there are thousands of people involved, so systems for communication have evolved and been used well.

The power of the Internet is limited only by people's imagination. Those with the ability to think laterally will gain competitive advantage. The Internet is clever, linking up computers on opposite sides of the world for the price of a phone call. It has managed to destroy distance. The worldwide web is rich in graphics, photos and sound, and exceeds most people's expectations, but they now need to learn how to use it well. It can be used to maximise profits, cut costs, improve customer service, enhance the company's image and maybe change the way the company works. The managers who make real progress are those who will be looking outside their own company, and the Internet is extremely useful for this. E-mail is ideal for business: cheaper than fax, quicker than letter, and easier than the phone for speedy communications. It has become a fundamental part of busy lives even more quietly than the fax did. Plug in and you are your own manager.

Web sites are multimedia noticeboards. They are strong marketing tools and are as good as the company imagination used in them. There are now companies who do web site design and maintenance on an agency basis. Companies like Shell have extended their loyalty card points to the web, and many are following this example. Transactional web sites, where things can be bought, are still in their infancy. Yahoo is a group which manages the web engine and produces a huge number of web sites as part of its business. The biggest bookshop in the world is called Amazon and has 2.5 million titles on its list. It is overriding local bookshops internationally, and Barnes & Noble are endeavouring to combat its power. New virtual companies are exploiting the Internet but the conventional company is rapidly catching up, and realising the strategic value of the service. Blackwell On-line can now tailor information from their client list to provide tailored service. Catalogues of components, travel booking, hotel descriptions and booking, technical manuals and encyclopaedias, package tracking, financial services, medical and other research data are all happening on-screen. Many of these are dependent on the use of the credit card, and on-line payments are still under consideration.

The Internet is the world's biggest clearing house. It is capable of matching supply and demand in a way that was never dreamt of before.

Technology, Technology, Technology

The intranet facility is proving more pragmatic than networking information technology on its own. Another aspect of practical management is to have headings for particular knowledge, for example global leadership, and to create the head/champion of that area so that the intranet system can be supervised and kept alert. Support of senior managers is vital for the whole thing to work. Balancing information flows and encouraging sharing should be rewarded in well-run organisations by money or other benefits. No one expects to achieve, to produce, to contribute quite as much as the person employed to think ingeniously. And no one is as quickly alienated as the creative thinker who is not allowed to perform. Not to manage the knowledge worker for productivity therefore creates both the economic stress of inflationary pressures and the highly contagious social disease of discontent. Neither the productivity nor the satisfaction of the knowledge worker can be easily managed, but they need to be enriched.

Self-service has revolutionised many areas of business. Now it is coming into offices and shop floors too. About fifty large companies in the UK are considering using intranets to make it possible for staff to update and manage their own personnel records. It is in their own interest to have correct information and it will abolish an accumulation of paperwork. One of the big problems of the average Human Resources department (where they still exist), is the tracking of holiday entitlements. Software groups such as Compel, Cyborg and Peoplesoft have been popping into action to solve the problem. They have created electronic holiday forms. Other self-service applications come into play in large companies with a wide range of contract and short-term staff. Details of absences, salaries and training can easily be added to the basic employee information. All is easily checkable by assessment and analysis of the database. More efficient forward planning can take place, without the high cost of a dedicated personnel staff. Alarm bells will be activated when too many staff are planning their holidays at the same time and so on. Sensitive issues, such as employee confidentiality, can be overcome by the use of passwords and by limiting the amount of information that each individual can access. Such measures will probably result in a cutback in human resources staffing and increase efficiency, leaving more energy for communications, recruitment and training. The retail trade in general and the fast-moving consumer goods sector in particular has used self-service to advantage. The estate agent profession has now been targeted by Microsoft, who have introduced a new home-buying software provider. This Home Advisor has already been launched in the USA, is free to use at start-up and describes itself as a comprehensive guide to finding homes and loans on-line. Users are given a rough guide to the process of buying a house, and there is additional data on everything from schools to crime rates in the location concerned. The web site provides home listings and pictures, and allows visitors to specify their criteria so that when a suitable abode is listed they are e-mailed. On another site the purchaser can be vetted and supplied for a mortgage in fifteen minutes. Microsoft uses over 300 sources of property facts to keep the database up to the minute. Self-service is now also accessible to owners of digital camcorders which give high-definition pictures. They can edit home movies on personal computers and continue to add to their film and other related expertise. Sales are booming.

Most software applications perform well-defined basic functions such as word-processing spreadsheets or presentation graphics. But there are some more advanced applications that are intended to meet the needs of broader and more abstract requirements, such as decision support. Packages like these are appropriate for businesses that often need to filter large volumes of information before being able to arrive at any business decision. These systems are complex applications which are capable of extracting data from a wide range of databases, then assembling and comparing it in ways that make the interactions clear.

Databases and PCs give competitive advantage by allowing users access to information that is available to everyone. Their use conveys a professional image, improves personal productivity and makes the user more self-reliant and less dependent on positional resources like secretaries. They make it possible to do the same work from different locations. PCs also enhance the thinking process: being able to think about the content rather than the mechanics of a task helps to crystallise ideas. The technology and software aid better decision-making, give a more objective over-view of the business and test assumptions more readily. Using PCs gives the individual a better grasp of new technology's potential and enhances relations with other techies. Directors and senior managers may be more reluctant to use PCs than employees, but personal satisfaction comes from the acquisition of new skills and abilities. Fundamental learning guidelines can help:

1. Prioritise the tasks you perform frequently and select the top two or three.

2. Get help from those who know what they are doing with computers and who also know your personal style.

3. Establish realistic goals for the next nine months which reflect the level of your PC skills to date, what is achievable and the learning time available.

4. Develop confidence and competence with the appropriate software in a step-by-step fashion based on goals which you have set yourself.

5. Know that the paperless office is a dream which is not likely to come true.

6. Accept that standard and other documents (for example, legal documents) are expected to be available because the technology exists, and details within them will be fuller and more numerous for the same reason.

The increasing power of computers, the growing sophistication of software and rising associated costs, have led the industry to look for alternatives to the PC. The most popular solution is a dumb terminal which relies on a powerful server for its applications. The network computer and the Net PC are in competition for the next wave of users who are graduating from their PCs. The Internet has become the ideal tool for businesses wanting to get their message to manifold users as cheaply as possible. It is a chaotic medium and is unpoliced, with connections prone to being busy or being interrupted at the salient moment. Access to the Internet is by attaching a modem and telephone to your PC and paying a subscription to an Internet Service Provider. A web browser also needs to access the worldwide web, the main part of the Internet. The main providers are the Internet Explorer and the Navigator. It is also possible to develop one's own web site. Intranets are rapidly gaining in popularity, using Internet technology for internal company purposes. In this way, sensitive company information can be communicated. E-mail is available as a stand-alone package and is rapidly becoming the most used form of communication.

Technology growth has led to the need for security, within both computers and software, and in any connections that are added. Computer theft is rife, and specially designed office security is now part of daily life in most organisations. Microsoft has tried hard to find out what people want from technology so that they can interpret what sells best. Technical people despise aspects of technology which are produced for the masses, and those of us who struggle to keep on-line and up to date with software development find much technology too complicated. Understanding the customer is the essence of delivering modern technology for future users.

Supply chains through the Internet are getting more and more sophisticated. The electronic bazaar is working. One example is in the trading of 3-D computer generated designs into models. Global PR uses the web site called Cyberbuild where they can see designs submitted by manufacturers, with Global PR setting the price. It has to be high enough for the manufacturers to produce but low enough to make the job worthwhile for the prototyping companies. The ultimate 'bazaar' model is the on-line auction. Interactivity and the ability to change information instantly combine profitably with a huge potential audience. Airlines use it for tickets, computer companies for equipment, and others will follow this line of lateral thinking.

The Knowledge Team

Time, distance and culture separate many staff from their managers, if not from their colleagues. Heavy workers and time targets mean that managers have to find ways of checking and keeping in touch with their teams. Hewlett-Packard is leading the way in training for managing at a distance, communicating by telephone, e-mail or whatever connects the individuals with their tele-coaches, who help them to assimilate and implement the learning. They have provided a global pool of knowledge of best practice which is continuously updated. This saves hours of travelling for face-to-face meetings and speeds up the level of insight necessary for managing from afar.

The cross-culture implications of the Brit in charge of the sub-continent supply of process, or the American responsible for the

Italian markets, for example, expose habits and stereotypes which have to be considered if everyone is to work well together. Hewlett-Packard discovered that by giving the teaching and information in small-sized bites, more was understood and transferred. They have proved their cost effectiveness by the decreasing need for longer training courses out of the workplace. They are achieving a competitive edge on all they do by their intranet efforts. The ability to give tele-coach sessions while the recipient is in a traffic jam or waiting to contact a client is very useful. Programmes are entered at the convenience of the user and are not intrusive for others. The programme has been so successful that the company has decided to increase the original pilot scheme worldwide. Virtual management is accepted more readily by some cultures than others. Latin and Asian structures find it more difficult to assimilate because both rely heavily on personal relationships in business, but they provide excellent centres for process and database work. Motorola and Unisys have put virtual training in place for their European operations and see managing remotely being relevant for small local teams as well as international teams. Any organisation that believes that personal development is linked to business objectives will be looking for ways to help the employee manage the balance between time, work and home. Team dynamics, based on numbers and culture, can affect communication. Managers who are comfortable with productivity overriding activity will be aiming to foster trust. They are taught to do this by listening, being clear and direct but not aggressive, and by defining limits so that decisions can be taken and reported back. The intention is to help them find solutions which suit them and to find a way of working which is not only directive but helps them to build relationships for multiple business purposes.

Mitsubishi Electric have set up an intranet where they advertise all vacancies, training available and current strategies and targets. This has brought people together and has increased the number of thriving promotions. AA Insurance have three years' experience of communicating with employees in this way and have maintained their critical competitive edge through using their intranet well. When people are involved in decisions, they're more likely to be happy and work better. AA Insurance found that when telesales teams were linked directly with senior managers, quotations and deals were completed more quickly. Marketing people then joined in and added seminars and conferences to continue and consolidate the vertical and horizontal connections in the organisation. They also added dress-down days and theme days to add to the fun element of working in insurance. They won an award for their communication systems from the Cranfield School of Management and *Human Resources* magazine in the category of excellence in the year 1997/8.

Key Communications, run by Colin Kent, helps organisations to use intranets effectively. It costs companies a lot of money when they do not build a team-working environment within which change is easily managed. Key found one company which had spent £800,000 on the annual recruitment budget and £50,000 on listening to their existing staff, even though they had spent £10 million on communications systems. When money was diverted from external focus to intranet obligations, the balance was changed dramatically. Intranets are used to spread gossip as much as straight information, which is fun, unless destructive elements invade. One of the best ways of exchanging information is through story-telling and gossip, so this is an accidental advantage of the intranet. Senior management therefore needs to keep an eye on the screens and check misinformation before damage is done. The intranet can be converted to reassure people too, with the middle manager having the important role of supplying the links around the organisation. When British Gas set up its intranet in 1997, it opened the lines between 19,000 employees, including those working overseas and the 2500 who are constantly on the road. The head of knowledge management, Tom O'Connor, is delighted with the money and time they saved. When they put group-based vacancies on the system weekly it helped people to move upwards, sideways and other ways which they would not have thought of otherwise. As organisations get flatter, this is a helpful device. Discussion forums, on or off line, add to the support that people can find in the group. They are working harder and smarter as a result of knowing more. Training and helplines are popular, and the organisation wins by providing access at all times.

What happens when clients have access to every move? The concept is simple: to link the company's internal communications and data network, its intranet to the extranet – an external network involving clients as well. To make the project work, all the staff have to acknowledge and accept working in a transparent way. The programme has to increase client satisfaction to make changes worthwhile. Unless staff commitment is total, clients may be alienated rather than attracted. The downside is enormous if it does not work because of the difficulty of dismantling the systems. Another drawback is that it opens up the creative areas of competitors. Advertising, PR and other such agencies are having to consider this way of working right now as their clients and markets need speed and change to such an extent that only a set of lightning responses is useful. Working efficiency is improved and the ability to have ISDN and world web sites is expected. Implementation of step change is difficult and requires the leaders to have nerves of steel while everyone involved learns to commit and come on board.

Knowledge is a source of personal as well as corporate competitive advantage, so how do people manage to share it? Having a personal game plan will be overridden by the corporate objectives unless the individual recognises the dangers involved in their personal agenda. Lack of co-operation may stem from the old industrial model of knowledge-as-object. The view was that by sharing, the value of the knowledge was cheapened. Knowledge management gurus argue that the opposite is true. They believe that sharing increases the influence of the individual.

The Internet is the best way of demonstrating the maturing collective intelligence. Information is recycled and multiplied so that more people in the team can be included by sharing and application. This can lead to problems. In large groups it is easier for the individual to hide, to minimise their contribution and to maximise their own inflow of knowledge. Leaders do not always take into account the need for communication when setting objectives and sometimes overlook the need for collective effort, forgetting that it is not possible for even the smartest individual to 'do it alone'. Encouragement of teamwork and very clearly set out rewards systems help to overcome these dilemmas. For those who find it easy, or have been trained, to be part of a team at all times, the benefits of sharing are second nature. Another frequently occurring problem is that of subordinates having the ideas and doing the donkey work while their seniors receive the accolades. One way to check that achievements are being properly divvied up is through 360 degree feedback. Questions like, Are they open? Are they good listeners? Did they take all team members into account? should give good indications. So says Joshua Jampol, a Paris based journalist who writes for *The Times* (London) and the *International Herald Tribune*.

Financial rewards are pertinent for encouraging sharing of information and latest developments. Charles Galunic, Professor of Organisational Behaviour at INSEAD, who specialises in consulting firms, says they frequently use subjective assessment of IT systems, for example, basing 20% of the employee's annual bonus on their contribution to the corporate intranet. At the US headquarters of the Swedish Company, Skandia, employees are asked to vote twice annually on the top thirty best sharers. The top three have their certificates displayed and earn a bonus of $1000. Skandia maintains that the acknowledgment is worth more than the money. In the future it is hoped that an open office culture giving competitive advantage will increase the development of new ideas and new products.

Digital Revolution

Nicholas Negroponte is the founder and director of Massachusetts Institute of Technology's (MIT) prestigious media laboratory. 'Computing isn't about computers any more – it's about living' is his main theme. Computers have already entered the workplace and people's jobs and are about to encircle and invade personal lives. He describes wearable computers: computers so small and so personal that you carry them with you all the time. Working prototypes are being tried out by the media lab and they have highlighted the potential of the lifestyle. 'Early in the next millennium the right-hand cuff-link or earring could communicate with the left one through low-orbiting satellite and have more power than the present PC,' reckons Negroponte. Such satellites are already being put into production by the merger of the interests of Microsoft and Motorola with the Iridium project. Many people interact with computers already (apart from areas in the world where the telecommunications and geographical features keep people isolated), but not everybody likes them or knows how to use them to the full. They do not understand or really want to know about the linkage from the PC to the world of the digital and wired position where everything is passed through or governed by the computer. Every decision or function will become more and more affected by the elaboration of ideas and systems.

Negroponte refers to the 'digital homeless' who refuse to grasp the extent of the information and economic revolution on which the world has embarked. With an enormous economic trans-formation under way, such clouded vision, or wilful covering of the eyes, is a short cut for the unemployment heap. People down the line from senior managers who do not accept the premise, will suffer too. By failing to appreciate the imperatives of the digital economy, and the urgency with which it must be embraced, people will be discarded by future successful organisations.

Your job, or career for life, is no longer an option. Charles Handy, Peter Drucker and all the other gurus have made this clear already, but Negroponte has linked the changes more closely to the technology that underpins them. Reflecting on what jobs will remain in the future, he argues that the biggest global employer in years to come will be oneself – but it is what people will be doing to earn a living that is more remarkable. Markets are different and you will be looking for large and small openings to sell your experience and knowledge at all times. Your strategy must be to embrace digital change in advance and not to be overtaken by it:

- Lifelong learning is accepted but what people need to learn has not been fully addressed.
- What worked in the past is not relevant for tomorrow. So, flexibility, education and awareness must win out over fear,

ignorance and doubt.
• The battle for people's hearts and minds is slow and difficult.

Negroponte has an illustration of the complexity of future conceptual thinking which he calls 'atoms and bits'. He describes the physical world and the goods that people buy and sell within it as 'atoms'. 'Bits' refer to digital information or data. The former passes from one person's possession to another, whereas information can be owned/used by many simultaneously. 'When I give you a piece of information, you have it, and so do I,' he points out. Negroponte does not rate on-line chat rooms, games and channel surfers. In his opinion, the main benefit of cyberspace is that it speeds up research, communication and consumer purchases, popularly known as 'e-commerce'. This will be an enormous marketplace from now on. Microsoft has the monopoly at the moment, and Bill Gates is looking for more and more innovation in the industry. However, it is likely that Microsoft will soon break itself up as it is too big to control and its location in Seattle is no longer practical. The main difficulty is the poor quality of the software. Every generation of software is worse than the last, and the programmes are too padded with options which few people want or use. Windows is the most popular system, but even that is too cumbersome. Whoever simplifies it will win top place in the market. Negroponte is Chairman of Digicash, whose product is electronic cash since credit cards will not be able to support all the transactions on the Internet. E-cash is a virtual debit card which allows firms to charge purchasers to a pre-set cash account. This protects the individual and keeps their anonymity. Although some firms do respect the privacy of the individual and do not use their knowledge of the individual's buying habits, lifestyle and so on for their own benefit, this is not the norm. Information is freely spread and sold for e-mailing and other contact and direct mailing lists. What is landing some users in trouble is their small purchases, because they then get bombarded with offers that are beyond their commercial level. This is the population that will value e-cash most.

Netscape has got off to a complicated and acrimonious start, and browsing the Internet remains a laborious chore. The prediction is that the biggest growth in the next decade will be in the developing countries. In the next five to ten years the most commonly spoken language on the net will be Chinese, not English. Then the dilemma with the low bandwidth will be apparent. This is the pipe through which digital signals must travel to reach their destination. The narrower the pipe, the slower the delivery, and it is most narrow between countries. Esther Dyson, in her newsletter *Release – 1.0* (the vade mecum of the Internet fraternity in the USA, according to Charles Handy), has said that with all the new developments and inventions, the average user will still need help to interpret all the information that is at the fingertips of everyone who is wired up to e-mail, web sites, voice recognition computers and cars that drive themselves, to mention just a few applications. The new technology is more than most people need. The world is becoming digitally over-engineered and in due course most people will select what they need and overlook the rest.

The digital revolution will not necessarily improve productivity. There is a high rate of obsolescence which detracts from the overall value of the technology. Updating equipment, constant training of users and the expense of inherent mistakes will all take their toll. Little quality control for information is possible because of the information overload and the cost and low availability of editing. At the moment the Internet system is virtually free. It is a loss leader, getting as much technology into as many offices and homes as possible. The predicament that is caused by tedious log jams and overuse builds up the less visible cost – the time of those using the systems. More and more organisations now operate round the clock – there is no end to the day for informed workers and professionals. Global competition and the need to access data keep up the momentum. One consequence is that quality of life for the 'whole man' is seriously affected. Ironically, statistics show that there is no measurable increase in productivity in USA in the nineties.

The dataholic has a typical pattern of living. Most evenings are spent in front of the screen and late nights tracking information are usual. Some even get up in the early hours to check their e-mail. They are permanently tired, irritable and on a short fuse at work. Social life is virtually non-existent because the virtual world has become more attractive than the real one. Friends disappear after many efforts to engage the dataholic in normal active life. The phone is always engaged as the computer goes on-line, and gradually the dataholic is in danger of becoming an outcast. Mobile phones are useful for the dataholic to keep in touch with other such affected geeks. According to research published by Reuters in 1998 based on 1000 executives worldwide, the warning signs are:

- Spending hours looking for information
- Lying to friends – and to oneself – about this
- Constant anticipation of the next on-line session
- Finding it easier to talk to people on-line than in reality
- Physical problems after sitting badly for a long time
- Constantly checking e-mail
- Skipping meals, events and family appointments to go on-line
- Having mixed feelings of glee and guilt
- Experiencing cravings and withdrawal symptoms when away from the computer

There is a fine line between having sufficient access to information and having too much. Constant search can lead to stress and cause problems at home and work. Seventy per cent of those surveyed reported a drop in job satisfaction, while eighty per cent said that they needed to have the information to keep up with customer and competitor activity. Your self-discipline has to be used to cut down the search for information and to spend more time with real people. Only by acknowledging the limitations of the technological revolution will the dataholic begin to be cured.

Recruitment in the Information Age

Time and time again the need for IT experts is talked about. Anxiety about the millennium bug and the speed of change within the industry has meant that there is a cry for installation and support from nearly every business and operation in the land. Cap Gemini is a leading computer services and business consultancy. It has stated that it will be recruiting about 2500 people annually (500 graduates) to keep up with the demand. Best People was set up in 1997 with offices throughout the UK to find IT specialists with the qualifications who need more experience. Training faltered during the time of the recession and now has to be made up. Best People are bringing recruits in from South Africa and the Philippines to help swell the numbers in the UK who are ready to do the clients' work. Simultaneously, much of the routine work is sent to the sub-continent for processing. Best People has inaugurated its own training courses to speed up the bank of skills in the UK. They accept graduates even without IT skills or background and train them up. They act on behalf of their client companies and build up relationships with the universities to find suitable people.

Declare is a small company which runs computer centres. Two INSEAD MBA graduates had the idea of catering for small businesses and the self-employed who want to produce posters, brochures and marketing plans without having to invest in the technology for themselves. Since their inception in 1993 they have moved into larger premises and have opened further studios in Covent Garden, Camden Lock Market and Neal's Yard. They are planning more. Declare has matched customer needs for training, too. Chosen candidates who pass their assessment tests go on courses which have already been tailored for the companies that will be employing them. Both partners have a similar background in engineering and provided their own start-up money, backed by a loan from NatWest. This has been repaid and further loans are in the process of paying for themselves. At first they had seven computers, two printers and one scanner. Now they have more than fifty workstations, fifteen printers and five scanners. They have increased their staff to fifteen and their revenues have increased twelve-fold. This is less than they had expected, but they reckon that the two first years of setting up have been tough and that from now on they should reap the rewards. Workstation hire is their core activity and they have increased their services to meet the requirements of customers. They also provide image setting, producing film and bromide, for magazine, newspaper and book production. In addition to Internet access they provide web-site design, maintaining the full commercial site for Faber & Faber as well as training and commissions on the open market. Clients can be corporations who send individuals, or individuals investing in their own skills to maintain or increase their employability. Their business plan is on a careful step-by-step basis from planning the project to opening the centres. In the longer term they want remote stations and have identified eight more centres for capitalisation. What drives them is the knowledge that they are setting up a new industry, and belief in their growth.

One of the effects of market uncertainty is consolidation. There has been a flow of mergers and acquisitions where the outcome has been to strengthen the financial position of the resulting organisations. The examples of Swiss-Bank and Deutsche Bank, Price Waterhouse and Coopers & Lybrand are two examples. One of the other effects is the resulting shake-up in the merged IT departments. As companies come together, their computing infra-structures are likely to be disparate, so work has to be undertaken to ensure that integration runs smoothly. This means that there is an ongoing demand for middleware skills in areas such as trans-action processing. Database integration through dedicated gate-ways is particularly popular. Those who can present themselves as the logistical glue within a merging IT department, having linchpin roles for communications between a number of vital functions, will be in a strong position. Those who are unable to adapt to new situations will find their status in the merged business entity weakened. Other trends in the IT sector show movements between consultancy and banking jobs, from bespoke systems to packaged applications and the development of existing systems to include the latest packages. Maintenance will always require heavy staffing to facilitate the business.

An unexploited and little explored niche within the whole world of IT is software testing. Software development process is seen as mundane and is left to the members of staff who have the least say. With emphasis on error trapping, software testing is becoming a priority. Many financial houses, for example, and banking and insurance businesses in particular, use testing as the focal point of their relationships with software development companies. Often they use their consultants as external staff members and keep them occupied with their internal problems. There is a shortage of testers and there is still a limited range of experience available when recruiting does take place. Increasingly, mature, competent testers are needed as opposed to a few smart staff who are asked to check after sales. Testers have to have an understanding of the automated testing tools, and the management level of testing is being paid at a level comparable with other senior staff. The increase in the number of trainees in response to corporate frustrations is affecting the lower pay levels too. Testing is seen as boring because it requires sitting down and using long lists of figures and letters to check the formulations, but the manual process has been almost completely automated and the computer itself can be given the tasks. Testers see the fun part as being the programming of the scripts which show the data needed for testing. The year 2000 and Emu have already stimulated training growth in the providers of IT support. Any IT executive prepared to invest in testing in the long term prepares trainees on testing before coding. Systems that have been certified as millennium bug-proof have mainframe testing and then others covered. Functional testing tools, static analysis software and other development products are being used widely and usually to great effect. Instead of being an add-on, testing is becoming an inherent part of the software development process. The problem remains of the lack of an appropriate qualification to verify the competence of testers, as there are no benchmarks available against which to be measured. In 1998 the Information Systems Board, which is part of the British Computer Society, began trying to bring out a qualification that would standardise levels within the testing market.

Companies will spend £340 billion on IT in the current year in the UK. It is a large part of the workplace with the potential for problems. The central help-desk is already a reality for many companies, but the system introduced has to be well thought through to get the best out of the staff who will be responsible for it. One way is to encourage IT staff to have a wider overview of the workings of the company. British Airways always takes new recruits to different areas of their business so that the IT people have a feel for the high density of people in the terminals, and have some inkling of the impact that an unsolved technical hitch can have on the speed and efficiency of the whole operation. The most common complaint is that the printer is broken – most often this is because it needs toner cartridge or paper. In fact they are tough and reliable machines. Panic arises when the user thinks that a file or folder has been lost, regardless of the number of challenges on-screen to prevent this happening. Approaching deadlines and impatient bosses lead to irrational operator behaviour. When the keyboard conks out, it is usually due to spilt coffee or crumbs, and the keyboard should be turned upside down and shaken rather than waiting endlessly for its replacement. When an application freezes or crashes, fax or e-mail the help-desk so that they can get on with fixing the problem rather than spending all their time replying to network users. Why are there no e-mails for me today? Either it is a lack of popularity or the system is down.

Historically IT support companies have looked at the client's business solely through the eyes of their IT departments. Clients now need a new kind of support which is business and IT consultant combined. This type of relationship is exemplified in outsourcing. For a client to entrust a fundamental part of the organisation to a third party, that party needs to understand the issues driving the business – its customer relationships, competitor issues, strategic alliances, and so on. Equally important, the client needs to believe that the IT support company will be as passionate about their business as they are themselves. To ensure this, outsourcing relationships are increasingly becoming true strategic business partnerships where the clients' risks and rewards are shared with the IT consultants. Such business partnerships also give the client company the opportunity and resources to explore new areas – be they new channels to market or new market areas.

Companies are looking for staff with IT training and expertise, and this has forced recruitment agencies to grow and develop international capabilities. Robert Walters, a provider of temporary IT and finance staff, has joined forces with the US recruitment group Staffmark in a £110 million merger to reinforce the facility to supply a client in whatever city it has offices. The merger gives chief executive Robert Walters (the founder) a paper windfall of £27.5 million, and the other directors on both sides will benefit too. Walters announced to shareholders that they would all benefit from the ability of the new group to deliver worldwide integrated solutions to clients. Morgan and Banks, the Australian recruitment consultancy, is planning to merge with TMP, the US on-line recruitment group, which together will create a £620 million company. In the nineties, headhunting and recruitment companies and partnerships have been following the general corporate trend to get bigger. The competition between the USA/UK group Korn Ferry/Carre Oban with Heidrick and Struggles to be the biggest headhunting group is endlessly fascinating. The break-up of Norman Broadbent and the NBS group has led to a more splintered approach. Just how large the growth has been in this marketplace can be seen from looking at the directory *Executive Grapevine*, which lists search and selection, recruitment, interim management, international groups and IT specialists as a series of directories and CD-ROMs. Ten years ago they had a single printed list.

The shortage of information technology skills reached a critical level from the autumn of 1998. Despite large cash rewards, there were more than 50,000 vacancies in the UK, forcing firms to look abroad. The weekly rate for contractors is over the £1000 mark but still the demand outstrips the supply. This situation has been exacerbated by preparation for the millennium bug and adapting IT systems for the euro. Salaries have risen on average by 9.5% recently and are forecast to go up by 20%. People from other industries are looking into retraining in IT. The South East is the hardest hit, with 40% vacancies. To make up the shortfall, staff are being recruited in all five continents, with Finland, South Africa and Italy as the favourite countries.

Working in a permanent post can be frustrating, especially when consultants and freelance specialists, such as IT specialists, work alongside earning much more for the same job. Nevertheless, it can be daunting making the jump between the security of a permanent job and the instability of the contracting world. One way of making the transition is to log on to the Internet job sites and test the response while you are still in your job. The more detailed your requirements, the more sensible should be the replies. Remember that you have to hold on to the electronic address which is known to your contacts and where you can be found by a headhunter.

· 6 ·

Positioning: In the Global Framework

A revolution is sweeping the world of work. It is changing the understanding of what is meant by 'work', 'the workplace' and the job. There are three main influences. These are: the globalisation of trade, the shift from the manufacturing economy to an economy governed by the use of knowledge and the provision of services and the development of information and communications technologies.
David Puttnam, RSA Report *Defining Work*, 1998

Where Is It?

The global village is becoming a reality as raw materials, intellectual capital, finished products and financial services are interchanged at high speed round the world. There is a steady development in the capacity of manufacturers to make their products fit the profiles of local markets. The national markets are becoming ever more similar. Simultaneously many tariff and non-tariff barriers are being demolished. Such technical developments as the CAD/CAM (computer aided design/manufacturing) and automated order processing, along with the impact of the Internet, are altering world trading possibilities profoundly.

The cost of capital is important, and forecasters are struggling to predict movements up or down. Global sourcing offers organisations the opportunity to optimise the positioning of their operations. For example, an American based multinational company can carry out leading-edge research in Silicon Valley, with product design in Italy, engineering in West Germany and assembly in South Korea. The advantages of this type of global sourcing far outweigh the liabilities of currency volatility and political friction.

Businesses that once were domestic will be forced to move their processes and suppliers to wherever there is the greatest advantage. In the integrated global economy, profits are inextricably linked to currency fluctuations and the employee pool can be across many countries, so a completely new approach to the best use of people is being adopted. One consequence is an increase in sociocultural interchanges between groups. Another is a high turnover of executives as the global economy shifts and turns. The requirement for talented executives with the abilities and background necessary to run new businesses is at a premium. The strategic thinking necessary to meet these dilemmas requires the following:

- Recognising that human resource planning must be an intrinsic part of corporate strategy. The HR department, in close collaboration with the CEO, will be constantly assessing the executive skills and aptitudes that are compatible with new markets.
- Making the HR Director a member of the top management team/board. It is essential that people with responsibility for managing others in the organisation have a direct reporting line to the top. As hierarchical structures change into more amoebic-like project teams, the amount of oversight needed increases.
- Using the personnel function for processing pay and rations for employees and outsourced people. HR thinking, development, adjustment, recruitment and training can then be linked into higher echelons of the firm. As corporations will have to compete more aggressively for talent, human resource leaders will have to look far and wide, and laterally, to find who they need.
- Emphasising training and development for all managers, especially for potential global chief executives. This includes placing the most talented managers in difficult roles, to test their abilities in rigorous situations and to glue their loyalty to the

core of the organisation. Adding to the bottom line is important, and how these people achieve this is equally important.

- Ensuring the unity and growth of the organisation by choosing leaders and managers who internationalise corporate cultures, values and goals. Aside from careful selection and continuous training, the best way to make sure that the chosen executives fit into the corporation is to measure their world view, temperament and business philosophy to match the organisation.

Winning teams in global companies are made up of players from different nationalities. As the hunt for management moves to more international requirements, the techniques of recruiters and headhunters are changing. The 1998 report from the Economist Intelligence Unit, *Building and Retaining Global Talent: Towards 2002*, says that 'the shortage of executive and other specialist talent is a worldwide phenomenon and is the major concern of the chief executives of the 150 global organisations surveyed'.

Global databases for senior positions and systems for international co-ordination are now fundamental in search firms. Russell Reynolds and the other big five international search and selection firms are also creating or joining international professional networks. Appointments are predominantly filled by nationals, especially in Western Europe, but the searchers look throughout the world to find good candidates.

Personal networking is successful too. About 42% of senior people are aware of upcoming jobs through their own contacts, and 24% find them by replying to advertisements. Knowing the competition and meeting colleagues in their sector at conferences or on the tennis court is helpful for increasing knowledge of movements in other institutions. Focused use of the Internet and e-mail is beginning to be established as an alternative route for finding people. The EIU report confirms that the preferred way for finding people is still by talking to sources who are already known to the headhunter or the employer, but this is changing.

A rich spread of talent is building up in the big global organisations. They note the movers and shakers in their industries so that when the need arises they can be approached. Discussions with suppliers to the big firms is another way of finding out who is effective in their roles. Advertising agencies, marketing consultancies, management consultants, accountancy firms and the like are all fertile sources of information. You have to be aware that your performance and talent is being noted all the time in many different ways. Looking for people who will fit into a national culture or a particular relationship makes these observations even more important. The ability to speak an appropriate language is part of this.

The company that anticipates their senior appointments as opposed to waiting for crisis in recruitment is going to have a wider choice and more opportunity to consider the implications of the role and its potential. Sharing information within and without their own structures makes the search more extensive. Non-executives on boards are also useful sources.

Recruiters and headhunters are better placed to find successful people when they have a strong working relationship with clients and when they really understand the company culture. ICI has always given their fast-track employees the opportunity of overseas postings as part of their development. They can then place them effectively, having seen how they have reacted and performed in specific circumstances. Diversity in recruitment and adding new blood at certain times is the other component. The importance of planning succession, of preparing for structural change and for the impact of worldwide boom and bust cycles, all have to be taken into account when contemplating the expensive task of employing people (and their dependants). Colgate-Palmolive have frequently reviewed their succession planning. Personal achievement and results matter to them, and so does the ability to fit in and the reputation that has been built up wherever the executive has been working. All are attached to the perception of the talent of the individual under consideration.

Global Scenarios

The future will be shaped by three powerful forces: liberalisation, globalisation and technology. There is no alternative ('TINA') to adapting to these forces. There are at least five areas where TINA means that there is no 'business as usual'. Radical transformation is needed in: European welfare states, the Gulf economies, Chinese politics, Japanese regulation, and former communist and state-owned enterprises, particularly in India, China and Russia. TINA also shows that failure to learn leads to economic, political or commercial underperformance. Other forces, such as cultural, social and political influences, all interact with those of TINA. How to exploit TINA in order to maximise outcomes is important. A Shell Scenarios document gives two suggestions:

• Just do it

Success comes to those who harness the latest innovations in technology to identify and take advantage of fast-moving opportunities in the world of hypercompetition, customisation, self-reliance and ad hoc informal networking. This allows the fullest expression of individual creativity and offers a large stage for the company to explore visions and to find new ways of doing business and solving problems.

• Da wo ('Big Me')

Countries and companies have discovered that success calls for a committed investment in relationships, where relationships of trust and the enabling role of government provide the long-term strategic advantage. Asia has already had the advantage because it has a society where the individual ('the small me') understands that their own welfare is inextricably linked to the welfare of the whole.

The next few decades will be about learning which of these two ideologies is best practice. The World Business Council for Sustainable Development has drawn up three scenarios for the years 2000–2050.

The first framework is called First Raise Our Growth. Many nations experience a fair degree of economic success, and economic growth is the major concern, with sustainable development acknowledged but not pressing. In this scenario, people react like the proverbial frog: when placed in boiling water, the frog leaped out of danger; but placed in cold water that was gradually heated to boiling point, the complacent frog was boiled to death. Globalisation and liberalisation of markets, along with the pressures of rapid urbanisation, have raised the degree of social inequity and unrest to a level that threatens the basic survival of both human and environmental ecosystems.

The second framework is Geopolity, which begins with a succession of signals showing that an environmental and social crisis looms. Governments are revived as focal points of civil society. They seek to work with markets rather than to displace them, and take the lead in shifting the structure of economies towards sustainable development.

The third scenario is called Jazz. This is a world in which NGOs, governments, concerned consumers and businesses act as partners – or fail together. Together they learn effective ways of incorporating environmental and social values into market mechanisms. Jazz encompasses a widespread availability of information about the ingredients of products, sources of inputs, and companies' financial, environmental and social data.

Marketing

The globalisation process is not a single set of activities or a single one world movement but a number of partially interlocking global networks. We live in a planet-wide economy, and humanity is heading for the worldwide rule of Coca-Cola and Microsoft. It is the universal presence of branded goods that is making us all more alike and recognisable to one another. According to the analysis of the late Robert Rapoport (a social scientist who died in 1996), globalisation is analogous with the seven rings of Gaia (the earth mother):

1. The political, which includes the interaction of national governments, the EU and the UN, as well as the World Bank and the International Monetary Fund. These have a strong US profile – even when its dues are left unpaid.
2. The economic, which contains electronically joined equity trading and investment banking, plus worldwide corporate dealings. An indicator of influence is the fact that the labels on

goods are the same from Tokyo to Timbuktu.

3. Non-governmental agencies, such as Oxfam and the Red Cross.

4. World religions.

5. Science and technology.

6. Arts, sports and leisure, including entertainment, in which the USA is predominant.

7. Criminals, drug-dealers, terrorists and other international gangs. This has the mirror image of the law enforcers who chase them. Not only are there mafias and yakuzas but web frauds are on the increase too.

These rings of activity are the bindings that are bringing us closer. There is a movement towards greater scrutiny of governments, and a belief in democracy as a good thing. Greater attention is being paid to the principles of equality of opportunity, non-discrimination by race and gender, care for the environment and the protection of children, but they have all to be established. All remain idealistic and optimistic. Are they being proved real and practical? Alas, most of these worthy principles are still being disregarded. Travel, trade and telecommunications will continue to bring international trends to bear on national and tribal patterns.

A new breed of European manager is emerging – younger, more aggressive, and transnational in outlook. In the UK, the first wave has taken place of top appointments filled from the wider continental supply. The UK has to shake off its insularity, penetrate the pan-European structure and use it as a springboard to global power. The launch of the Euro economy was followed by international interchanges, such as Chrysler and Daimler-Benz staying on one side while Rolls-Royce and Bentley were split by Volkswagen and BMW. European Union provisions now include equal pay for men and women for work of equal value. In 1995, the EU amended UK law to grant employment protection rights to all workers, however many hours they work, and regulations concerning the minimum wage have since been added. Money from the EU's large social development fund has been set aside for people wishing to return to work or who need reskilling training.

It is now possible for a subject of the UK to live, study and work in Europe – and even to be involved in the politics of the country concerned. Job-seekers who can prove that they are actively looking for work and have paid the relevant tax and insurance to date, can move anywhere within the European Union and still receive unemployment benefit for up to six months. Families can move to any country within the EU and receive the same social benefits as local people.

UK managers may be left with little choice. They have to become globetrotting Euromanagers in order to succeed. The larger and richer continental companies, with their economies bouncing back, are proving more aggressive in penetrating markets globally and are boosting their senior management prowess to achieve their objectives. By comparison the UK is still looking complacent. German firms, especially in auto-engineering, had long been self-regarding, inner-directed and paternalistic, and their recent transformation is dramatic and unprecedented. The whole motor business has gone from being a high-cost, high-priced, up-market manufacturing one to being a full-line supply of vehicles competing all the way down market. They have advanced in the new worldwide age through teamwork and supplier partnerships. The USA is rising to the challenge, and the UK needs to wake up. British industry has the habit of narrowing rather than broadening markets. ICI is now divided into specialist firms, including Zeneca. Robert Heller has pointed out that GEC is concentrating on defence rather than 'majoring in the opportunities that abound in civilian electronics and telecommunications'. He also says that 'specialisation does little to relax the imperative need to command the heights of well-found markets'. New age specialisation can be beautiful and big when the trend is bucked: for example, Siebe has acquired British Eurotherm and become the world leader in process automation. Geographically and strategically the need to become established in continental European markets is strong. When borderless Europe and the euro are up and running, then the days of national marketing and manufacturing will be numbered. Corporations as well as countries will have to lower barriers and allow the free flow of investments and revenues. New-style managers will no longer be able to run overseas interests as outposts of the British empire, because that will slow down their international impact.

Domestic markets have less meaning, and the UK has always suffered from a small home market anyway. The USA has always had a vast economic safety net in the scale of its home market, but the evidence is that even so America is stepping out globally – for example, Wal-Mart expanding into Germany from its base in Arkansas. Global management skills are a core part of corporate and employee development programmes. Recruitment will have to be opened out now that competition is coming less from Japan, more from the USA, and definitely from a cheeky and resurgent Europe which is already crossing boundaries in many ways. You need to play the new world game to win your position.

Flexibility

Flexible working allows companies to adapt to changing demand quickly and efficiently. It allows time zones to be understood and serviced with round-the-clock operators. The stock markets are an example of attention paid to activities in different centres at different times.

With growing emphasis on striking a balance between home and work, flexible work practices are key to fostering a sense of empowerment among employees. However, there are still mixed feelings about flexibility. Employees find that they have to live with unequal pay, reduced career and training opportunities and increased security and stress, and employers find that it complicates their training programmes and internal communications. Job sharing, flexitime and home working are becoming more popular. One in four companies find flexibility difficult to manage at this stage because line managers are unprepared for 'extra' requirements and some employees try to resist change. The use of call-centres is an example of a new working method. Callers do not know that they are speaking to people in a call-centre rather than in the company itself, which means that they can be working at unusual hours. All this is for the benefit of the customer. Teleworkers may miss the social side of the office and will have to make the effort to keep in touch with corporate development and any possibilities of promotion. Firms like the Prudential help by appointing team leaders to keep in touch.

City lawyers, in London, have declared that they want a better balance between home and work. The latest survey has illustrated that one in four professionals (men and women alike) believe that career progression and family life are proving incompatible in the working climate of the nineties. In City law firms there is a competitive culture and a habit of long hours, so the balancing is complex. National and international clients demand a high level of commitment from the fee earners – which is measured by the number of hours worked. The present targets of 1200–1800 billable hours are commonplace. World time zones affect the hours worked on any project, since lawyers often have to talk to clients and offices around the world. This is exacerbated by the need to market their services, so it is becoming more and more impossible for them to 'have a life'.

Women now make up more than half of the new professionals, and, like Parliamentarians, they balk at the constant requirements of late-night sittings. Flexible working is therefore beginning to be studied more closely by law firms as a possible solution. They are anxious to retain carefully recruited, highly trained and expensively developed people, and now realise that something must give. Men still outnumber women on a 10:1 ratio at partnership level and are the main decision makers. Wilde Sapte work on the basis of time off in proportion to intense transaction time worked; Berwin Leighton has a part-timer process in place; while the top six firms are still working on a case-by-case basis. Until the City values people in ways other than by the number of hours worked, there will be movement out by those who want a different lifestyle.

Despite increasing recognition that staff given the opportunity to work more sociable hours are often highly productive, motivated and loyal, there is still considerable resistance to flexible working. One argument is that clients are unhappy when they cannot reach particular people, but research by Linklaters shows that clients can understand, especially when the office is efficiently managed and they receive a high-quality service. For some who are seeking to leave the conveyor belt, the answer lies in setting up as independent firms. This works best for niche specialists. One good example is within media and entertainment law, which probably has the highest global movement of clients who need constant contact. Clients are not necessarily interested in palatial surroundings, but they certainly want immediate and high quality action from those who know their business as well. All firms start with good intentions of looking after their family/other life, but few achieve this balance as business grows. The current argument is that with the help of technology and with determination, it should be possible to enable even lawyers to have a better lifestyle.

SOL is a Finnish cleaning company where staff bustle about in smart yellow livery, carrying laptops and the latest mobile phones as well as their heavy-duty vacuum cleaners. They contribute to the £60 million annual turnover by working at times they like. The owner is Lisa Joronen, who enjoys keeping fit with cross-country skiing, and she is a believer in freedom in the workplace. She has thrown out traditional management styles and hierarchies in favour of 'people motivation and the strict auditing of targets'. She believes creativity is restricted by routine. She knows that a fun atmosphere is worthwhile. Personalised training and quality consciousness, along with paying attention to customer feedback, are the areas of development which work best. Territorial space has been abandoned and a social playground with bright colours, trees and animals, a nursery and games is in place instead. No one has been allocated tasks. There are no secretaries or assistants, anyone makes the tea and the headquarters is open all the time. The staff who work from home are telelinked. The 3500-strong workforce is distributed between 25 branches and operational independence is at the customer interface. New attitudes and skills have been learned and added to, ever since Joronen split off the cleaning from the original family laundry business. Employees are enjoying flexible thinking and the company is continually expanding.

Mobility

International Secondments is an initiative set up by the Department of Trade and Industry in the UK and managed by PricewaterhouseCoopers. The programme offers small businesses the chance to send key staff abroad. The aim is to help British companies increase their competitiveness by learning from world-class companies overseas and to understand foreign business practices by experiencing them in their own contexts. Many links have been formed, leading to business alliances and opportunities as a result of personal contact. One family business with six staff which is based in the North East of England and specialises in marine engineering wanted to expand into more sectors and to learn more about management practice and successful production techniques. They benefited from the secondment of one of the owners to Norway, and the DTI funded a temporary manager in his absence, who has stayed on as a permanent member of staff. When he returned, the director put his new-found enlightenment into play and looked at the original business in a different way. Previously the company had been run informally, but now the introduction of production-control systems achieved an even spread of trading activities. The Norwegian group is giving support and providing technical know-how and spare parts, and the turnover has increased.

International secondments last from three to twelve months. The scheme provides free advice on how individual companies can gain advantage from and help in finding a host company elsewhere. Companies of any size are eligible but those employing up to 250 staff receive extra financial help. The host company provides accommodation, and replacement staff are provided if needed. There is also the possibility of qualifying for language and presentation-skills training. This is a way to accelerate into world markets.

There is an increasing number of European and American managers targeting the UK for jobs, because they see the advantage in gaining international exposure. Finance, information technology and telecoms are the most popular businesses. By not underestimating the need for familiarisation and the cultural issues involved, the mobile executive stands a better chance of success. The Centre for International Briefing at Farnham Castle in Surrey has been used by Shell, Unilever and many of the top 1000 companies to initiate and brief their employees on their moves. Currently they provide more information and orientation programmes for those who are coming to the UK than for those who are leaving. The mobile manager needs to think of financial planning, career positioning, and negotiating for an income that is appropriate to the local cost of living as well as taking lifelong expectations into account. Most of all you need to know how to exit from your current role to the overseas scene as well as plan for return job availability in the same company. This will need to be agreed before embarkation, and checked on from time to time.

Companies spend a lot of money sending people abroad to gain experience, but many leave within a year of their return. There is not enough thought given to repatriation in many cases. When John Smith returns, to the USA in particular, he finds that his credit rating is in trouble because of having been away. Just buying a car is a problem. House prices in all commercial centres will have risen and it is difficult to get back into the marketplace. Companies should help their senior people to keep a toehold in the property market of their home country so that when they return or retire, there is not an insurmountable gap in the prices. Home can be a foreign country for the returning executive. Even after a short posting, familiar landmarks will have disappeared. Work colleagues move too, business focus is different, speed of life will be strange and family arrangements will be traumatic initially. The relocation package is a help, and an efficient and helpful partner is a godsend. On the other hand, the situation can be complicated by a partner who is also trying to get back into their own workplace at the same time.

The demand for global managers with international business experience is growing, and the clarification of the employee's position, wherever they are, at any stage in their career, is the new company problem. It is about balancing investment with the best use of senior people. 'Out of sight, out of mind' will be your main concern when you are away from Head Office. You have to work hard to keep in touch with the situation regarding plum jobs, relocation of main operations and so on. Voicemail, e-mail and intranets are useful communication aids. (The Diplomatic Service has only just replaced the telegram service with electronic secure systems.)

People becoming satellites in orbit which never return to earth is a commonly held view of expatriates. Smart companies send their best people abroad, so they will always be in contact and be highlighted when promotions and performance records are noted, no matter where they are. The deadender or ignorable executives will be overlooked anyway. Organisations should start the repatriation process before making the original appointment. You may be motivated by the possibility of earning well, acquiring experience or solving a mid-life crisis, but the employer needs to know what will be the outcome of their good faith.

Managing Global Executives

- Select the best available people for the job
- Plan the end game from the beginning of the assignment
- Arrange a mentor at HQ
- Use multimedia and other ways of constant communication
- Ensure sensible timescales for briefings on the countries/ cultures where the work is, for all the family
- Create strategies for re-entry and integration, both abroad and at home
- Share knowledge and experience throughout the working teams

With more organisations extending their operations across the world, the management of global teams is becoming a challenge. When the team is spread across five continents, the use of technology is helpful but not the full story. Remoteness is difficult for those involved, and few multinationals have come to grips with this problem. Anyone being recruited or promoted into this situation needs to be aware and prepared for a different way of thinking.

Ford Motor Company shows how it can be done by running a complicated design and engineering process with nearly 1000 participants on a worldwide basis. The senior manager of the project is based in Detroit, with direct managerial responsibility for twenty-five people. The project is divided into five territories headed by project managers, and they have fortnightly telephone meetings and weekly videoconferencing, as well as virtual meetings. Input from designers, engineers, suppliers and staff is encouraged. They achieve about 90% of the process of building the car on-screen, including doing crash safety tests. Trying to glue everyone together is the main objective. Their boss visits them once a year and everyone enjoys the contact. The contribution of the team and their creativity is encouraged.

Hewlett-Packard tries to have face-to-face meetings regularly throughout their teams to enhance their motivation and to make sure that they are all heading for the same goals. Time zones are still a difficulty, but if peak performance is the object and if a sense of loyalty and community is to be retained, then this has to be overcome. Like the politicians in the European Parliament, many managers are accused of 'going native' and forgetting that the main loyalty is to 'Head Office'. Paying attention at all levels to relationships and different styles, with an inbuilt balance between national and international emphases, is the answer.

Partners/wives/husbands with career interests of their own, or who manage the household in strange and sometimes hostile environments, can be the root cause of failure for the global executive. You will have the familiarity of the workplace to soften the jolt of changing lifestyle. You will have the continuity of daily activity, marketing the same products or services, langauge facilities and colleagues. Your trailing 'spouse' has to find out ways of communicating and often has no friend or supporter to open doors. How to occupy yourself when waiting around in hotels or at the new home for the main worker in the family/partnership is a huge dilemma and often leads to discontent. Immigration rules and labour laws can mean that a wife has to give up her career if her husband is moved. The ECA International survey of UK 500 companies and Shell International, who manage 5500 expatriate workers, agree that about 20% have working partners who have to sacrifice their prospects when they go abroad. Gemini Consulting is trying to incorporate family thinking into international movement of employees. They have inaugurated a loss of earnings payments system, career advice and further education costs to encourage people to accept the travel abroad. Procter & Gamble offers partner payments, and Lego has compensation provisions. Other companies adjust pension plans and provide family support to help. Language skills are imperative in most situations, and companies have been giving teaching and courses for employees and their families for some time. People who adapt best to working abroad are those who are flexible, tolerant, open-minded and curious, and already have comfortable relationships.

Diversity

People
'The Third World may be full of poor and under-educated people, but don't write it off. There's a huge amount of talent out there,' says Andrew Young, the first black mayor of Atlanta, USA. He believes that it is the under-developed regions which offer real opportunity for healthy growth and have vast amounts of untapped human potential. They make up about 70% of the geographical world. Companies that recruit the young from these countries and train them have the advantage of accessing emerging markets later. By mining the diversity within the organisation and the community local to it, the stepping stone to further global markets is formed. The example of the Chinese students employed by Coca-Cola who later helped them to open up markets in their home region is pertinent. The World Bank, the Southern African Enterprise Development Fund and the Brazilian Development Fund are only three examples of myriad bodies that exist to help raise awareness of potential trade and expertise available elsewhere. The sub-continent (India) is now the most used location for basic database and auditing technology for worldwide operating organisations.

Taxes and lack of jobs are the main reasons why there has been an influx of workers from France to the UK recently. The number of young people seeking work in 1998 in countries bordering their own has risen by 50% and is seen to be due to the opening up of Western Europe under EU provisions. People have increased choices for where they want to live and work.

Products
One of the most challenging decisions confronting an organisation is whether to diversify or not. General Electric, Disney and 3M

have all succeeded in increasing their product lines, but when Quaker Oats tried to enter the fruit juice business with Snapple, it did not succeed. RCA made an unsuccessful attempt to expand into computers, carpets and car rentals and quickly retreated. Detailed financial analysis is essential before the decision to diversify is made – it should not just be enacted on the hunch of the board. Constantine C. Markides, associate professor of strategic and international management at London Business School, reduces the gamble for managers by assembling six questions for their consideration:

1. What can your company do better than any of the existing producers?
2. What strategic assets (such as Coca-Cola trying to enter the wine business without the knowledge of wine) do you need in order to succeed in the new market?
3. Can you catch up or jump over existing people in that marketplace?
4. Will your diversification split up strategic assets that need to be kept together? (For example, Swatch Design Lab + Bhamo put together their core competencies and were successful.)
5. Will you be a player or a winner in the new marketplace?
6. What will you learn by diversifying and are you sufficiently organised to learn it?

Organisations
Talented, hard-working individuals have many options. Competition for talent is going to intensify, as the balance of power shifts from the corporate to the individual. In *The Dawn of the E-Lance Economy*, MIT's Tom Malone and Robert Laubacher demonstrate that 'companies grow when it is cheaper to exchange information and do business internally . . . they shrink them . . . when dealing with outside parties'. Powerful personal computers and electronic networks are giving the smallest of companies access to information, expertise and capital for the first time. Well-equipped individuals find it easy to work outside the organisational structures now. This is the way that many creative people currently work within the global marketplace, and they do

not subsume their individual thinking to workplace practices and policies.

· 7 ·

Positioning: For the Top

We have faith in leaders because of their ability to make things happen in the larger world, to create possibilities for everyone else, and to attract the resources to the organisation.
Professor Rosabeth Moss Kanter – Harvard Business School

What Goes On Up There?

Not everyone aspires to be chief executive or even boss. It depends what career success means to you. Knowing you have achieved and have job satisfaction are the most quoted reasons for perceptions of career success. Challenging roles are there at all stages. Succession planning depends on identification of potential high-fliers early on in their time in the organisation as well as clear thinking about the best use of senior people. Succession planning is not only about top management but should be a key issue running through the firm. Until recently, most sizeable organisations had it on the agenda and had development programmes for key people to ensure a supply of individuals for the top. However, with global and local economies affected by an increasing speed of change, it has become more difficult to forecast short- and long-term strategies.

Transfer of power from one leader to another can have a major impact on the morale and business performance, as well as the share price, of a company. Many people with a good track record and performance are moved along just because the new boss wants to make an immediate impact and insists on producing 'his own people'. The other side of this is persuading an incumbent to go at the right time. Some of the greatest leaders have shown their blind spot when it comes to handing over the reins. Some may be genuinely irreplaceable. Those who have played a dominant part in the growth of the company may be regarded as so inseparable from it that the risk of change is too much.

Companies may think they are working in teams, but this is rarely the case. Real teams require a well-defined discipline to achieve performance potential. Performance is the key issue, not just empowerment, sensitivity or involvement. Good leadership differentiates between team and non-team opportunities and then acts accordingly. To be effective at the top, a leader has to be able to assess which work is better done by combining teams rather than by using just one person, and vice versa. Leadership has to be appropriate for the situation, and flexibility gets the best use of each of the senior managers. They should be taking joint responsibility for corporate results. Individual leadership skills take a long time to develop and refine, and working within the top team can be complicated for the newly promoted or appointed executive. When team structures are created with the leaders being given the wherewithal to lead well, the system works and individuals benefit. Rigid boundaries are diluted by this practice and soon internal networks are established. Each person is focused on company goals, and improved competitiveness results. Often management has come to work this way after a crisis situation, for example, Leyland Trucks after having a tough financial time.

Even when there is no shortage of technically competent accountants, recruiting a good finance director is still complex. Looking for requisite qualifications plus evidence of good management and understanding of the institutional demands is the headhunter's job. Candidates must have at least five years of wide-ranging experience and should have up-to-date knowledge of accounting standards. Anyone of director level calibre will have been accustomed to budgets, forecasting auditing, investment and banking, plus tax, legal and compliance issues. The recruiter will have to talk to colleagues, customers and professional advisers as well as accepting your CV. Candidates have to be a neat fit for senior management teams – then they will be able to contribute to the strategy, give leadership and be generally useful at the top from the minute they join the company at that level. They have to be internally astute and externally aware. It is helpful to have senior connections elsewhere and certainly to know about world movements and issues. It is also necessary to have a particular interest or speciality to contribute to company thinking.

In the UK they are seen as Fat Cats; in the USA they are Heroes. Top-earning executives are viewed with suspicion, probably because it is not understood what they actually do. Entrepreneurs, such as Richard Branson, are looked at more kindly, especially if they smile their way beyond the inherent motivation of 'making money'. There is a change in attitude to high-profile leaders, evidenced by the focus on the personality of the deal-maker when BP and Amoco announced their mega merger. Sir John Browne hit the headlines and was not the target for snide remarks by the media on this occasion. The late nineties corporate culture is that of winner takes all. The elite top managers, unrestrained by regulation, hostile taxes or shareholder pressure, reward themselves ever more handsomely for achievements which are more often to do with financial dealings provoked by bankers in the City or Wall Street than with the efficient making and selling of useful products and services.

The ninety-nine per cent who are not the elite have been destabilised in their working lives by the cost-paring and merger-synergy which have been prevalent since the eighties. The stock market is predicted to fall sharply before the end of the decade. The emphasis on short- rather than long-term investment and innovation has been fed upon and caused the meteoric rise of the stock market to date. The boss of BP earns sixteen times more than the average BP employee; chief executives in the UK, on average, earn eighteen times more than their employees' take-home pay. In Germany it is 11, in France 15, in the USA 24 and in Hong Kong it is 48 times more, so the UK scene is about average. This is a vast improvement on the previously highly restricted rewards systems which did not recognise the wealth-creating capacity of the 1%. An argument is that the time has come to balance the situation more fairly. Where does the company stop, either in the heights to which rewards can rise or in the lower levels which are acceptable as income for the staff?

The new type of chief executive is encouraged to act as owner-boss rather than just maintaining the operation during their period of tenure. The main part of the remuneration package has changed from salary to share options or bonus calculated on share performance. It is forecasted that as the share market falls so will the remuneration of that 1%, the top dogs. Employment lawyers have become very skilled at writing employment contracts so that the individual does not suffer from the foibles of the market, the board or company behaviour to any great extent. Golden hand-shakes, golden parachutes, handcuffs and similar devices have been instituted to prevent pain. It will be the coming tough economic climate which will make it obvious which CEOs are earning their keep. While dividends are buoyant, the share-holders relax, and the opposite happens when dividends fall. Genuine achievement is laudable. The marketplace pays well for a track record of success. 'Fat-cattery may be offensive but to try and restrain it by regulatory interference would do more harm than good. Unfettered capitalism is, after all, the best engine of prosperity yet invented, but no one has said that it had to be universally fair' (Martin Vander writing in the *Independent*). David Varney is combative, driven, brave and busy. He left Shell after twenty-eight years to head up British Gas. Even his own chairman agrees he is a maverick, but the Chief Executive of British Gas has been a breath of fresh air for the demerged group. He does not feel like a fat cat and says that he has a fairly robust attitude to all that and has managed to get both the Government and the City pinstripes on his side. He has also managed to increase both the figures and the goodwill for the group.

Women are at last breaking through the wages barrier and there are now more than fifty women in the UK who earn more than £1 million per year, with many more coming up the ladder behind them. You have the examples of Jennifer Richards-Stewart, who has made a fortune selling Actua Soccer computer games, and Marjorie Scardino, who came from the USA, and has proved to be a successful CEO of the Pearson Group (media). There is also Pat Grant, who owns the freezer group, Norfrost, and Amanda Thompson, who is in the middle of converting Blackpool Pleasure Beach into a modern theme park. Then there is the remarkable success of Helen Fielding, who earned nearly a million by writing the best-seller, *Bridget Jones's Diary*, and has seen her fortunes augmented in the USA too. Denise O'Donoghue regards herself as very astute, intuitive and an unsystematic risk-taker. In the independent television production sector she is a star. She is Managing Director of Hat Trick Productions, the company responsible for *Drop the Dead Donkey*, *Have I Got News For You?*, *Father Ted*, et cetera. She comes from a family of strong women and after graduating from York University in politics and having a spell as a management consultant at Coopers and Lybrand, she got a job running the Independent Programme Producers' Association. She and her business partners, Jimmy Mulville and Geoffrey Perkins, each own one third of the company, which is worth around £35 million. Very focused on her career, Denise likes to be 'at the coal face' and wants to continue doing what she does well.

Women in the UK continue to earn more than ever. The glass ceiling has turned into the glass elevator. Mary Dobson started her business with £500 in her mother's garage over twenty years ago. Now turnover is £29.3 million per annum. She is the 'tsarina of signs'. Her company Spandex supplies signs for stores, high streets and everywhere that signage is used. She and her husband have sold out their shares to the American company Gerber Scientific and now she is busy creating new ideas. The top ten women in this context are: Mary Dobson; Linda Jacobs (Raines), dairy food entrepreneur; Evelyn Stewart, nursing homes entrepreneur; Vanessa Wynn-Griffiths, nursing agency entrepreneur; Carol Moffett, engineering entrepreneur; Carol Galley, fund manager; Enya, pop singer; Ally Svensson, Seattle Coffee founder; Ann Gloag (Stagecoach), transport empire; Bridget Blow, CEO of ITnet. These are followed by the Spice Girls, the All Saints, Barbara Taylor Bradford (author), and Natalie Imbruglia (pop singer). So nursing and singing are the most profitable pursuits at the moment.

The organisation which is dedicated to best management practice and the use of innovative ideas will deploy the latest communications systems and other techniques to lift middle management out of isolation and unleash their talent. Companies or organisations employing up to 300 people and with an income of between £5m and £50m, which is the middle market group, have the challenge of a DTI initiative called Partnerships with People (1998). (This covers six out of ten employees in the UK and contributes two thirds of the Gross National Product.) The initial investigation discovered that these managers are so busy working that they do not have time to keep up to date with either their competitors or the latest thinking in their own organisation. Owner-run organisations rarely survive beyond the third generation, so the concentration on managing talent is timely. Managers who see their people as contributing more possibilities than just their forty hours per week will benefit.

Guidelines from the DTI Innovation Unit (1998):

1. Shared goals: The whole organisation should know where it is going and everyone should be involved in developing the vision. But it should happen gradually – to rush is to court disaster.
2. Shared culture: Staff should be managed to ensure that everyone understands the company's values – not just towards customers, but also towards suppliers.
3. Shared learning: Staff should not be neglected in corporate thinking. Unwilling, unreasonable and unresponsive workers (for example, teachers at the 1998 conference reacting to David Blunkett, the Education Secretary of State) can undermine the best strategies – but well-founded career and development plans will increase loyalty when they are agreed.
4. Shared effort: Teams are the building blocks of innovative businesses. Training is vital. Teams should not be competing with each other. Over time, they should be encouraged to lose rigidity and to adopt a more flexible and more efficient learning approach.
5. Shared information: Tell the truth at all times without undue optimism or pessimism. Avoid corporate bureaucracy and excessive use of meetings.

Asked what success depends on, 68% of top companies agree that it lies in developing the business abilities of employees along with their personal ambitions. Nearly all of them say that people management is top priority now, and that training is the way to make employees feel valued and so be successful. An ex-Cadbury Schweppes executive said, 'It takes guts to let people have an input to targets and budgets. It involves sharing power. The owner manager in particular has to let something go. But once they have said "I can trust people" the financial side becomes less of an issue. They discover, in fact, they are reducing risk by having more people at the sharp end who know how things really work.'

Managing Imagination

Talent, imagination and creativity tend to be associated with the arts, and are thought to be the expression of highly original ideas. However, to be useful, an idea has to be appropriate and actionable. It must influence the way business gets done and be able to benefit every single function and process. Within every individual, creativity is a function of three components: expertise, creative-thinking skills and motivation. Managers can influence these through workplace practices and conditions, bearing in mind the following:

- Expertise is knowledge: technical, procedural and intellectual.
- Creative-thinking skills determine how flexibly and imaginatively people approach problems.
- Motivation is not always driven by personal gain. The urge to solve the problems at hand leads on to other solutions even more creative, and can be more satisfying than other rewards, even money.

The latter can be most influenced by the workplace. The first two are harder to manage. The manager who recognises the triggers which help creative people will hold their attention and may retain their contribution to the organisation. Challenge, freedom, resources, team flexibility, encouragement from above as well as below, together will achieve the corporate goal of keeping the people assets creative. There has to be a safety net in place so that everyone can fly high with their ideas and not be controlled by fear.

How to harness talent was shown by the enthusiastic Ian Hardcastle, managing director of the services business in ICL, the leading European IT systems firm. He is a computer man with a mission to galvanise employees to enjoy their work. He found out at Logica that staff see service industries as a sweat shop, so you need loose decision-making within tight boundaries to change their perception. He positions people to meet customer requirements and to ensure future career development for each member of staff. They are free to move around the company to maximise experience and to have space to grow. He believes in living life to the full and encourages people to have interests wherever they are. Personally, he is mad about motor racing and American Football.

Managing talent works best in a shared working environment. Executives who keep staff informed about their performances have learnt that this increases effort and stimulates interest. At the same time, the MD does not have to suffer heart attacks on a daily basis. Sensible companies do a SWOT analysis (listings of strengths and weaknesses) before initiating changes with everyone involved. Entrepreneurial managers are usually the most sceptical, but they are pleased when they note increased activity, excitement and output due to improved communication and team effort. All the people involved have to acquire a tough edge and the whole thing is challenging, demanding and stretching. Now that traditional hierarchical structures within organisations are rare, it is no longer possible for you to keep your head down and work on without being noticed year after year. With the flat structures of today, everyone is being given freedoms and responsibilities. When everyone is team-focused there is great peer pressure to perform, most especially on the newcomer to the group. There can be a high drop-out at first – up to 25% of newcomers in the first six months of employment – unless you are accustomed to being valued for your contribution rather than doing what you are told. Some organisations invite potential employees to work with teams for some time before they are appointed. This way you can test yourself and find out if you like this exposed way of working. Equally the teams can decide if they want you to stay.

Managing talented and creative people well requires top executives to have a clear understanding of corporate goals. They need to adopt a strong leadership style but not to dictate the vision or the terms of the company culture. The great unifier for everyone in an open, honest corporate environment is the customer. Multifunctional teams will work best when they are focused on serving and delivering to the customer.

Sector Crossover

1. Private to Public Sector
Private Sector managers seeking jobs in the public sector must be prepared to go through an alien recruitment process and follow it to the letter. They have to be aware of their own naiveté and to avoid being contemptuous of the conventions to which they are not accustomed. Headhunters such as Spencer Stuart, PricewaterhouseCoopers and Korn/Ferry always warn potential candidates to listen to their briefings carefully. One of the indicators of the preciseness of the procedures is that even the most senior roles are advertised, for two main reasons. The first is to ensure fair and open competition and equal opportunities. The second is the new rules of appointment and accountability which have been initiated by the Nolan committee.

In most instances an advertisement offers an information pack or a telephone number. You should take the opportunity for a conversation about the job. It makes sense to analyse the information before completing and sending off your CV. Packs will include facts and figures covering strategy, existing appointees, organisational structure, job and person specification and profile. The remuneration and benefits package, response instructions and interview dates will be outlined too. Addressing the criteria for the job is vital. Go through your basic CV and make sure that you have highlighted your experience which meets these best. The covering letter needs to be brief unless otherwise stated. In any event it is probable that it will be separated from the CV at some stage. Read the pack and then telephone and demonstrate that you have read the information, that you might be interested and see if they consider your track record to be relevant and at the right level. Then the CV gets finished and sent.

Even the most able candidates have to overlook the 'bureaucracy', which can be irksome. The language you use and the attitudes you expose matter too, as more than just political correctness, when dealing with public bodies. Civil servants, NHS staff, voluntary boards for quangos or whatever agency or department with which you are in discussion, have certain standards which must be adhered to at all times. Everything is recorded, often in triplicate. Make sure your application is clear and suitable for multiple photocopying.

Local government recruitment also expects professional responses, and again you must aim to match their criteria right from the earliest sifting exercise. Headhunters are invaluable in outlining the traps and other things for applicants/candidates to be wary of along the way. For example, in certain circumstances it is all right to meet with the existing incumbent. This is dangerous unless you are very clear about the situation, because you could be disqualified for lobbying if you approach anyone in any way having influence on the appointment. Talk to people already employed by or on boards of public sector bodies. They can bring you up to date with the current issues, pressures and sensitive areas. Prepare, prepare and prepare, because there is so much to know. Pressure is on the candidate to be aware. In the private sector the emphasis is more on company and bottom-line implications. The rigorousness of the recruitment process in local government is offputting for those who have never been through such a system before. You are confronted with assessment centres, panel interviews, timed discussions, presentation requirements and full statements which you have attached to your CV. Control of decisions is in the purview of the professionals initially but with the elected or ministerial or appointed in the final instance. Often there are observers at the panel interviews too.

It is common practice in the public sector to require references and a commitment to accept the job, if offered, well before the final interview. This is very daunting for most people, especially when there is any possibility of putting your existing job in jeopardy. A friendly headhunter can be a great ally in the timing of these aspects and in protecting your confidentiality. Sheila Drew-Smith, a member of the Nolan Panel on the appointment of the Chairs of quangos, who is Chair of Broadmoor Hospital herself, understands the resentment senior people feel about the endless filling in of forms when they wander into public sector appointments. They also resent the time waiting for feedback at each stage. NHS applicants have a duplication of activities throughout the appointment process for senior and non-executive positions, probably because of the numbers of people the NHS employs nationally. Many senior people have not been interviewed for a long time, and have not prepared a CV either. It is difficult to be tolerant about the ritual of forms, meetings, the different language and consistent referring back to yet more people. Headhunters and recruiters have to ensure that the employers have a realistic market-based expectation of applicants. They also need to check scales and salaries so that there is a cross-sector comparison which is acceptable.

A reduction in the success of private sector applicants in the public sector has been measured in 1998 and shows a drop of 24% in applications from business people. During 1995–8 there was a steady increase to 39%, while the number of women made a giant leap to 34% overall from 19%. By describing candidates in terms of their skills, experience and educational background, rather than the number of years they have spent at Civil Service grade-so-and-so, the public sector can attract more commercially practised people. The need to find a good public administrator is less strong now that the public sector requires business acumen and the ability to transform an organisation, not just maintain it.

Moves from the private to the public sector are increasing, whereas the previous pattern was a flow the other way. Both sectors have supplied the voluntary sector forever, either as volunteers or as executives. Most private sector managers recognise the important work to be done in the public sector. However, up until very recently, a move across was regarded by hard-bitten businessmen as an admission of failure or defeat. Why should anyone take the risk of reduced income in such a move? This is not necessarily the case any more. Neville Bain, ex-Coats Viyella Chief Executive, has arrived at the Post Office as Chairman. He aims to create great commercial success for the organisation but is confronted by government resistance on one side and fierce competition on the other. Cynics in both camps doubt his success.

The public sector is often more family friendly than the private sector, with provision of crèches, paternity leave, study time and a range of flexible working arrangements. There is a greater chance of having part-time work or extended leave in the public sector than within a company. Talk to a senior executive and often you will find a hankering for a role in some sort of public service. Sir Michael Bett, who took over as President of the Institute of Personnel Development from being HR Director of GEC, made a halfway step and has proved himself well, but it is his role as First Commissioner of the Civil Service which is impressive. Lord Simian of Highbury was one of the first to make a move from the private to the public sector after the last election. After a year he discussed his positive experience and concurred with the government policy of developing a real partnership between industry and government. He wants each side to understand what the other is doing, and he has shown that it is the job of business to deliver competitiveness and prosperity while it is the government's role to provide the background and architecture within which business can operate well. He talks about everyone living in an increasingly globalised business environment where the pace of change leaves no space for complacency. Everyone needs to improve their performance continually. He quotes Geoffrey Robinson, David Sainsbury and Gus MacDonald as other examples of businessmen caught up in public service.

Successful business leaders have been tempted by the part-time policy level appointments and, on the whole, have been effective in their new roles. The New Labour government has co-opted many business people to run or be on the boards of Task Forces, NHS boards, and other such committees. Barclays' Martin Taylor and Peter Davis from the Prudential are oft quoted examples. Most senior people have accepted more or less onerous roles outside of their income producing situation in order to give back to society.

The recent dramatic changes both in local and central government have given opportunities for a more entrepreneurial, innovative style of management. The government's initiatives to create a new culture to meet the push for best value, to deliver the service and to work in partnership with external agencies, all make more demands on managers. Forward-looking public sector organisations are keen to recruit financial professionals. They have to be technically competent, be able to work with senior teams and accept accountability and openness. They also need to be creative and innovative in managing money and finding new ways of dealing with public funding. Because of the rate of change the public sector perception of the corporate candidates is that it is too big a learning curve for them to manage when the job needs someone who will be efficient from day one.

The Civil Service used to be an obvious career for bright graduates. Today it is a less popular employer. It is a gruelling process to be accepted. You have to be good to get as far as sitting the examinations for the Civil Service selection board and very good to pass them and be offered the chance to go to the next stage. Excellence is necessary. Only 300 graduates a year become fast-stream entrants to the Home Civil Service or the Diplomatic Service.

2. Public to Private Sector

Public sector employees are prejudiced too. They regard themselves as followers of a superior calling. They tend to look down on the commercial sector as being short on integrity and intellectual challenges, not to mention grubby in its profit motive. Yet a move into the world of profit does not have the same stigma as a move in the opposite direction has had. Former MPs and civil servants have achieved a high-level entry and been involved shortly after leaving their high-profile office. Typical examples are Sir Peter Middleton, who joined BZW after being Permanent Secretary at the Treasury; and Kenneth Clark, who after being Chancellor went on several boards, including Unichem, British American Tobacco and Foreign and Colonial. Rigid divisions are slowly breaking down as the two sides start to accept that they are not on separate planets. The public accountability and lack of final decision-making that define the culture in the public sector are now being called for in the world of business. Living with the relentless attention attached to senior public sector jobs could benefit many of Britain's top business managers; equally, delivering a profit in a competitive market is beneficial to local and central government and other public bodies. In the USA and on the Continent, people move easily between the sectors on their way to the top, but in the UK it is most likely to happen near the end of a career. It would be much more valuable for talented individuals if they could transfer between sectors when they still had time to go back again.

3. Public and Private to Voluntary Sector
Charities provide an alternative workplace. Executives who want a challenging job but with less pressure are moving into the voluntary sector, where they are being well received for their commercial experience. One of the effects is to create a glass ceiling for the younger people who have been working in the charity sector for some time as the senior executives move over from the down-sized corporate sector. It is almost impossible for someone who has worked to a high level of responsibility in a charity to move the other way to a company, because of the existing perception that they do not understand the commercial and financial requirements. However, small- and medium-sized companies are starting to consider voluntary sector managers, because they understand that they can bring with them a wide range of experience.

Charities are no longer as easily pleased as they were. It used to be the practice that they would be grateful for secondment arrangements whereby executives would come and work for them at the end of their main career or when they had actually retired. Those days are over. Younger, bright and sparkling people are wanted to take on the onerous and publicly accountable roles in the newly competitive charity. For example, the work done within the Prince's Trust has attracted both champions from business and bright young things.

Bertie Pinchera, Head of International Retailing at Boots Opticians, is an example of the executive in his prime who has been appointed as chief executive of a charity. National Kidney Research Funding has welcomed him to develop their work. He sees the principles of management as being the same in both environments, and his new job provides a strong enough challenge for him to be excited. The job also fulfils his desire to cut down on international travelling and have time to spend with his family. He has already identified a problem inherent in managing volunteers and a restricted spending programme: there are not enough people with professional skills and they are not necessarily working for the same goals, so effort can be wasted. He has responded by clarifying the part that each member of staff can play in carrying out the charity's strategic plan.

The perception still exists that working for a charity means being paid less, being valued for the 'goodness' of the job, and being able to affect directly the well-being of the people for whom the charity is working. It actually requires a strong political sense and diplomatic management style, as well as stamina and an acceptance of a high public profile. Charity jobs are usually advertised internally, encouraging staff to move upwards from within. Budget constraints tend to limit external advertising, so it is advisable to approach the charities directly. Usually the more senior positions, especially the more specialist ones, such as property management, are advertised nationally. Most charities offer the opportunity for on-the-job vocational training, and usually NVQs, graduate placement and other work experience schemes too.

The Director of the National Council for Voluntary Organisations has identified the broad types of leader who are attracted to these jobs: the technocrats, the cause-related chief executives and the second career leaders. Only 15% of the present CEOs have come from the private sector nonetheless. As the average age of the charity chief executive falls, there will be an increasing pressure for cross-sector mobility. Women are pre-dominant in the voluntary sector staffs, but there are only fifteen female chief executives and they are in charge of smaller organisations. Only one of the top charities is led by a woman: Sheila McKechnie, at the Consumer Council. External challenges for voluntary chief executives are tough and clear. They will have to continue to cope with a more challenging funding climate, a decline in public trust, growing media scrutiny and increased competition in service provision as the boundaries between all sectors blur. 'It goes without saying that only the visionary need apply to climb this management mountain' (Barclays/NGO Survey).

Staff (6500 altogether), at a major utility group, the Eastern Group, are busy helping the jobless to write CVs, painting with adventure play groups or doing the books for a community project. HarperCollins have brought their American culture to the UK and require each employee to give a stated number of hours per week to community work. Charity work is often part of staff training, and Community Service Volunteers (CSV), the UK's biggest provider of volunteers, sometimes teams up with companies to carry out specific projects. In 1997, CSV placed 156,000 volunteers. The Prince's Trust Volunteers invites cross-sector volunteers to help in their projects combining employed and unemployed young people. Forward-looking organisations increasingly want their staff to widen their experience and life beyond their work stations. Volunteers pick up and pass on skills, and improve their own chances of promotion. For example: Anderson Consulting encourages staff to give regular time to charity work and to help functional staff in charities to be even more professional. This arrangement can be more productive than attending courses, because everyone is acting within a real working environment. Volunteers are often given access to all departments within their employer company and are given support for their community work. This increases knowledge across the firm.

Most volunteers get the opportunity to add to or balance the skills and training they already have. For example, Eastern Group employees are mainly technical, and by spending half a day per month on voluntary work they get the chance to develop non-academic, non-examinable and so-called soft caring skills. These include the ability to communicate effectively with a wide range of people, to work unsupervised and to be a self-starter. Volunteering is a growth area. Many young people take on charity work to get their feet on a career ladder. Sometimes they are kept on full-time. In any event, future employers are impressed and value volunteering on a CV. They see it as evidence of self-confidence and teamwork, with the development of above average time management and negotiating skills.

Leadership Model-building

Leo Murray started in business, ATKearney and Rothmans, before joining Cranfield to run the Business School. It was his global experience that identified him as a star candidate for the job. He found that university life is very different from commercial. He has become accustomed to the network of accountabilities and the use of influence rather than power to manage people who are essentially autonomous. He believes that the reason why so many successful people fail to make an impact on public sector jobs is because they have not understood this important distinction. The management of knowledge workers depends on creating credibility, having an overview of the whole organisation, using the influence of the top role and being very accessible. He has managed to lead the faculty into putting the university before the personal interests of academic stars. He is aware of the difficulties in managing egos, and refers to 'useless egos', which are 'selfish upholders of their own rights'. He aims to attract and retain useful egos. He believes that the role of the CEO is to listen but also to have a point of view and to give a lead. Teams can easily degenerate into committees. Although he has been approached by the headhunters on numerous occasions, as there is a worldwide shortage of capable heads for business schools, he has remained true to management education and Cranfield in particular. Above all, he enjoys his work.

Finance companies are in the vanguard of employers taking staff away from the office to foster better teamwork, communication and personal development. The focus is on mindset and team-building rather than just romping over them there hills. About 25% of companies using outdoor facilities are from the City and include insurance companies and merchant banks, with the retail banking sector following their example. Staff have commented that the practical side of these courses helps them to understand different points of view and to be more tolerant. Being an effective leader does not necessarily mean leading from the front, and they learn the value of delegating in situations such as trying to find their way out of a cave. Senior managers who often feel unable to ask for support find an exercise called 'the pamper role', which concentrates on physical exercise, helps them to do so. They learn to depend on team-mates while they are up the greasy pole or whatever. A scheme called 'Teamscapes' has proved popular. It is intellectually rather than just physically challenging. Teams are chosen and work together in competition to solve problems. They demonstrate communication techniques and find out that there are many different ways of solving problems. British Airways use the training for many parts of their organisation, including financial services. Managers in sales and operational are given insights into implications for the bottom line. For example: a large map of the world is spread out and a Lego model has to be made of specified areas. The teams have to earn each piece by taking a bucket of water across a stream or by climbing scaffolding, et cetera. The exercise shows how the staff interrelate with their tasks, skills and creativity.

Training that takes people beyond their usual four walls is useful in motivating staff who have been in the same job and may have got stuck over a long time. Traditionally long-term service was the norm in careers in building societies and insurance, and until recently there has not been much organisational movement. Sometimes new leaders are found through demonstrating what they can do on these training occasions. Bringing managers from different parts of the company together and team-building in different ways can generate a big change in their behaviours and confidence.

Disorganisation is Chaos?

Tom Peters claimed that a firm has to 'innovate or die'. At IDEO staff are encouraged to 'play' and the most important rule is to break the rules. So potent have IDEO's creative ideas proved that *Fortune* magazine described its seemingly chaotic design studio as 'one of Silicon Valley's secret weapons'. Its success, the industrial design firm believes, lies in the ability to sustain a culture of innovation. IDEO is the largest industrial product design firm in the world. It has been involved in such diverse projects as helping to create the first Apple computer mouse and the design of the 25-foot mechanical whale in the *Free Willy* films. IDEO has become a magnet for multinationals who wish to associate themselves with a consultancy that will enhance their own cultures and make them more innovative. It is a formula which seems to work. The UK office originated in 1969 when Bill Moggeridge set up the design company, which then merged with Matrix Product Design and David Kelley Design, and so IDEO was formed. It has a turnover of £30 million, offices throughout the world and 350 employees. It has blue-chip companies amongst its client list. Samsung has created a joint design laboratory, and Steelcase, an American furniture design group, has taken an equity holding in IDEO.

Tim Brown, the London director, says, 'Above all else innovation requires a willingness to embrace chaos. It means giving rein to people who are opinionated, wilful and delight in challenging the rules. It demands a loose management structure that does not isolate people in departments or on the rungs of a ladder. It needs flexible work spaces that encourage a cross-fertilisation of ideas. It requires risk-taking.'

Tom Peters visited the offices in Palo Alto, USA, and commented: 'IDEO is a zoo. Experts of all flavours co-mingle in "offices" that look more like cacophonous kindergarten classrooms.' IDEO believes in the ultimate innovation environment, and despite intense pressure and tight deadlines, the company maintains an air of creative anarchy. It employs an eclectic group that includes cognitive psychologists and computer scientists as well as industrial designers, who together create about ninety products a year. Staff work wherever they happen to be and scatter scribbled notes – to the untrained eye it is a chaotic mess.

David Kelley, one of the original directors, describes IDEO as 'a living laboratory of the workplace. The company is in a state of perpetual experimentation where new ideas are constantly being tried out in the projects, work space and culture.' It is a project-based organisation. All work is organised in project teams which form and disband in a matter of weeks or months. There are no permanent job assignments, and people wear so many different hats that job titles are meaningless. IDEO sends people out on secondments to offices so that they can experience other work-places, and they are free to move locations if they can find colleagues who are willing to switch with them. The company has a special approach towards brainstorming. At the start of a new assignment, project leaders call for a brainstorming session, typically between about eight people. This multi-disciplinary group will then scribble on white papered walls and surfaces and complement the low-tech with the high-tech of multimedia presentations using video and computer projections. They work towards their five principles:

1. Stay focused on the project
2. Encourage wild ideas
3. Defer judgement
4. Build on the ideas of others
5. One conversation at a time

The aim is to create a whirlwind of activity and ideas. Speed is essential to the process, and the most promising ideas are pro-cessed into prototypes within a short space of time. The outcome is a number of spectacular successes as well as the spectacular failures.

Being Eccentric

Demand for head-office managers is strong. Competition for the right people now focuses more on their 'softer' skills than on process management as companies look for people who are team players and are able to motivate staff. Insurance and investment companies, as well as financial recruitment consultancies, are looking for a new breed of manager – one whose people skills are every bit as good as their hard management experience. This is not a new philosophy of management. It simply means that, with the exception of highly technical roles, the operative word to describe a successful financial services manager has changed from functionary to strategist. In order to be successful in financial services, there is a fundamental need to avoid stereotyping, to try out new ideas, to challenge the status quo of the procedure manual. The term eccentricity has been coined to describe this approach.

The search is constant for the manager who is a lateral thinker, a good networker, a negotiator, business analyst and above all a leader and motivator of people. The new philosophy involves challenging the prejudices of managers about their relationships with their staff. Managers can no longer depend on being effective by being authoritative but must focus on developing the skills of the team, acting as facilitators and coaches. You can use your own reactions which you have experienced on your way up to encourage others. The ethos of compliance arising from the Financial Services and Pensions Acts has changed the focus of that industry; so has the obligation to reach a gold standard of customer service. There is not much difference between the products on offer, so it is essential to capture the customer by service and interface with sympathetic staff. Companies vie with each other in their battle to expand business. Compliance has also influenced the level of service demanded by customers. The media has contributed to this by showing and writing about practices of salesmen that have not benefited the customer. High-profile events such as the pensions mis-selling scandal have made consumers wary.

Another factor behind the new breed of head-office manager is the success of some companies in winning the trust of the public by being innovative. Psychometric and other testing is now used in recruiting programmes because employers are struggling to find the eccentric quotient and individualistic potential to add to their teams. Increased internal competition in companies that have been affected by the recent spate of mergers and acquisitions has led to differential assessment of the existing managements, which have to be downsized because of duplication and overlap. There is a huge skills shortage in industry which adds to the pressures. Just at the time when new ways of working have evolved, there are not enough people available to carry them out. Those who can be creative and stretch their imaginative management to make the company work better and more profitably will win. 'In the land of the blind the one-eyed man is king' principle can apply. So the eccentric can be successful.

Being Entrepreneurial

The entrepreneur is the object of envy and admiration, the mainspring for the private sector, the stuff of commercial legend, and the source of new companies, new products and new industries. Entrepreneurs act on their own logic and observation as well as intuition, and their plans, decisions and execution are controlled by methods that can be easily understood, described and imitated. Persistence is the single most useful attribute of the entrepreneur. Founder entrepreneurs are often people who have worked in an industry and seen the gaps in the market, then gone and taken advantage of them. The man who invented the sugar packet is one example; Michael Heseltine, who set up Haymarket Publishing for management, medical and other journals, is another.

Entrepreneurs who succeed are those who know their business, who target markets, jump over setbacks and find money when they need it. They do not give up. Once start-up difficulties have been overcome, ingenuity continues to be important. 'The more successful the business becomes, the more it faces a serious obstacle,' says Robert Heller, writing in *Goldfinger*. In the mid-eighties, Barry Jackson set up a small company called Sea-Band to make wristbands to combat nausea. It grew quickly and is still prospering. Annual sales are £3 million and it has a sales force of 89 people covering 50 countries, including the USA. The company has survived through the recession and against new competition by careful planning, by listening to expert advice when necessary and by understanding that it was really a marketing company. Sea-Band handed over debt collecting to a factoring firm, knowing that this would secure their cash flow while only marginally reducing their profits. Barry Jackson believes in spreading risk and in expanding to markets internationally. They discovered the value of the fax machine when selling abroad. It was early days and the sales soon covered the cost of this type of communication. They then set up a network of distributors and agents, and by 1992 they had an annual increase in sales of 20%. Jackson has kept the company lean at all stages. They have had to combat the effect of the strong pound, and have decided not to lower prices but are improving services by giving customers extra goods. Jackson monitors financial trends closely and jumps on accounts and other things quickly so that everything is put right before developing into a crisis.

A list of Britain's Top Entrepreneurs announced in 1998 shows that the new generation of whizz people are better educated than their predecessors. Many are graduates, six of them possessing doctorates as well, and one is a full-time professor of electrical and electronic engineering (at Leeds University). Many still describe themselves as graduates of the School of Life. The management style of these successful people is described as 'loose and cool'. They are keen to learn from their managers, inspire others with their success and have collectively created a quarter of a million new jobs in the recent past. Paul Brett, CEO at Thomson Travel Group, is a details man rather than having a grand strategic vision, but he is also clear about what he wants. He is a calm, low-key character in a cut-throat business. His philosophy for survival is to offer high-quality products and to control costs. He enjoys travel himself and spends any spare time looking around.

Many women, blocked by the corporate glass ceiling, have broken into the big time in business by becoming successful entrepreneurs. The majority of successful female entrepreneurs are not household names. They have moved on from retailing, fashion and food to high technology, recruitment consultancy and car dealing. Self-made women are the driving force in their companies and are very busy. Nicola Foulston inherited Brands Hatch and has put the leisure group, which owns four motor-sports circuits, on its feet. Anita Roddick goes from strength to strength with her flamboyant, environmentally friendly organisation, the Body Shop. Ann Gloag, living in her Scottish castle, is delivering a major transport revolution through Stagecoach. The City is full of intra-preneurs as well as entrepreneurs – Nicola Horlick at Societe Generale, for example, or Carol Galley at Mercury Asset Management. The new generation includes Dr Susan Kingsman of Biomedica, Jenny Richards-Stewart of

Gremlin, the quoted computer games company, and Karen Jones, who built up the Pelican Restaurant Group. For women who have taken the plunge into their own business, the rewards are satisfying, especially in giving them control. Jan Fletcher has a range of businesses stretching from MSF Motor Group to Bee Health, the natural honey/propolis-based product, and also owns fish and chip outlets and a haulage business.

Successful women, like successful men, have certain character-istics: arrogance, single-mindedness, aggression, strength and a competitive nature. Women tend to be calculated risk-takers, more secretive and more guarded than men. They are less volatile and bottle up their professional frustrations more too. Women support each other to some extent, but the higher up they go the more they are exposed. Increasingly entrepreneurs are talking to each other as they become accustomed to being owner-managers and have the need to share their ups and downs. They are characterised by sheer grit and persistence. As soon as they become serious players, they are taken more seriously: money talks. Female entrepreneurs see themselves as creators of jobs, while men rate themselves as creators of wealth. This shows the latter as being more concerned with profits (43%) while the former look for customer and staff satisfaction (28%).

Survival and success are the paradoxical components which drive the typical entrepreneur. In the UK there is a native suspicion of winning and success, so there is an inherent problem for the entrepreneur to cope with – jealousy and lack of under-standing for their drive. Small Business Management reports are published quarterly and track the progress of entrepreneurs in all areas of business. Manufacturers are consistently under pressure, with the retailers showing the greatest seasonal influences. The typical profile of the entrepreneur has certain common characteristics. They have:

- Business role models. They are often the children of business-men, and have been imbued with business thinking from an early age.
- Competitive tendencies. They need to win, whether it is the high-jump at school or the latest business success.

- No fear of responsibility, taking risks and projects that others often pull back from.
- A need to be in control, finding it difficult to be at the beck and call of others.
- A knack of knowing everybody, especially in the industry in which they are working. Networking is their lifeblood.
- Experience of rapid change and dealing with it successfully.
- Early success in whatever projects they have undertaken.

Some people cannot stop launching new ventures. They are ideas people who enjoy the thrill of building something up from scratch, and some of them have thrived in an increasingly favourable tax climate in the UK. Having made their millions, many are now moving on to become venture capitalists themselves, helping up-and-coming businesses. Chris Evans is typical. He is not the media star, but the scientist son of a Port Talbot steelworker who started up the successful biotech companies, Celsios and Ciroscience and took them public. He then moved into car security technology with Toad and founded a seed capital company, Merlin Ventures, for investing in small businesses. He has now been appointed by the government to head up an EU initiative to look at the ways legislation should meet the needs of the small and medium sized businesses.

Herman Hauser is another such person. He used his experience as a founder of Acorn Computers and has been involved in setting up 35 other businesses. Hugh Corbett is now the owner of Top Inns after selling out the Slug & Lettuce chain. Entrepreneurs thrive on discontinuity and are well represented in the electronics, bioscience and retailing industries.

John Bates, Director of the Foundation of Entrepreneurial Management at London Business School, argues that entrepreneurs are not so different from corporate executives. He compares the serial entrepreneur with the company doctors who go from one company to another. They are all people who lead from the front, like being in the start-up situation and get bored when it is all running well. Entrepreneurs have always been assumed to be loners who do not fit into the corporate life, but it is emerging that they are very good at creating teams and need partners who make sure that everything works. Money matters too and entrepreneurs are well-motivated by financial success.

A 1998 prizewinner is European Safety Systems which has revolutionised a whole industry. SE makes industrial warning systems and has advanced the technology by 20 years. They make the audible and visual devices which warn employees of hazards and are used when ships are being loaded, when heavy machinery is being moved in factories and on oil rigs which are being evacuated. SE was set up in 1992. Since then it has developed from three tone devices to 32 tones based on integrated circuits. Hazards can be defined more specifically and identified by precise noises. Gardner Energy Management is a company which deals with the steam loss which costs British industry £3 billion per annum. Gardner used to design industrial steam systems until it recognised that it is costly energy going up in thin air. The answer is a simple steam trap with no moving parts, requiring no maintenance except for occasional cleaning. There is a market for a trap that did not fail and which would not need constant replacement. The company started in a shed in Devon and won its first order before the prototype was complete. British Airports Authority had faith in the idea. Now Gardner has a manufacturing base in Newton Abbot and supplies customers within a week of their order.

Battles on the Way Up

Bullying exists in many organisations even though managers deny that it is happening or claim that it is part of a tough commercial world. Senior managers are sometimes fearful that if someone under them is labelled a bully, they could be seen as bad recruiters. Managers can eradicate bullies by developing awareness through policies and procedures which will be followed up by action. They need to define insidious behaviour which has come to be seen as acceptable and to change attitudes. They should alert people to report bullying and then do something about it. Bullying is a hidden problem that damages people and dents profits, but it is not being taken seriously enough. It is presumed that human resources professionals will deal with it, but senior managers do not always go to them for solutions. The Andrea Adams Trust carried out research in 1998 and discovered that 80% of organisations have a bully. Half of the respondents in the project claimed to have been bullied themselves but only 16% said that they would go to the personnel department. Even when there is a policy in place, it is kept fairly quiet, as organisations do not want to be identified with the concept.

Littlewoods believe that giving everyone dignity at work is important for the business to function effectively. They have set up supporters and investigators and trained them to their specific roles. Supporters are there to listen, analyse issues, then put forward options and go through the pros and cons of each one. It is for the bullied individual to make the final decision as to what should happen. The investigators handle the complaint impartially. Line managers who are neither supporters nor investigators are taught to recognise issues early and shown how to intervene and get people to work together again. They have had no tribunal cases and by dealing with the issues quickly they have not had to take recourse to formal procedures.

Staffordshire University School of Management have studied the position of the bullied. A quarter leave the job, and a quarter of those who have witnessed the bullying have considered leaving. It is not the big, dramatic incidents that cause the most bother, but the stream of small, insidious moments which may seem innocuous at the time but add up to a pattern. Eventually it undermines the victim's power and confidence. Psychological effects can last for ever, so the responsibility of the employer is to try and make sure that each person is able to do good work, experience success and enjoy outcomes and profits. The example of zero tolerance of bullying from the top helps too.

The glass ceiling is an invisible barrier on the way to senior management. It must also be said that when both men and women look up and do not like what they see in terms of responsibilities and corporate policies, they shy away from senior roles. The latest survey shows a conflict of perception of jobs at the top. Catalyst, a New York non-profit making research group, demonstrates that male chief executives blame the glass ceiling on a shortage of female senior executives. Women, in particular, respond by saying that they have not had the promotions and openings they should have had. Men believe that there has been a big increase in these opportunities (93%) but women are less convinced (60%). The problem is not going to be solved so long as few people agree on what the problem really is. The 'glass elevator' is now being used to move people quickly to the top.

It's Lonely Up There

Leadership can be a lonely business in any sector. Being at the top of a national charity is especially difficult. The chief executive of a private company, with a well-resourced senior management team, is answerable to the company, the employees and the share-holders. The head of a charity is alone in reconciling a multitude of competing stakeholder interests and has to act as an interface between managers and trustees. Chief executives of charities face demands for public accountability unknown to organisations with a similar turnover in both the public and private sectors, and will often need the political awareness of a cabinet minister and the strategic vision of a business school guru. It is an isolated role, exacerbated by the need to be operating as a large business while keeping the cause and the charity well to the fore. The price of failure is high, and this does not help to make it comfortable when you are in charge. Exceptional individuals, with a strong track record in general management, finance and volunteer under-standing are appointed from varied backgrounds to manage major organisations within the voluntary sector. They are still predominantly male, in their fifties, and have spent a long time already in the charity world.

After having created and developed a managerial team, the senior manager may find that they are excluded from subsequent strategic meetings and decisions. This is a form of rejection and is difficult to accept. The way to deal with it is to really believe that the new generation is OK and has its own talent to contribute, and needs to be allowed to grow and prosper. Strong leaders will have the wherewithal to share knowledge, give praise and encourage-ment to tomorrow's possible competition and move on when the time is right. If you regard the marketplace as a fixed entity then survival becomes your primary focus, and selfishness, greed and envy can take over. It can become a 'them and us' situation which can produce a 'night of long knives', and then the young potential will be sacrificed by the senior/stronger manager in the name of corporate ambition. Responsibility leads to maturity, and hope for a prosperous future lies in the hands of those who follow successful role models as well as taking risks and having dreams.

· 8 ·

Positioning: For Excellence

People are always blaming their circumstances for what they are. I don't believe in circumstances. The people who get on in the world are the people who get up and look for the circumstances they want, and if they can't find them, make them.
  Mrs Warren's Profession, Act 2, George Bernard Shaw, 1898

Finding and Managing Talent

Headhunters are popular when organisations find it difficult to identify and attract experienced and talented people. The rapid pace of economic growth, interrupted by the crises in Asian and other markets, has caused a shortage of key people to manage the new situations. The number of people in the UK aged between 35 and 44 years old will decline by 15% between 2000 and 2015, which will leave a significant shortfall. Securing and holding on to creative people is absolutely essential because:

1. Switching from industrial to mainly service provision in a knowledge economy means that more of the organisation's worth is tied up in the employee's knowledge than in tangible assets. When they leave, that goes too, and can be the means of transferring competitive advantage.
2. Hypercompetition. Once upon a time, having a good product line and a strong market share was enough to ensure years of trading. Now competition is so intense globally that companies and managers have to be strategically alert and actively smart.

3. Talented people discovered, after the lay-offs in the eighties, that they could manage themselves and be loyal to their own professional development without having to maintain company loyalty. The outcome is that organisations are having to think and act well to retain their best people. Employee mobility is top of managers' lists of concerns.

Employees with knowledge and talent go for the employers who have potential for further success. They have choices and are looking for growth and advancement, recognising that where there is big risk there are big rewards. People who want to save the world have to be convinced that the institution has comparable values. Those who are more materialistic want to see income and bonuses that will match their expectations.

An analysis of FTSE chief executives shows that it takes more than an accountancy qualification to reach the top. Ruthless determination and hard work are key qualities. Bosses of industry in the UK are chaps in their fifties with financial backgrounds. Most of the top one hundred captains of industry (Reed Elsevier has two) are more or less as predicted. Accountancy, finance, marketing and general management are the main routes to the top. Scientific and engineering qualifications feature in CVs, too. The job for life – a whole career spent with the same company – still shows up, with the examples of Ladbroke's Peter George and Marks & Spencer's Sir Richard Greenbury. Work intrudes on every area of the lives of these people – family, friends, play and holidays are subsumed to the main pleasure of work for the company. The main motivator is being Number One, even though they do all have magnificent financial packages as well.

They are driven, single-minded people, with an Olympic ideal. Many make enormous sacrifices on the altar of ambition. They work constantly, sit in aeroplanes and go home at weekends. John Viney, Chairman of Heidrick and Struggles, the large international headhunters who found Pehr Gyllenhammar for insurance giant CGU, says, 'You must remember that most people who get to the top of businesses give up almost everything else to get there. They're pretty well short of a bundle – psychologically unbalanced even. I would say what they need to get there means that in other areas of their life they are probably eighteen years old or less – and they are eighty years old in terms of their business.' Bill Gates has reflected on his years spent living in motels, eating pizza and putting up with sweaty companions. People frequently tread this route to the top.

Power is the other motivator. Nigel Nicholson, Organisational Behaviour Professor at the London Business School, points out that this is what is holding women back from being at the top: 'They just do not want to play these games.' The state of the economy inevitably affects the attitudes of people looking for a CEO to run the business. A recession atmosphere needs the safe hands of the accountant type, while the boom situation will seek a marketer. Viney is conscious of the rarity of long-term thinkers such as Richard Branson and his empire-building. Allen Yurko, the American CEO at Siebe, reckons that 'Britain's managers are the world's best at engineering and restructuring. Americans with their growth mentality and their faster growth economy are more size orientated.' UK businesses hunt worldwide for CEOs to lead cosmopolitan boardrooms.

New recruits do not have amazing security – there is a reasonably high turnover of CEOs just like other senior managers. In the UK, there were 35 changes in 1998, and the year before there were 56, due to a mixture of reasons: retirement, city objections, shareholders' reservations, internal board wrangles, or the individual's management style which ousted them in the end. (The autocratic style of Lord Hanson, the 'thou shalt not speak to your subordinate's subordinate' thinking demonstrated by Sir Clive Thompson at the CBI, could well be outmoded.) Outgoing CEOs are often well heeled. Most of these clever, able people soon stand down when they recognise that they are in the wrong place at the wrong time. Those who have actually created something are different and rare. Two examples are WPP's Martin Sorrell and EMI's Sir Colin Southgate – and they are both very busy being successful. The British respect for 'the containment of risks' is more prevalent than entrepreneurial flair in CEOs.

Organisations try to stay ahead and not lag behind competitors in products, services and management techniques. Everyone, including the middle manager and advising professionals, can make pivotal contributions. Top management directives to open new markets or to cut costs will mean little without the managers below reacting quickly. They have to be able to imagine the future, design the projects and processes, carry them out and redirect their groups accordingly. As a potential innovative manager, you have to have your finger on the pulse of operations, listen to customers and communicate well. You have to conceive, suggest and set in motion new ideas. Now you can test yourself and see how innovative you already are. You should be:

- Comfortable with change and confident that uncertainties will be clarified. You are the sort of person who has the foresight to see difficulties as opportunities.
- Selecting projects carefully and using a long-term viewpoint to minimise setbacks on the way to achieving goals.
- Preparing well for meetings and professional in presentation. Acquiring and using strong political skills.
- Actively encouraging subordinates to participate and be part of a hard-working team, with rewards they appreciate and promises which you deliver.
- Persuasive, persistent and have discretion.

There is a strong association between carrying out an innovative idea and using a strong collaborative leadership style.

Using Creativity

Creativity is the key to business success. Lew Grade started a new film venture when he was in his nineties, which is the living proof that good ideas, allied to seemingly limitless energy, are the vital ingredients in the formula to create and grow world-leading companies. Clearly you are never too old to be a success in business. Creativity is needed in all industries – organisations need good ideas to stay ahead in the competition. In the knowledge economy, ideas are being promoted in every kind of group, from General Electric to the smallest company. Some ideas, however small or large, will change the business forever. Creativity is vital for progress, but many companies unwittingly kill it by crushing their employees' intrinsic motivation. The employees' strong and instinctive wish to follow their passions and interests can be undermined by an exclusive concentration on the business objectives of productivity, efficiency and control – which is what most senior managers demand. To be creative, the individual person has to have expertise and be able to be flexible and think imaginatively, as well as being self-motivated. Managers need to provide challenge and freedom to experiment, to have workteams instigated for that purpose, and to give encouragement and corporate support all the time.

Invention, innovation and creativity are the nineties buzzwords. The next century will be dominated by brain, not brawn, with creativity and knowledge as the tools. Arthur D. Little, management consultants, have published a study on innovation which shows that there is much lip service and little evidence of innovation as a priority. The report concludes: 'By its very nature, innovation requires "out of box" ideas, but not so far as to conflict with the vision and the mission of the organisation. Put simply, innovation should be part of the long-term strategy of a company. For it to succeed it needs support from the top.' Generating new ideas is one stage, then comes implementation, which has to be in tune with the existing corporate structure, including cost implications. Risk-taking leads to success or disaster. Malcolm Hatton of the Green Hat Company, which deals in ideas, says: 'The British business loves ideas . . . when it comes to action there is always prevarication.' Empowerment strategies must be used to harness the resources of the company, and everyone should be involved in order to achieve the company's goals. Professor Richard Duggan of Salford and Liverpool Universities is adamant that ideas have to be managed. He has proved the premise that it works to give each person three pieces of paper: one for themselves, one for the progress chaser and one for the senior manager. There will be varied responses, but the point is to encourage and reinforce the notion that ideas do matter.

Creative types may not be the best innovators. They are great at ideas, but poor at implementation and a bit woolly on the details. Ideas take time and money to come to fruition: they can transform the company, but there has to be an urge to take the whole thinking throughout the firm. Edward de Bono, the guru famed for the teaching of lateral thinking, uses his company, the Holst Group, to recognise and use creativity. He makes a distinction between innovation and creativity: the former is the process which makes new, unexpected ideas useful, while the latter generates them. De Bono believes that chairmen, chief executives and other 'adaptor-innovators' can train the brain to be creative. Richard Branson follows this line of thinking but goes on to say that success is the combination of good ideas, motivated staff and an instinctive understanding of what the customer wants. He is proud of having changed a two label recording company into Virgin, one of the world's most recognisable companies, and states: 'The most important time . . . the manager has, is to have the time to find good people . . . to give the company a staff to be proud of and customer satisfaction will follow.' It is a brave organisation that takes the risk of using new ideas when finance is tight and there is a smell of bankruptcy around. Considering the downside, including everyone in the equation and then going ahead fullheartedly with whatever decision is made, seems to be the way out of this type of bind.

The Wow Factor

In his seminar, Tom Peters describes the arrival of the creative amoebic team: the single-team approach for big projects. Collaboration between all the parties involved in large projects not only makes it possible to meet deadlines but also makes a serious bottom-line contribution. This was the approach adopted after there was a serious tunnel collapse in the Heathrow Express project. After repairs were organised it was decided to strengthen the team structures too. The most fluid of arrangements can provide the opportunity to be creative and to contribute. Cultures change only when senior managers are involved and are themselves willing to alter their habits of a lifetime. The starting point has to be that senior managers accept that they are just as susceptible as the next person to human imperfections. Top managers can work with a coach to create their own strategy. In order to gain the trust of everyone in the organisation, it is essential to build trust at the top first. The issues of group sizes, meetings, ideas, bonding and other ways of getting together need to be addressed in order to encourage the airing of thoughts and grievances.

Sometimes there has to be a capital outlay in order to achieve a time efficiency. For example, the short-term measure of putting extra people on certain aspects of the job at the right time can have long-term benefits. In certain situations frontline teams have to be given priority over the top senior managers, so that is where efforts and energy should be focused at that stage. Alongside planned activity there has to be an acceptance of the no-blame culture so that there are no mistakes or hold-ups in the progress necessary to meet targets. What has to be done gets done. Who has to do it is not the question. Encouragement and recognition at all levels of the team keeps up the momentum and makes the challenges and dilemmas solvable. Talking rather than memos, negotiation rather than holding one's corner work best. Close senior management involvement also speeds up the project to success. Where there are many companies involved at any one time the same principles apply. Keeping everyone appraised of developments and communicating at a fairly detailed level become the norm when the single team idea is working well. It helps if the various levels of management and staff are located together.

Project managers, professionals, managers and workers flow in and out of the total single team as priorities require. Support and solutions work better than finger-pointing and problems. The single-team approach often creates a culture in which each person gives a remarkable degree of personal investment to the project. Most notable is the day-to-day visibility and commitment of the senior managers in most cases. Regular contact with the front line and constant communication with suppliers and external people all help the project to meet the specified outcomes on time. The better people know each other, the greater will be their tolerance for idiosyncrasies and anxieties. There will be room for hunches and insights as well as judgement, work experience and natural wisdom. Concentration on the single-team approach leads to success, completion and satisfaction both corporate and personal.

In the future individuals will have to take responsibility for their own personal development. Just working hard does not necessarily mean that you will get promoted or appointed. In a competitive market you need to use a different set of rules to ensure that you will be noticed. Try these tactics to impress those who count:

1. Find out who the decision-makers are and watch how they react.
2. Learn how to be a team player.
3. Arm yourself with allies. It is counterproductive to impress your boss if others consider you to be rude, aloof or not a good colleague.
4. Analyse the position above the one you want. Look at the skills required to get there, measure yourself against them and do whatever training or learning that is necessary to achieve your objective.
5. Never upstage your boss.
6. Put forward your own ideas at meetings or wherever it is likely that they will be noted.
7. Talk about the organisation as we or us rather than it or them. This reveals that you are identifying with the corporate profile and indicates your loyalty and responsibility.
8. Ask for feedback. If there is no appraisal system in place, ask if there can be one. In any event show that you are keen to know how you can better your performance.
9. Display a positive attitude. No one likes a moaner. You give off all the wrong vibes by complaining or talking down the company.
10. Show you are above office politics on occasion. In a conflict situation act as a mediator or peacemaker rather than taking sides.
11. Moving sideways, either internally or externally, can sometimes be the way to move upwards the next time. This is marketing your skills and experience so that you are constantly visible.
12. Look for ways to be helpful beyond your job description, for example, participate in trade fairs, conferences, presentations,

sports events or linked community work. Volunteer for anything where you can learn more and be useful.

13. Put yourself in situations where you can bump into people.
This can be anything from the restaurant to the washroom, the
deliveries department to the car park. Playing golf has long
been a well-used way of meeting senior people on neutral
territory. Do not beat the boss on a regular basis.

14. Seek the advice of the people on the next rung. Shadowing
and mentoring schemes will give you this opportunity.

15. Know your worth and make sure others do too.

It is not so easy to be upwardly mobile in the lean, mean company
structures which now exist. Sometimes it is better to move sideways than to wait for the rare opportunity above. Elaine Ratcliffe
is a good example. A business continuity project manager with a
health trust, she took a six-month secondment to a London-based
high-street operation, to sort out their IT strategy. This gave her
extra knowledge which led to promotion on her return to her
original employer. Secondments, provided they are for a
stipulated time, give you opportunities to acquire different skills
without risk, and often lead to further recognition and promotion.

Being Non-executive Directors

Everyone seems to want to be a non-executive director. You may
think it is a highly prestigious position where you can contribute
from your career experience to date, but there are far fewer
openings available than all the keen candidates believe. Very few
companies and organisations will pay professional fees for search
and selection to find people who match the vacancies on the
boards. Stork and May, headhunters, reckon that the board often
balks at the prospect of paying ten thousand pounds or more to
find an NED, and they know that advertising for NEDs is not
effective. However, some executive search and selection agencies
do undertake to match available executives who have agreed
fifteen or more days off from their work, to be on a compatible
company board elsewhere. Public appointments have to be
advertised under the current Nolan requirements, but the boards

of quoted and other companies rarely advertise at this level. Successful non-executive directorships (NEDs) constitute that rare phenomenon – a win-win situation. Objective and independent non-execs can contribute anything from restraint to radical new ideas. In return the non-exec gains exposure to other corporate cultures and challenges which will increase their own experience, visibility and promotability. Being on a board is a great way to gain active management development.

Traditionally, chairmen's friends have filled boardroom seats; increasingly, this has been supplemented to include associates of existing board members. Occasional search for specific knowledge and professional qualifications is added from time to time. The safety of appointing those who are already on boards, plc or otherwise, has led to the same people being used over and over again. Fast-track, senior executives have been given opportunities by employers to acquire junior board level experience and in a small number of instances, this has led to more senior board appointments.

Gianni Agnelli, the legendary boss of Fiat, is said to have advised, 'There should always be an odd number of people on a company's board, and three is too many.' He was ruthless and autocratic, so it would not have been much fun to be in a boardroom with him. There are fewer Agnellis in business now, and the boardroom is an ultimate goal for many people. NBS Selection/Arthur Anderson published a report (1998) about the path to the top, which reveals how companies select, develop and motivate their top managers and directors. One third of these were recruited from the outside as opposed to being promoted. Dr Elizabeth Marx, NBS, said that a wide range of methods was used to find people, and a more rigorous process was applied to external than to internal candidates. Only 15% of the surveyed companies used a regular, systematic review of senior managers by auditing their performance in order to progress them to the board. The level of professionalism in UK boardrooms has improved dramatically since the Cadbury Report, even though there has been little alteration in the number of formal inductions available for NEDs when they are introduced to the board. In the *Sign of the Times* report (1998), carried out by the Institute of

Directors and commented on by its director Tim Melville-Ross, it was discovered that only 27% of NEDs were given any training before starting. The report also shows that 'strategic awareness' and 'leadership' are the current buzzwords in the boardroom, and 'satisfying customers' is the top business issue.

Professionalism is expected of non-executive executives, and organisations are having to be more formal in the search for the right people. The great and the good are considered in conjunction with the gaps in the board's expertise. Sometimes complying with the wishes of the venture capitalists is a reason why companies opt for particular non-executive directors. Implementing the best practice of corporate governance is another. Many are appointed in any case for the general management experience which they can bring to the table. It is reassuring to have an experienced NED join the group to add credibility when discussing sensitive issues, to bounce off ideas, and to get a rational, unbiased and experienced opinion. It is a bonus when they fit easily into the established corporate culture. The boardroom used to be the repository of the old boys, but those days are nearly over as the Cadbury, Hampel and other reports and requirements are now accepted. All too often it is people who are already known, convenient, of a certain age and locally conversant with the activities of the firm, who are invited to join. 3i's Independent Directors Programme is a scheme with a pool of 500 to 600 NED candidates who have been vetted and recommended by venture capitalists. Run by Patrick Dunne, the Programme supplies client companies. In the case of a start-up, buy-out or buy-it merger or acquisition, it makes sense to find people who have been through a similar process already. This is described as situational not sectoral matching. Age can be an issue, as organisations look for people with significant financial independence and wide experience before they are admitted to the programme.

The ideal candidate is aged between 45 and 52 because of their blend of gravitas, energy and kudos, and it is helpful to have been an executive director. However, this is changing with the increasing need for the NED to be comfortable with worldwide communications, IT and other systems, so companies may take the risk of appointing someone without the years but with the nous to advance their objectives. The younger the candidate, the more likely they are to be in tune with the fast-rolling marketplace. The freedom to resign should such an action become necessary is the underpinning of the true independent director. Knowledge of more than one sector, main board experience elsewhere and sound public profile add to the attractiveness of the NED candidate. Often the chairman will specify that they are looking for a financial director, but this may be to cement and upgrade the work of the executive financial people, which is not a viable motive for the appointment.

There are many databases listing people who want to be NEDs which are maintained by professional bodies, the Institute of Directors and some search and selection consultancies. This is an expensive way of getting general lists, which still need assessment and checking in depth. The launch of the Internet will increasingly affect the sourcing of active key people and radically reduce the costs of searching for them.

Management Today's checklist for the appointment of non-executive directors is revealing:

- Each appointee should have a letter of appointment setting out the expected duties.
- Plan a helpful induction course.
- Even if the NED has been imposed by the venture capitalist they should not be regarded as a policeman.
- Insist that board meetings focus on board matters, not on the immediate problems facing the executive directors.
- Ensure that NEDs are given adequate time to read the papers to be discussed at the next meeting.
- Hold board meetings at appropriate intervals. In a small company, bi-monthly meetings may be sufficient if complemented by a monthly executives meeting.
- Non-executive directors should not be overlooked at the time of appraisal.
- Think about paying NEDs at least partially in shares.

Recruitment costs for finding NEDs are getting less expensive at the same time as the fees for NEDs are increasing. The volume of appointments remains static. Many small businesses believe that non-executive directors are an expensive and interfering irrelevance. The Cadbury, Greenbury and Hempel reports focus on corporate governance of non-executives in public companies with responsibility for protecting shareholders' interests, but they have a different but equally valuable place in small- and medium-sized enterprises too. Patrick Dunne argues that a non-executive in a small business is like a teddy bear: 'someone in whom you can confide your greatest ambitions and worst fears'.

There are key stages when non-executives can contribute: raising capital, credibility, and growth. They should not be on the board for ever but appointed for the duration of their usefulness. What do board members do when there is a clash in the boardroom or with the chairman? They may find themselves extra to requirements after a merger or acquisition as well. Many set up conversations with headhunters. Anthony Saxon and Stephen Bamphylde set up their group after careers in the Civil Service so they are well equipped to find candidates in the public sector as well as the commercial. If they are fortunate, they will know John Stork, who heads Stork and May and believes in being realistic and in giving creative appraisals of career options for them. He takes sensitivity into consideration when advising the individual who is looking for pastures green. This is another side of headhunting, which has to be handled carefully so that there are no conflicts of interest between the individual and the corporate clients. Knowing what is expected at board level is imperative if successful appointments are to be made. The executive search firms, Heidrick & Struggles, Spencer Stuart, Korn/Ferry Carre Oban and other big groups, have the advantage of experiencing a very wide range of clients from all over the world and understanding what they need when they set up searches for board members. Conversely, they are always noting the people who have potential, whether it is for the Top 1000 companies, the plcs or others.

Boardroom practice is taken seriously, and directors know that they need preparation and training to perform well and keep up with corporate demands. This usually takes the form of ten sessions with a personal coach in the year plus a telephone help-line connection. Often the cost is defrayed by the organisation that is enabling the non-executive director to be effective. Coaching is currently focusing on preparing people for organisational change and helping them as business leaders and team players to adjust to new roles and to ensure that top managers are performing at their best. To get promotion, or to be a good director, you have to understand what motivates you and have a high level of self-awareness as well as seeing how others perceive you.

Having a safe place to test ideas and learn to challenge yourself and face reality is helpful. It forces you to plan and helps you to make an impact in the early stages of the new job. During conversations with the coach you will learn how to set clear goals and measure the effectiveness of the measures. Personal relations and training get sorted out before a problem arises. By understanding what is happening in a range of industries, and not just your familiar surroundings, the coach can alert you to choices and practices which have been effective. The coach acts as a conscience, prompting when the agreed deadlines and objectives start to slip. Realisable timetables have to be set. Then, as roles change, prepare to move on, either internally or externally. Many people reach the top and discover that they are stressed, pressed and isolated. They have to create access to training and development without showing vulnerability. Seeking coaching could be seen as a sign of weakness, but you can see it as a sign of self-confidence. The usual solutions relate to:

- Changing the management style to suit the need; for example, from aggressive to using a lighter touch
- Dealing with a shift in numbers; for example, from 20 to 1000 and vice versa
- Breaking down barriers of communication
- Reducing the levels of reasoned scepticism and believing in the project, the people, and the customer
- Reducing stress by having a game-plan
- Gaining insight into others' agendas and motives, which aids co-operation
- Using the coach as an opportunity to explore further than the individual could do by themselves
- Gaining an alignment across the needs of the individual, the job

and the organisation
- Ensuring that the coach is not too alike . . . so that the grit remains in the relationship in order to create the pearls

Improving Internal and External Communications

Making presentations has always been something of an ordeal for most people, but managers now face an additional challenge. Organisations are realising that the message gets across only when the presenter really connects with the audience. They are demanding advanced presentation skills. It requires courage to learn to do less, but this is what works best. Relying less on material and more on your own personality is the secret. It is better to get 80% of the content across and have an impact. Being nervous is helpful because it adds an edge to the presentation. The increasing emphasis on garnering and disseminating knowledge within and without the firm is putting pressure on managers to express new ideas quicker and in a confident and creative manner. Most people in senior jobs have technical skills and are looking for a way to make the desired impact. Slowing down, looking at the audience, remembering the six most important points and talking with people rather than at them all helps. Communication is the most important part of your working life, and being able to spread ideas in a compelling way is a winner.

Public speaking by key people in a company is one of the great undervalued secrets of a successful business, and it works no matter what size the business is. Good delivery on conference platforms and elsewhere invigorates customer service and ups the profile of the group. Conference organisers, trade forums, membership organisations and internal presentations are all looking for good speakers – and it will enhance your personal CV as well as giving organisational exposure. Good-quality public speaking opens doors, which can be local or global depending on the targeted audience. The guidelines for good feedback and outcomes are:

- Identifying the audience and what it wants to hear
- Beginning powerfully to catch attention and then holding on to it

- Engaging imagination by dramatising it
- Not selling on the platform but having a supply of information
- Finishing on time

Delivering an effective and memorable business presentation is a challenging task. For those who need to show accountancy and finance information, it is doubly difficult. Dr Max Atkinson of Henley Management College teaches techniques for delivering speeches and presentations. He has written a book called *Our Masters' Voices* which analyses the rhetorical techniques used to good effect by politicians. He followed this by demonstrating on TV how an inexperienced speaker could get applause and a standing ovation at a conference with the right help. Financial data is hard for the audience to retain. He says that the written word is the wrong medium for the presenter. 'People don't understand the difference between the spoken and the written word. We have become so dependent on the written word that we have forgotten how to speak effectively.' Written words are unduly formal and uninteresting when recited aloud. Many of the rules of oration are the reverse of the written word. For example, a good writer tries not to repeat themselves, whereas a good speaker uses repetition frequently, to provide emphasis or contrast. The spoken word is not a good medium for getting across complex ideas, so simplification is the name of the game.

Financial data can only be simplified to a certain degree as numbers are already precise. Audiences prefer to concentrate on trends and relationships rather than the numerical aspects. Simple graphs and pie charts are useful, provided they are kept simple. For small meetings the old-fashioned use of talk and chalk is still the most effective way of unrolling the information. It is better to unravel the formulas a step at a time rather than using pre-made glossy slides which take the audience to the conclusions too rapidly. Overhead projectors are the biggest obstacle to successful presentations. They may be blackboards on a different scale, but they annoy the audience by being too quick or too slow in revealing the information, and they leave the audience in the dark. Computer software that unveils points line by line as the presenter uses the mouse is more acceptable. The combination of high-quality, professional images and interest through colour is now expected by senior people at the presentations they attend. Contrasts in speech and demonstration, analogies and metaphors, anecdotal information and well-told stories work well too.

You communicate best when you are relaxed and confident, so prepare. Most people find it terrifying to stand up in front of an audience, but presentations are used all the time as a way of communicating, and any senior person is expected to be capable of talking well in public. Thinking about the audience and preparing with it in mind prevents the first mistake, which is to be too focused on yourself. Thinking about how the audience will perceive you – your voice, body language and facial expression – needs to be considered and then forgotten as you deliver at the podium. Here is your checklist:

- Hold your head up.
- Remember a cogent, no-nonsense style works well on most occasions.
- A well-prepared, logical progression in the thinking is valuable and will hold the audience's attention.
- Start the presentation strongly. State the key message and back it up with evidence or specific examples.
- Humour is high risk and only to be used if the speaker is well practised and it comes naturally.
- Use familiar skills and words rather than using a new box of tricks.
- Breathing is very important. There are trainers who help people to overcome nervousness and project well.
- Eye contact is both essential and helpful for coming across well.
- Thinking of best and worst scenarios beforehand helps the speaker to gain confidence. Often having notes to hand as a crutch but not to be used is useful.
- Scripts should be in large writing and easily turned or put aside.
- Overhead projectors and other visual aids *always* need checking.
- You may know you are sweating but the audience is usually unaware.
- Verbal and visual messages are strong if they coincide. Politicians have a problem with this: no verbosity.

- Use a small message and motivation of the audience to activate it.
- Thinking of the audience as You, You, You is a strong reminder of focus.
- When possible use anecdotes (not jokes), especially if they are about the speaker, since they encourage empathy.

In business meetings, don't wait to be asked to speak – you may not be. The last person who waited their turn is still waiting. The idea that the chairman will be even-handed and let everyone have their say is not the usual situation. Use an opportunity to get into the discussion, make clear points and get out again. Getting attention in a busy meeting can be difficult. Clearing your throat, coughing, even spilling your coffee are old ploys which can be necessary. High-impact openers are useful. The correct turn of phrase, flattery, and mentioning money are potent. If your voice is not enough, then create a diversion. Use a flip-chart; stand up when all are seated; or whatever makes you noticeable. Being brief and to the point is good. Whingeing and moaning is bad. Positive solutions are attractive and may even encourage your colleagues to seek your advice.

Entering the Virtual World

Electronic commerce and the digital society are operating along with the sped-up time of the Internet. There are rogues, heroes, philanthropists, entrepreneurs using the system as well as the applications being accessible for you. There are big winners and big losers, fortunes made and lost, and the killer applications provide possibilities for unregulated and random activity. Technology is now the central driver of the business economy. Cyberspace may already be the home office of each local and every global enterprise. Michael Porter's *Competitive Advantage*, published in 1980, states that traditional strategic planning is still necessary for sustaining above-average performance and that you have to have the facilities and the will to implement it. Analyse market conditions, assess competitive strengths and weaknesses, and develop and monitor your long-term strategies, then you can enjoy your leisure.

Now you can go out and play because you have so many choices in the virtual as well as in the visible world. The time you spend on 'work' and that you spend on other things which interest you will probably be intertwined and not possible to separate. The answer to that is to enjoy everything and only deal with crisis when it actually happens. You have probably suffered the effects of re-engineering, total quality management, mission statements and all the other strategies described by Scott Adams in *The Dilbert Principle* – and look how he deals with the outcomes. Laugh.

· 9 ·

Positioning: Never to be Ignored

The important thing is this: to be willing at any moment to sacrifice what you believe yourselves to be, for what you could become.

Charles Dubois

The Present is the Future

Charles Handy, the management writer and social philosopher, reacted to receiving a business card with just a name and an e-mail address by saying that 'the future is now the present'. He is unconvinced that the digital age is going to revolutionise everyone's lives although it has increased processing power. Most people will continue doing much of what they are doing at the moment. They will be driving lorries, building walls, repairing pipes, packing cartons, eating, drinking and making love. Life revolves around the visible world, things and people, as much as the virtual world. He continues that the digital world will happen, but it will not change lives as radically as that other revolutionary product, the contraceptive pill.

'In the turn of the [twentieth] century organisation and its scientific management legacy, individuals constituted not assets but sources of error. The ideal organisation was designed to free itself from human error . . . management was there to handle a few unexpected events that could occur.' Rosabeth Moss Kanter had the foresight to write down the series of complex ideas which she has developed with a steady sense of evolution over thirty years while she has been a professor of business at Harvard Business School, and which will apply to the twenty-first century. In *World Class*, she coined the phrase 'the Global Village', which is now in common parlance. Kanter travelled throughout the USA in the eighties and discovered that the recurring question was about how to get more innovation, enterprise and initiative from the people at work. This was a siren call from bureaucratic business, post recession, who had prospered in the days when organisational structures underpinned success but were now facing the need to use and talk to their people better. Kanter analysed that corporations can be divided into those which are segmentalised and those which are integrative. The former will always be against change and have a narrow, compartmentalised perspective on corporate problems, and suffer as a result. Integrative companies will encourage innovation and prosper. She defines innovation in the broadest possible way as comprising microprocessors and computer-related devices rather than tax laws or the creation of enterprise zones or problem-solving task forces. Maybe you need a combination of them all. Kanter's innovative pro-change organisations are now commonplace – she saw them before any other business guru.

Work is now multi-layered. Moving from industrial output to service and technical plus intellectual knowledge means that employers expect familiarity with all areas. People are different from machines and systems because they require education and training, healthcare and have to pay taxes. This is causing friction.

Value systems are being challenged too. Your status in the organisation is probably more dependent on short-term projects and on your position within the team responsible for their com- pletion. Whilst you have access to systems you are in the competitive game; otherwise you are digitally homeless. You must learn not to be put off by uncertainty, to enjoy change and to proceed forwards. Are you daunted or excited by this? Opportunities are there for you to exploit, so be aware of them and know what to do – and how to do it.

Planning your 'Career'

Stage 1
In your twenties onwards, you need training, a good employer and the chance to gain experience, technical know-how and professional self-confidence in the best circumstances you can find. Pay is not as important as creating a good 'career' foundation.

Stage 2
In your thirties you are in the 'onwards and upwards' mode. You will have increased energy and earning power. Your leadership qualities will be tested and you will negotiate for the rewards you deserve. This is the time to accumulate the wealth you need to increase your choices. You will consider whether you are a corporate person or an entrepreneur; whether you are an employee or a boss.

Stage 3
Reaching the top may be one of your goals. By keeping your options open and retaining flexibility you will progress. Eventually you will have to arrange your golden exit or continue your working life doing what you like, when you like, for as long as you like.

- Know who you are and what you have to offer. Define and assess your skills, abilities and interests. Knowing your own strengths and weaknesses is the best starting point for 'career' planning. Then define your marketplace position by deciding what kind of work will suit your interests and abilities best. You could surprise yourself.
- Undertake research and use any source of information, from newspapers to professional and academic directories. Network with friends, colleagues and people working in your chosen area so that you are aware of opportunities. Keep in touch with recruitment agencies who seek people for the organisations you are targeting.
- Examine your finances and be hard-headed about what you need to earn. Find out what the realistic income ranges are for

what you have to offer.

- Review your CV and make sure that it has plenty of hard facts about your achievements to date and highlights your potential. Show what you have had responsibility for and how you dealt with given situations.

- Make the most of your present job/projects. Don't assume that you have to move to improve your situation. Consider ways you could make your current job/projects more interesting or challenging by working with different people in the organisation, taking on a different form of work or by learning a new skill. Volunteer for external possibilities like sport or community work which is recognised by the firm.

- Follow the five-year rule. Some people stay in the same job too long because they fear change. However, if you have become too comfortable, if there is no sign of promotion or significant new improvements, then it probably is time to move on.

- Brush up on your negotiating ability. This will be useful for reviewing your salary, benefits and holiday entitlements. Know the organisation's policies and those of your sector and industry. There is greater flexibility in the packages prepared for the individual than there used to be, so check that you have maximised everything, including pension and healthcare. This could alert you to possibilities elsewhere too. In any event, you want to have your job description checked frequently, as things are constantly changing at work.

- Persistence, performance and creativity are the most valued attributes in an employee or potential appointee. Make sure that you are known to have such aspects in your working record.

Understanding Management Thinking

By knowing about and having some insight into the whole panoply of management thinking, it is easier to position yourself and to be alert to predicted trends and take steps accordingly. Well before modern management gurus emerged, Machiavelli had a great deal to say which still influences thinking today. Even in the fifteenth century he had worked out that it made sense to make difficult decisions first. There is a practical aspect to this: 'He [the boss] must inflict them once and for all, and not have to renew them every day. In that way he will be able to set men's minds at rest, and win them over to him when he confers benefits.'

Adam Smith influenced the Industrial Revolution when he worked out that manufacturing could be broken down into a chain of complementary functions, which were later converted by Henry Ford into the production line. Thus management progresses. In the twentieth century there have been two great shifts in management thinking. The first was Scientific Management, a theory conceived by Frederick Winslow Taylor, the original management consultant who was a bossy, opinionated engineer who believed that efficiency could be improved by observation, analysis and measurement of working procedures. He wrote *Principles of Scientific Management* (1911), which stated: 'In the past, man was first. In the future, the system will be first.' The second big theory, related to Taylor's scientific management, was the time and motion ethos which measured processes. Then, in 1993, the idea of re-engineering was launched by Mike Hammer (MIT) and James Champy (consultant), who expounded the idea that most jobs need less of everything - less brains, less muscle and less independence. Industrial psychologists announced the discovery that people work better if they are treated well and considered as people rather than as robots or units of production. The pioneer of this thinking was the Harvard professor, Elton Mayo, an Australian who came to the USA and set up a five-year programme in 1927 observing groups of women workers in Chicago. The Hawthorne Experiments showed that management's attention to the workers made the biggest difference in their positive responses.

In the 1950s, Douglas McGregor, working at the Massachusetts Institute of Technology, came up with Theory X and Theory Y. He died in 1964 with his book, *The Human Side of Enterprise*, largely unread. According to Theory X, most people only work because they have to; they dislike responsibility and require constant supervision and rewards. According to Theory Y, most people have a psychological need to work, look for fulfilment in it and welcome responsibility. He promulgated the idea that unless people were given the opportunity to achieve and earn the respect of their peers, they felt deprived and behaved accordingly. All of this is familiar today and accepted as fundamental for good management. Abraham Maslow was not convinced at the time when McGregor was teaching, but it was proved by Procter & Gamble that Theory Y did work, because McGregor implemented the ideas into his project work with them in 1954 through a student. The plant, run by self-managed teams and without hierarchy, consistently outperformed other Procter & Gamble plants by 30%, but they did not reveal their methodology until 1994. This was revealed in the book *In Search of Excellence*, by Peters and Waterman. Charles Handy in the UK and Warren Bennis in the USA fully acknowledge Theory X and Theory Y in their work. They talk about the value of self-managed teams and the consequent empowering of employees to release their initiative and creativity.

As discussed in Chapter 1, Maslow and Herzberg identified people's needs and what motivates them at work. 'To avoid pain and to grow psychologically' remains the cry. Herzberg invented the concept of job enrichment. The unwritten agreement, the psychological contract between employer and employee as to what they expect from each other, was simple in the 1960s. There was the possibility of a secure career in return for loyalty and hard work. In the 1990s it is very different. Edgar Schein, in his invention of this 'contract', had bridged the gap between companies treating employees as production fodder to their valuing them as assets. The Learning Organisation is one where everyone learns from each other and shares knowledge for the good of the enterprise. From this has sprung the concept of 'knowledge management', which is the 'capturing and storing [of] the wealth of expertise and experience locked away in people's heads'.

Peter Drucker remains the century's most eminent and long-lasting management guru. He is famous for defining the tasks of a manager. He was the thinker who said that a business begins and ends with creating customers, that management works well with objectives, that commercialisation of public bodies is privatisation, that flatter structures could be orchestrated by the CEO and the rise of the knowledge worker (which he had foreseen in 1969). Philip Kotler, the Illinois business school professor, has turned marketing into a science, and still preaches customer focus and development. The quality revolution was ignored by US industry when W. Edwards Deming began teaching it in 1942, but the Japanese seized on it when he went to Japan to help with post-war reconstruction. The statistician Walter Shewart used his expertise to add to the quality debate and told everyone that it was about committed people. Quality control is proving itself in all types of business activity and is not even superseded by the current cry that 'brainpower rules'.

Archie Norman, ex McKinsey, Chairman of Asda, claims that the culture of hierarchy and status is now a thing of the past. The example of St Luke's, the prize-winning advertising agency which has a totally open culture, is a reminder that a small group of talented individuals will always have the option of organising themselves just as they want at any one time, especially in a start-up situation. 'Hierarchy is not dead, it has merely changed its form. The trappings of the modern workplace may have been toned down but the boss is still the boss' (*Management Today*, 1998). Back at Asda, everyone has a different job to do, and for some it is the role of leadership. While Norman encourages everyone to 'call me Archie' and has open access to his office, he relies on the 217 store managers to be the mouthpiece of their colleagues. At Rentokil, in contrast, the idea of 'a place for everyone and everyone in their place' is the current ethos. It is the opposite of Asda as far as the senior management is concerned, because they do not believe in the open door policy. Rentokil is run on military lines, with eight layers of management between a service operative and the top boss. The hierarchy is still strictly observed. At Asda, they encourage informality and believe in egalitarianism, but Charles Hampden-Turner warns against confusing this informality with the end of the organisational pecking order: 'Any smart person wanting to get the best out of a person treats them as an equal.' He maintains that the more skilled the company's work, the fewer tiers of management and the fewer managers should be required. At the main Microsoft operation, with 25,000 employees, they use e-mail as the main communicator. Open-plan offices (which are detested by many employees in all countries) are frequently cited as the great corporate equaliser. Denmark comes top for truly egalitarian behaviour, with Korea as the most hierarchical. UK firms are in the middle of the range, and France and Germany are more structured.

Overcoming Resistance to Change

'The only person who enjoys change is a wet baby', according to Mark Twain. Everyone who gets comfortable with life's routines has the tendency to tolerate a bad situation rather than to risk something new. This is because change comes with many unknowns, and the fear of the unknown has a paralysing effect on the human will. Change is happening at an unprecedented rate, and for you to adjust you must acknowledge this and take charge, not become invisible. There are negative reactions to change – natural resistance and lack of trust. Resistance is universal and can be overcome by careful strategic planning, agreement and hard work together. People agree to change when it is clear what they can become or achieve. They have to be convinced that change will be of benefit to them or those about whom they care. Along with the benefits of changing, it is also wise for you to point out the cost of not changing. Resistance to change can be overcome by keeping people involved, informed and encouraged.

Your success in persuading people of the value of change will depend largely on your ability to convey your message. A conflict of communication styles frequently appears in meetings. Your vocal tone can negate your message. Research by the Institute of Personnel Development estimates that in a face-to-face conversation, 7% of the total message is conveyed in words, 38% by vocal tone and 55% by body language. Someone pointing a finger at the group and saying 'That's nonsense' is much more aggressive than the same words being uttered by the person leaning back in the chair, apparently relaxed. Equally, someone saying 'That's a great idea' in an enthusiastic voice will have a different effect from the person who drawls out the same words. In addition, the awareness of gender norms needs to be considered: how women speak, how laddish the culture is, what the expectations are that affect the people involved. Female surgeons who copied the style of their male colleagues in one experiment were seen as bossy and demanding whereas the men were seen as professional. Turning it the other way round, if persuasion, requests and soft tones are used, then the senior person is not necessarily taken seriously.

Get to know your colleagues outside the workplace and understand their foibles. Understanding cultural rituals is imperative. Look at people carefully. What do they value and how do they speak? It is worth taking the risk and really listening to them, asking questions and being open to changing beliefs about them. It is not sensible to become hypersensitive or overawed by political correctness. Conversations that sound attacking, whining or plain nasty need to be stood back from and considered before taking the burden of their content personally. Is there any other explanation? Process/result are inextricably linked. In any work group there will be those who focus on the process and those who like the results. Dissect the evidence and use it to help you integrate and to motivate others.

Men are the doers and women are the carers is a strong perception. In reality everyone is probably a mixture. Daniel Goleman has written in *Emotional Intelligence* that in a team, both issues of process (relationships) and results (tasks) need to be addressed, and a working balance secured. He gives the example of engineers at a research firm: those who had the best people skills obtained the best results. When these researchers ran into a problem, they asked a friend for help and got a speedy response. Those who did not know their colleagues well enough sent memos to strangers, and these were often ignored. The implication for the workteam is that everyone needs to be helped to work towards a result that has been agreed and clearly understood, with the process for achieving it put in place. That process has to be able to cope with any conflicts arising from disagreements about data or facts, and this works best when there are common acknowledged values. People have many unspoken values which need to be ferreted out by the group leader. Most people want to be consulted and to have interesting work just as much as they want money or benefits. Underlying values in the organisation will determine the success or failure of any conflict resolution or communication programme. Good outcomes from communication seminars are augmented when the employees consciously look for honesty, respect and fairness. If these values are not evident in the firm, no amount of talking about them will have any effect. The office grapevine is usually pessimistic and fearful of the unknown. The more transparent the thinking and activities, the more individuals can buy into them and make good use of the conflict/communication systems in a creative way. Fairness is embodied in policies and procedures and in the culture of the workplace.

The UK comes second to Japan in inscrutability. American gurus encourage shouting and sobbing 'to act as pressure releases while freeing up the communication channels'. Here are some guidelines to prevent you regretting your actions:

- Only use emotion in a workplace where it is happening already.
- Emotions are a knee-jerk response that do not stand up to retrospective scrutiny.
- Emotions are also time-consuming: afterwards you have to spend more time on damage limitation until everything is calm again, and of course, time is money.
- Anger and upset make you look and sound ugly, and visual messages last longer than verbal ones. Do your suffering in private to remain effective.
- Describe how angry/frustrated you are instead of demonstrating it.
- Give solutions rather than dwelling on problems.

Increasingly companies are seeking workers who can join small, flexible teams and do any job that needs to be done. Task-based teams will lead to the development of working communities where people will join without being given any specific job or title. When the American power company AES sets up a new plant, they usually hire about thirty people and wait and see which are the natural leaders. Each person is given the chance to become a rounded business person, being offered varied roles which are not based simply on their work and professional qualifications to date. So a plant leader who is involved in operations, is surprised not to be continuing work on development projects – he is also in charge of public relations and the environmental implications for the plant. The company is driven by the philosophy of devolving the maximum amount of responsibility to the individual. This is designed to develop commercial awareness and self-reliance. They try hard to cut out bureaucracy and have complex but clear lines of communication. Amoebic teams enable people to come together to meet corporate needs while encouraging creative thought and job satisfaction through achievement. The teams flow together as required and do not need static frameworks. They last as long as they are necessary and re-form to suit the next idea or chore. Underpinning team ethos are the values encapsulated in fairness, integrity, fun, social responsibility and more fun. People should be able to recognise and fit in with this culture so that they can enjoy working in autonomous atmospheres. There can be an impression of chaos, but the players soon manage to turn that to their and the company's advantage. Staff levels are kept to a minimum and topped up only when necessary.

Recruitment has to reflect the ebb and flow of team arrangements. Headhunters and recruiters are accustomed to the model of the single-track career, but now they have to change and think about finding the appropriate person to complete team dynamics at any stage in the team's development. Clients have to brief their agencies well so that they can be on the alert for people who will be keen and available at short notice.

Networking

For many, networking is the elixir of life. Societies and business contain networks of many kinds which act as informal connectors for information and influence. Women often complain about the 'old boy network', ethnic minorities help each other this way, and other ways of keeping in contact are demonstrated by the Mafia, the Mormons and the Masons. Many economists and business gurus have studied the role and structures of networks as model-building exercises for corporate structures.

Formal or not, most networks work horizontally rather than vertically. You keep in touch with your peers more than with your superiors or staff. In the 1970s, Anthony Judge, then of the Union of International Associations, compared human networks with railways, pipelines, transactions and commodity trading. He also compared networks globally and showed how the volume of networks of ideas and problems were linked, how networks of organisations overlapped and how they all interrelated. KPMG, through its work for businesses and governments worldwide, has developed methodology for identifying hidden networks within giant firms and political parties.

You can see the telephone and the computer on your desk, but you cannot see the networks that connect them to the world. Morse, Western Union, Bell and others who set up networks through wires did so without really understanding what they were doing. Now networks crisscross the planet with wires and impulses reaching into homes and offices. Complex switching systems, transmission technologies, terrestrial and satellite communications are among the techniques which have produced smart and intelligent networks. Many of these you now take for granted. Intra-intelligent networks deliver the message precisely as sent. The fax has been the most recent innovator of this type for most of us. For the headhunter it has meant an instant response to ideas for contacting people and for carrying out instant checks. The extra-intelligent networks go beyond just transferring data, being able to analyse, combine, repackage or otherwise alter messages, creating new information as they do so. As electronic networks expand, power bases change. You can use networks of all kinds to enhance your visibility and make other people aware of your presence and capabilities.

Getting to know people is always scary and exciting at the same time. Your success will depend largely on your expectations of the business, social or other situations where you are included. Being alert and aware of the vibes, others' expectations and generally open to opportunities usually means that 'things happen'. Coincidences are rarely accidental. Recognising the linkages in conversations, experience and relationships is not just the prerogative of young lovers. It is possible that the deal of your life comes about this way. Keeping your addresses and contact database is as important as having your CV to hand at all times. You can never predict when you will need it.

Positive Thinking – Beating Failure

To get rid of your Automatic Negative Thoughts you have to recognise that they exist. Here are some helpful hints:

1. Make a list of your concerns; for example, it is a foregone conclusion that you are not going to get the job.
2. Re-write in a positive mode.
3. Before sleeping, review your day's activities. Collect three strong, good and positive things and retain them. Next morning, these are the things to dwell on before starting the new day.
4. When your self-esteem is at a low ebb, think of yourself as your best friend. Tell your 'friend' all the good things you know about them. You will be surprised how long the list will be. This distancing is helpful because we are geared to think of ourselves as less capable than other people.
5. It is not necessary to feel like doing something in order to do it. In fact the reverse is true. It is the doing which will give the sense of achievement which will spur you on to do more and more. Even when there are setbacks – which there will be – use them as stepping stones rather than barriers and you will be able to progress. This habit of 'doing' will lead to success.
6. Use your anger creatively. Sportsmen, business people and others turn anger into energy and so use a negative as a positive. Use your talents in music, art, scribbling or whatever to go from frustration to outcome.
7. Learn to say NO. This is the first step to valuing yourself. Visualise someone else standing up for themselves and saying no to a proposition, then transfer that to yourself. Practise until you really mean it. It is OK to act in your own best interests. Establish what it is that you really want to do, at any stage, and do it. This is the way to build up your self-confidence and respect.

Your brain weighs the same as a bag of sugar (2 lb or around a kilo), which is 2% of body weight. It accounts for 20% of the body's energy needs. A trillion nerve cells are packed into the head and there are as many cells between the ears as there are stars in the major constellations. Each of these cells is linked up to 100,000 others, and just counting each possible connection in the human cortex, the outer layer, at the rate of one per second, would take 32 million years. It was Plato who first recognised that it was the brain (and not the arms or legs) which housed the 'originating power of perception, hearing, sight and smell'. The massive mental power of homo sapiens is unique in the world.

The immune system can be eroded by physical overwork, but being a couch potato has detrimental side effects, too, so it is sensible to strike a balance. Pliny the Elder, the highly revered academic of his day, died on the slopes of Mount Vesuvius because he had let his physique deteriorate and he was unable to bear the strain of the mountain climb. You can look after your body at the jogging track and the gym, but aerobics of the mind are also important. Chess, Go and backgammon are popular in Japan and have spread steadily westward. Many doctors and psychologists believe that by playing bridge, Scrabble, word puzzles, draughts and other mind-stretching games the chances of a longer and healthier life are maximised. The Book of Genesis states that the human life-span is 120 years but in the New Testament it was reduced to 70. Current life expectancy rests at 79.5 for women and 73.6 for men. Medical experts forecast that with the increase in healthcare and the improvement in lifestyle there will be an increase in the numbers of those who live to be 100. Insurance companies and actuaries are continuously investigating the possibilities of longevity. They reckon on the family history and the lifetime of the parents as key data. From their questionnaire on activities and habits they have surmised that 11.5 years can be added by being mentally alert, agile and curious.

Brain cells do not die off because of old age. The theory that they disappear at the rate of millions per day and especially after a drink is apocryphal. Instead the scientific evidence suggests that brain power and agility can increase with age if constantly challenged. Professor Arnold Scheibel, former Head of the Brain Institute at the University of California, asked the question: What can the average person do to strengthen their minds? Anything that is intellectually stimulating can serve as an incentive for dendritic growth, which means that it adds to the computation reserves in the brain. Doing puzzles, playing a musical instrument, following the arts, and anything else which activates focus and thinking is good. All of life is a learning experience because of the brain needing constant challenge and building on to its circuitry. It is never too late to do more. Trainers who help football teams to play better football by teaching them chess is an obvious example of connecting mind and matter.

George Bernard Shaw was fascinated by brain power. For example, he compared the effect of listening to Mozart's Sonata in D Minor for 2 pianos with a relaxation tape and silence. He came to the conclusion that Mozart raised the IQ scores by 9 points and the others did nothing. The House of Lords has requested that mind sports be put on a parity with physical sports in the national curriculum. The proof of interest came when 35,000 children from 1000 schools entered for chess championships. An American survey carried out by Syracuse University in 1997 showed that 92% of women are attracted to intelligent men rather than just to good looks.

Having Fun

Headhunters are impressed with the 'whole' person. Often it is your interests, sports, mad collections and attributes that make you stand out in the pile of candidates. Having a life outside the office is a very good idea. It also helps you to shine at corporate and client dos if you can perform when requested and join in with whatever serious or silly activity is proposed.

To conclude with the words of Bill Gates, writing in *The Road Ahead*: 'For me, a great part of the fun has always been to hire and work with smart people. I enjoy learning from them. Some of the people we're hiring now are a lot younger than I am. . . . They're extraordinarily talented, and they'll contribute to new visions of what Microsoft can achieve. If Microsoft can combine their ideas with the contributions of our talented veterans and keep listening carefully to our customers, we have a chance to continue to lead the way. I believe more than ever that this is a great time to be alive.'

· 10 ·

Positioning: For Changes and Consequences

Knowing is not enough
We must apply.
Willing is not enough
We must do.

Goethe

Using Resources and Short-term Solutions

The nineties have seen a growth in the provision of interim managers and staff. This is a short-term contract arrangement whereby the recruitment agency has people on their payroll and sends them to organisations who need professional help on a fee-paying basis. Interim management started in Holland in the 1970s with PA Consulting and EIM (Executive Interim Management) both claiming the kudos for inventing the concept. Now an increasing number of companies are outsourcing their recruitment needs. Some agencies specialise, for example in banking, finance and commerce, and find that they have to branch out to supply people with other experience to maintain their clients. The new idea is for one agency to contract with the client to manage all their recruiting needs, in which case the agency will liaise with other agencies to ensure as wide a range of people as possible. This helps the company to do final interviews and appointment without spending a long time sourcing the agencies themselves. These wide recruitment portfolios are emerging after the demise of personnel departments and with the agencies looking for more and more business. From the consultant viewpoint this is good news, because it attaches a wider management responsibility to their role.

The focus is changing from just selling to delivering a consistent service. Recruiters who outperform competitors do well. Some agencies are setting up partnerships with old competitors to cope with the shift in the marketplace. Success is based on neutrality, control and the recycling of skills within the client organisation. Underpinning these is a highly developed database system and software which enables recruitment activity to be tracked, recorded and reported. Marketing and other statistics can be extracted, and individual statistics can be ready for the client too. Working in the City may not be the first choice for people who want job security. Economists, analysts and investors are divided over whether the British banks will follow the example of the USA down the mega merger route. The same is happening with companies. It is hard for the individual to sort out the possibilities for work in the City in the short- and long-term framework. So far, corporate restructuring has had even more impact than the crisis in the Far East. This is when interim work can lead to contracts.

Judith Mayhew, chairman of the policy and resource committee of the Corporation of the City of London, says that the overall employment picture is still extremely positive. International services are forecast to grow 7% per annum for the next 25 years. London is the financial centre with deep liquidity and an enormous volume of international trading. It is more stable because of the links with the global economy. Workers have little to fear from the rash of mergers, because after rationalisation there is still rapid movement into other jobs. Judith Mayhew believes these mergers can be beneficial: if two separate functions come together the result is probably to increase the dynamism within the new organisation. City employment is improving as employers realise that training and development have to be systematic and that a constant check on the supply and demand for certain skills is crucial.

Whether the interim people call themselves business coaches, company doctors or interim managers, they are here to stay. This is particularly true of the small business sector. These advisors help growing firms through the stages of diversification, flotation and crisis management. They are sounding boards for owner-managers, who are so involved in day-to-day business affairs that they find it hard to step back and take an overview. Each organisation believes in its value and uniqueness, but they have to overcome their resistance to letting outsiders into their companies, be prepared to face up to challenging questions and embrace the concepts that used to be the preserve of the larger firms or were deemed too risky. The company doctor brings comparative experience, and often turnaround situations can be created in small firms with the help and influence of the outsider. The advisor will also bring a fresh perspective to the mundane issues. Coaching and side-by-side advice is a product of the 1990s and is now an adjunct of the whole management consultancy business, but the process only works if people are encouraged to solve their own problems. There are times when it is productive for the advisor to be confrontational and provocative, as there is no point in being a pal when fees are high and the client is seeking profitable outcomes.

The interim manager can step in and hold the fort when there is a change in company circumstances: a merger, a major programme of change, the loss of a senior executive, a recruitment gap or a short-term project. Temporary executives often represent better value for money than equivalent management consultants. The benefit of having an outsider with applicable experience who is accustomed to handling change is obvious. They prevent the 'drama turning into a crisis'. Stuart Rose is a high-profile interim CEO who stepped into the breach at Argos during a takeover bid. This sort of arrangement helps to fuel the belief that short-term troubleshooters belong to the world of major corporations. In fact, they are frequently used by small companies too.

Candidates can find the list of headhunters and recruiters from the Association of Temporary and Interim Executive Services. Then the CV has to be prepared with the specific firm and role in mind, so the candidate is dependent on an accurate briefing from the company or its agent. The candidate needs to be given a written report which defines the job and specifies the skills and personal attributes required. Negotiation will take place about reporting lines, duration of employment, the level of authority involved and the allocation of sufficient funds to enable the interim manager to be efficient and effective. Both employer and employee need to agree on how the work will be monitored, positioned and completed before handover, when the final outcome of the assignment will be set against the original requirements and analysed before signing off.

Interim managers provide senior skills on tap. If there has been a financial or other dilemma, the appropriate interim manager can be set to work very quickly. Chris Beehan, of NB Selection, has placed interim managers in many client firms. The big difference between the use of a consultant and the use of an interim manager is that the former is an adviser and the latter is a doer. He reckons the best interim managers are in their fifties, have reached a notable board level in their career to date and are financially independent and available at short notice. They are able to assess the crisis, approach it dispassionately and have the experience to tackle problems with confidence and speed. Senior managers may be anxious that the growing use of outside service providers could damage their promotion prospects, but there is an argument that it actually increases their power. Catering, IT, telecommunications and back-room operations are the favoured areas for finding external suppliers. Managing service providers is legal and contractual. It is not easy to fire them and it is impractical to walk away from them at certain stages in the relationship.

Headhunting consultancies and recruitment agencies have a fixed income from interim management candidates from which to deliver the service to the client, and to make a profit. It is a tight margin. Manpower Inc. is the largest employer in the USA. In the UK, Manpower is the leading company in providing managed services and they have the responsibility to provide the right people with the right skills. They have 40,000 people working on contract at any one time. It gives a different type of career path for those who are on contract to the agency as opposed to the client. There is variety and security at the same time.

Jumping off the Treadmill

It is often during a holiday that you realise your work has slipped into rat race mode. You have been talking about it and may now decide to take action. Opting out of jobs with long hours and heavy responsibilities and into simpler jobs which leave some time for a wider life is a popular practice in the 1990s, but there is a price to pay. The cost of a better quality of life is often a lower salary. As well as pay, personal status could drop too. The other risk is that by jumping off the ladder once, it may not be possible to get back on again. Even so the trend is for people of all ages and career levels, especially managers and City types, to prefer less to more. (There are also more people with zillions in the bank due to mergers and acquisitions – and to the Lottery – and many of them are no longer looking for work.) Decisions are often made when there are redundancy proposals in the firm. You may be tempted to take the chance to pay off mortgages, school fees or other burdens. The other use of redundancy payments is to provide rainy day cash and investments.

Anyone wanting to get off the treadmill has to check some possibilities before jumping:

- Look at personal priorities and seek jobs that might fulfil them.
- Have an objective assessment done by a career psychologist or similar before making the final choice. Everyone needs a career check regularly.
- Really analyse if living on less is realistic when responsibilities are costed. All the extras and bonuses which are attached with more senior roles may disappear lower down the scale.
- Your family and others who depend on your income need to be consulted for support.
- Where possible, use secondment or other ruses to find out what the new job really feels like. It can prove a very valuable check.
- The choice to reduce strains is helped considerably by having a fall-back position or nest egg in place.
- Talk to outsiders and see how they react to the new label you are considering. This will give an insight into whether or not it is bearable and appropriate.

- Find out from ex-colleagues who have already taken the plunge whether they are pleased they did.

Telecommuting is regarded as cost-effective but still attracts suspicion from above that you are not doing real work when you are based out of the office. As home computers, fax machines, new telephone technology and other gismos develop apace, the ranks of home workers are growing about 15% per year. Telecommuters save approximately ninety minutes per day travelling. They save their employers around six to twelve thousand pounds per annum in fixed costs (office space, equipment costs, et cetera), plus there is evidence of increased turnover and productivity. The existing scepticism about whether you are really working when you are at home can be combated when you keep a daily log showing the time you spend on such items as reading and replying to e-mail and voicemail, producing a certain named report, checking in with the designated office contact, making conference calls with the marketing team, and so on. Moreover, you can list customer contacts, if relevant to your work, and the irony is that the customer doesn't care where you are sitting, so long as you are in communication and ensuring he receives his orders.

Being able to concentrate better, have few interruptions and so be able to produce consistent and high-quality work are proven advantages in teleworking. The drawbacks of isolation and lack of corporate identity can be addressed by away days and regular office meeting sessions.

Being Owner-managers

Small companies employing 250 or less are estimated to provide 10 million jobs, which is around 50% of the private sector. They generate about £145 million in sales, which is 40% of the national total. The sector is increasingly important with the downsizing of the large corporate sector, and the government is being more sympathetic to those who are providing employment and keeping the unemployed totals down. Thousands of small businesses are suffering the effects of the strong pound and rising interest rates which are detrimental for growth. Professor David Storey of

Warwick University stated in June 1998: 'It is of paramount importance that the Government has a policy, because if it does not it will waste public money and reduce the potential of small firms.' Welfare-to-Work schemes are now in place, and small firms are being asked to take on the unemployed concerned. Entrepreneurs would prefer to employ people who can already do the work rather than have to wait and pay for the training which the individual needs to get up to scratch. Now that the over-fifties on the dole are included, the necessary skills and experience are more likely to be available. There is untapped potential amongst 'grey labour' who have proved to be more reliable and efficient than younger workers but have suffered from being overlooked. Criticism is coming back from the companies involved in the Welfare-to-Work scheme as they claim that the quality of the job seekers is lower than what they need. Many in the SME sector are reluctant to get involved because of their earlier knowledge of youth training schemes.

When Peter and Lorna Ashton consolidated their insurance arrangements they made a substantial saving in their annual premiums. They are in their fifties and run a graphic design business in Leicestershire based in their home buildings. Three years ago, Homeworkers Insurance Services replaced their three policies for buildings, contents and business and computer cover with one policy. They have acquired inclusive cover for their client work, travelling and goods in transit. When working from home you need to consider public liability, business equipment and other cover. All these costs can be charged against tax when used solely for business purposes.

City Herbs was set up in 1984 by John and Maggie Lawless. Previously she was a geography teacher and he served fruit and veg in a supermarket. They had three children. The risks were high, the expertise low. Originally Maggie wanted to set up a business growing herbs hydroponically in the new Docklands Development area. She could not get permission. Nor could she get backing from her bank. The bank manager who was interested suggested that she prove her market first by importing the herbs. This she did by collecting them from Heathrow Airport every evening. rebundling them and delivering them to customers around West London early in the morning. She set up the company in their double garage at their home – they could hear the answering machine below from their bedroom as the London restaurant chefs found out that they supplied herbs. Through the night the orders came in to be filled in the morning. She sold £84,000 worth in her first year even though a cold spell had wrecked a tarragon harvest. Fourteen years later the original family camper van has grown into a fleet of ten 7.5 tonne trucks with the familiar logo. Four more are on order. The eighty staff now work in a refrigerated warehouse with state-of-the-art facilities and twenty-four-hour service. City Herbs has spread its range to other products. After herbs they went on to unusual salads and then to wild mushrooms. Now they include unusual plants which they have sourced from around the world – cloud-berries from beyond the Arctic Circle, Welsh red onions, red round carrots, and sea holly are some of the foods being researched. Maggie Lawless recognises that with the greater freedom comes greater risk. Businesses devour more and more capital when they expand, and personal risk often gets overlooked until it is too late. More companies go broke in expansion than at any other time. Bank managers are vital but they are there to make money, not cosy friendships. They are not risk takers. The family home should only be used as capital for the business in the very last resort. Family businesses consume money, time and energy, and divert concentration from the children to the market. This is not what everybody wants to do, but the backbone of the UK commercial sector is made up of the Maggie and John Lawlesses who go ahead, work hard and breed success.

Many owners of small businesses are happy with the company as it is and do not want to join or re-join the rat race. The threshold for registering for VAT is based on turnover and is a severe controller of the unambitious. The same applies to employment regulations where, for example, disability rulings do not apply if there are fewer than twenty staff. They have a set of customers and suppliers with whom they deal, and are not concerned with expanding the size of the firm. The view that 'You don't make money if you stand still' is still prevalent, so most SME directors have to consider whether:

- There is a person available to deputise for the boss for holidays, relief and so on
- Awareness of the marketplace is active so that products can be adapted according to demand
- The client/customer list is upgraded constantly in line with company objectives
- Prices remain competitive to retain existing customers
- It is possible to replace customers who have switched allegiance
- Someone is keeping an eye on the financial health of the customers so that any hint of failure is detected before non-payments occur

Careful growth creates opportunities and retains good staff. If the situation arises, a growing company is easier to sell than a large one. However, achieving successful growth is never easy. Only one independent UK business in 3000 makes a profit over £1 million per annum. The Cranfield University School of Management report *Barriers to Growth* reveals that the growth prospects for owner-managed firms are particularly slight. The vast majority of these companies are small – 95% employ ten staff or less – and most remain so. Research suggests that significant growth only ever occurs in 4% of these firms, and over 55% have no plans for growth anyway. The rules need to define the differing roles of family members, either as managers, shareholders or simply 'relations'. They should be agreed rather than imposed. Common sources of conflict include questions about who can be a director or shareholder, dividends, strategy, putting capital in or taking it out, and rewarding management. Good communication between members of the family, the board and management are a must. Family dynamics can make or break a family business depending on the level of goodwill or bad will. Common barriers include mismanagement, poor setting of objectives, lack of strategy, inadequate planning and muddled marketing. Many SME people do not know what they do not know.

Any training or education of these owner-managers does pay off. Opening up awareness of management principles and market orientation help enormously. Financial controls and raising finance are absolutely necessary parts of growth, as are company strategy and market research. A sample of students on a Cranfield growth course shows that they had grown their firms four times faster than their comparables, and they were twice as profitable. Entrepreneurial people are sceptical about management training, but the proof of bottom-line improvement will encourage them to participate and make the time to stop and think.

Many small businesses think that acquiring another company is the easy route to rapid growth. But an acquisition can distract management from running existing business and subsequently lose good customers. It can over-stretch the management team as they attempt to integrate the two businesses into an enlarged one. It can also cost too much and drain working capital resources. But if the owner wants to grow the existing business rapidly in order to float it before they grow too old, joining two companies can bring significant economies of scale. Another factor may be that the company needs the critical mass to deal with customers on an equal footing. Management needs to check the timing, and the capability and corporate culture of the targeted company. It is a major drain on management time, so it has to be a viable proposition or else it will affect the existing business badly.

The challenges of running a newly acquired company, especially across split locations, may necessitate an acquisition team in addition to the original managers. The incoming executives have to be studied carefully: will they meld into the old company, or will they become a fruitful addition, or do they need to go now? Just as the serial entrepreneur is trendy, the acquisition is believed to be a way to success and financial power. The entrepreneur gets his kicks from taking a business, whether start-up or existing, and making it work well, so the company acquisition needs to bring many advantages and not be a series of problems. There are always teething problems with people who have done things their own way, then join a larger organisation and realise that the product that was their be-all and end-all is now just one among many. Sorting out the people in the merged situation is a serious dilemma with long-term implications. The employer needs to select the candidates for redundancy from existing and incoming staff. Incoming staff are covered under the

Transfer of Undertakings (protection of employment) Regulations, and the purchaser has to clarify the details of employment terms and conditions. Apart from compatibility, strong funding, people transfers and added income, tactical planning will be crucial for success. In the words of Colin Barrow, Head of the Enterprise Group at Cranfield School of Management, 'The more you do it, the better you get at it.'

The impact of the European currency system on the small business will be seismic. SMEs are being encouraged by the banks and the accounting firms to be prepared and prosper, or ignore and perish, but a survey produced by Grant Thornton, accountants, in 1997 showed that only 315 British businesses had made any preparation for using the euro. Until the present, exchange rate risks have been held within the multinationals, but if they are trading in euros, that risk will be passed on to suppliers, which are often small or enterprise firms. Most profiles show that SME firms have two or three large customers and many smaller ones. The change to the euro for the larger customers will require updating of accounting and computer systems. PricewaterhouseCoopers point out positive sides of the changes and emphasise that the costs of going international will be drastically reduced. The European single market will become the domestic market.

Many small firms are being crushed by the burden of regulation. Over 500,000 small businesses were set up in 1997, creating more than 900,000 jobs in the UK with a further 750,000 part-time jobs, according to research by Barclays Bank. There are more than 30,000 enforcers responsible for ensuring that businesses meet the requirements of the regulations. There are currently moves to reform the system with a code of practice that will make the regulators more sympathetic to the needs of small business. The government's task force, chaired by Lord Haskins, has the brief to deregulate as much as possible. The Access Business Group, chaired by Peter Kilfoyle from the Cabinet Office, is working hard to tackle the problem of over-zealous officials. A new code of practice is emerging and some important principles are being discussed:

- Service standards to be discussed with the business sector before enforcement. Then they should be published clearly and monitored.
- Plain language information and documents with advice to be available for business queries.
- Officials to wear name badges and to have accessible contact numbers and addresses. Visits to be agreed and arranged for mutual convenience.
- Proper complaints procedures to be mutually agreed.
- Reasonableness and common-sense to be applied where practical, for example, to the placing of first aid kits, the sizes of kitchen fittings, et cetera.
- Requirements to be consistent – not attaching the finest details of the regulations to one firm and not to another.
- Care to be taken to distinguish between that which is legally required and that which is best practice.

Balancing Work and Play

During the sixties the prediction was that there would be time for leisure activities because of the effects of automation. Fear of unemployment was counterbalanced by the thought of more time to play. In the seventies industrial unrest and conflict created an anxiety about what to produce and how to produce it. During the eighties (the Thatcher effect) the enterprise culture dominated working life. People worked harder and longer for their individual success and to gain material rewards. The nineties brought the shock of the 'big bang', and a trail of privatisations, process engineering, mergers and acquisitions, strategic alliances, joint ventures and so on, which have continued to the present time, transforming the workplace into a hothouse, free market environment. Economic competitiveness improved working conditions for a time. Then the stresses and strains began to show. The recession outcomes of downsizing, short-term planning and contracts began to affect recruitment and security of tenure.

There are fewer people at work, doing more and feeling insecure in their roles. New technology has added the burden of information overload, as well as accelerating the pace of work and increasing the level of expectation from the employer. The inauguration of the fax machine in the eighties brought the need for instant response, and e-mail has added to this pressure. The whole atmosphere of job insecurity has created a climate of presenteeism – the need to be seen to be there. The old trick of leaving the jacket on the chair is no longer enough. Individuals vie for recognition of their commitment and they demonstrate their loyalty to the company by the long hours they spend in the work-place. The trend towards outsourcing and market testing is leading to more short-term contracts and freelance forms of work organisation. The media industry is famous for this. The privatis-ing of the public sector in the eighties has led on to the privatising of the private sector. More and more employers refer to a flexible workforce – meaning those off the payroll. The implications for the family are complex.

The relationship between employer and employee in terms of reasonable permanent employment for work well done is being eroded, and few employees now regard their work as secure.

The statistics prove the point:

1984–94
1. The number of men working part-time doubled.
2. The number of people employed in firms with 500+ people slumped to one third of those employed.
3. The number of self-employed rose to one in eight.

The implications are enormous. Already conclusions can be drawn from the evidence:

A. The increase in the number of self-employed and those who work from home plus those who are on short-term contract or work part-time contributes to the rise of the virtual organisa-tion. The big question of the future is how such a dispersed workforce will be managed. Communications difficulties are apparent even within the real organisation, so the chances for the wider workforce to be able to keep in contact with each other seem questionable.
B. The balance between work and family is being disturbed by

the number of dual earners and the overlap of the use of the home for both family and work. Then there is the shifting between the roles of men and women. The search for flexibility by employers could lead to their employing more women, since women have traditionally shown how flexible they can be.

C. Since the Industrial Revolution there has not been a continuous problem of little employment for the white collar or professional worker. Even blue collar workers have been able to recover after times of recession and low employment. Now this has changed.

The UK is moving towards a contingent workforce quicker than any of its European partners. *Quality of Working Life*, a survey carried out in 1998 by the Institute of Management and the University of Manchester Institute of Science and Technology, covered 5000 managers and revealed that:

60% felt they were unaware of their organisation's strategy for the future
48% had as their biggest worries the security of their jobs and their employability in the wider job market
89% considered that they need to develop new skills (IT and financial management in particular)

The prediction is that most organisations will have only a small core of full-time, permanent employees working from conventional offices. Most of the necessary skills will be bought in as projects require on a short-term basis. Top managers want to safeguard their flexibility so that they can meet the needs of the fast changing marketplace. There will be more time to play golf or follow other pursuits.

There is an upside, according to Cary Cooper, Professor of Organisational Psychology at the Manchester School of Management and UMIST. He reminds managers that they were complaining in the seventies, eighties and nineties that they did not have control of their working lives. Now they can take control of their more independent positions. Taking responsibility for your career rather than depending on the company, the boss and the corporate life is possible within the growing freelance and contract culture. An ever increasing range of skills will be necessary to maintain flexibility for the future of stable insecurity, freelance and independent work, and the recognition of the virtual organisation. It is all about the individual creating opportunities for growth and development.

Rebranding Retirement

In the retired population, 95% are under 65 and two thirds start to draw their pension before the age of sixty. Even more remarkable is that many will have begun to draw from their company pension scheme from the age of fifty. In 1975, 94% of men in their fifties were busy in the workplace but now this figure is closer to 65%. The Incomes Data Services 1998 survey analysed that eight in ten workers in the UK now retire early. A pattern of second careers or portfolio occupations is rapidly being established. The state pension age (65) is suddenly irrelevant. Portable company pensions have allowed people to select their next step, whether they have chosen or been asked to go by the company where they worked full-time. They have been able to top up with their own contributions and have moved on.

Planning for the pre-retirement period is now in corporate consciousness, and the individual benefits from thinking ahead and preparing both financially and mentally. Corporately, the age mix in the workforce has led to new strategies for promotion prospects as the average is lower, and the top end is reduced. Companies have realised that early retirement causes them to lose irreplaceable skills and experience, even though there is a cost-effective reason for encouraging it. Retirement planning has moved away from the traditional view that full-time work is followed by full-time retirement. Progressive companies are filtering their people into a more gradual retreat from work, but restrictive tax rules make the process more difficult. Marks & Spencer offers financial planning training for staff of all ages, so that appropriate savings plans can be put in place early on. KP Foods, like many other companies, offers individual counselling services for both blue and white collar workers.

Group courses are popular with potential early retirees. They look at possibilities and opportunities for their life hereafter, whether it is a new career, volunteering, at home or abroad, a return to education or pursuing other interests. The voluntary sector has had to be proactive in seeking those who have things to offer charities and campaigns. Ford set up a centre at their Dagenham plant for volunteers, manned by ex-employees. Transitional secondments are being used more and more. The Prince's Trust and Business in the Community have set the example of benefiting from the time, energy and expertise of busy people paid for by their employers. Barclays Bank has 100 or so senior managers on these secondments at any one time. MSL, the recruitment and career agency, devised group working packages and were amazed by the power of the discussions and outcomes. People were helped to look at their interests and passions and relate the activities to secure environments. Once they were involved and became aware of their options, they were creative and excited by the possibilities ahead. By dispelling fear among staff, the process of change became easier. Kent County Council had to merge two departments and use the group work model. They had 85% of the staff staying at work while the rest went off happily to do their volunteering or part-time roles with glee (and an agreed package).

Sally Greengross, heading Age Concern, has led the way in setting up Age Resource to enable active oldies to be useful and to sparkle. Not only does it have national information networks, a new industry sector offering education and work for retirees, holiday schemes and financial advice, but it has engendered a high level of participation. Having made the decision for retirement, or having had the decision made on your behalf, you face probably the greatest change in your working life. It can be daunting or exciting depending on your mental attitudes and preparation for 'free' time. Without the pressures of full-time work, your new skills can be developed, your lifelong dreams be indulged and you can travel near and far. To make it all worthwhile there are some guidelines to be followed:

- Redefine priorities.
- Minimise tax liability.
- Maximise income from pension and other sources.
- If working as a volunteer stick to the time it should take.
- If setting up a new business, be precise about viability and costs, and use a business plan.
- If checking the possibility of another job, be sure it is really appropriate and not just following the habit of a lifetime.
- Make sure that your home base is still the right size and area, and appropriate for your new lifestyle.
- Really enjoy holidays, hobbies and friends to the full.
- Join suitable groups/activities for company and fun.
- Arrange wills and the passing on of estates carefully and effectively.
- Above all, your health is worth monitoring and tending for the benefit of all.

Niccolò Machiavelli (1469–1527) wrote: 'Princes who have achieved great things have been those who have given their word lightly, who have known how to trick men with their cunning, and who, in the end, have overcome those abiding principles.'

Having Career Checks

You need to do a career check every two years, just as you would have a health check. Courses are being aimed at ever younger groups to prepare them for their next steps. The result of a lower average retirement age, combined with improving health and longevity, is a complete rebranding of the concept of working life.

There are key times for taking stock, and the opportunity of catching a glimpse of future corporate life will help people to plan for themselves. Already 40% of larger organisations have formal arrangements for management development and 45% give it high priority. This transformation over the past decade has been enhanced by the 69% increase of executives who are women. The continuing theme is stress, which is caused by the changes brought about by growth: the information overload, long working hours and the sheer amount of work needing to be completed by the individual in the emerging lean and mean companies. The most important element in your development, of keeping on track, being active and succeeding in whatever you are doing, is real life experience. You are the outcome of your childhood, your early working life and current concerns. It is also true that you have to have the important quality of 'getting things done' regardless of obstacles or in spite of them.

· 11 ·

Positioning: Keeping on Track

It's no use saying 'We are doing our best'. You have to succeed in doing what is necessary.

Winston Churchill

What Do Employers Seek?

People who can be trusted to work with minimal supervision and employees who follow the example of their bosses are still what most employers seek. Employees who can step into a leadership role when necessary and consistently behave in a responsible way are highly sought after. Employers are people who are responsible to customer demands and are agile in the face of changing technology.

The Industrial Society study, *Liberating Leadership*, showed that 13% of respondents identified leaders as people who were not only in a position of authority but were inspirational. 'Human skills of management are as important as technical skills. They need to be developed by practice, improved by comment, sketched by example. They have to be worked at,' says Charles Handy. High-performing managers achieve results through the integrated application of the 'core' management skills of finance, marketing and managing people. Of these, managing people is key. There will be many job opportunities for those who keep up to date with technology, both in the office and in general. Those who can use and interpret the enormous amount of information available and who can turn it into commercial products are at a premium.

Consultancies of all kinds are going to grow more and more popular as a way of servicing all businesses.

Education is being changed beyond recognition. Teachers will be more like coaches than authoritarian figures, and schools will become work/learning stations. It will take another generation before the turnover in subject delineation will be completely absorbed. Learning is paramount and is continuous. Ideally there would be a worldwide open society with communities flourishing within it. Charles Handy has predicted that 'the ultimate payoff may not necessarily be better businesses but better democracies. This is an outcome not to be sneezed at but don't count on getting richer while it happens or on having a simpler life.' Education and training are the ways that employers and entrepreneurs can keep their people up to date in the world of work.

If employers looked at the older, economically inactive people (55–64 year olds) they would find that less than 60% are working. Business has recognised the power of the grey pound but tends to ignore the experienced labour market. A radical new approach to recruiting and training would utilise the potential out there. Demographic change will result in a drop of 21% in the number of 25–34 year olds by the year 2006. Companies such as B&Q, BT, British Airways, Littlewoods, Marks & Spencer and Unigate have found that a mixed age workforce can be highly advantageous. Littlewoods have recruited people in their sixties to work in their call-centre in Sunderland, and they have shown a tremendous commitment to the job. The American company Wal-Mart actively looks for people in their fifties and sixties. Mature staff have better people skills and show more empathy with customers, an ability that will become more important as the market grows older. The Employers Forum on Age (EFA), says that there is a growing awareness of ageism, especially in the finance sector. In the eighties and early nineties many institutions downsized too quickly and weeded out a whole stratum of staff of a particular age. In doing this they lost a vast amount of knowledge and damaged the future of the business. Now many are looking to bring in new people with experience to try and regenerate and improve creativity and motivation among existing staff.

For good customer service, the staff should reflect the profile of the customer. In McDonald's it is expected that you will be served by a bright young thing, and at B&Q the expectation is to find a DIY expert with years of experience. Older people need to sharpen up their skills. Legislation will counter ageism practices to some extent, but the person who is alert to current thinking, strong on computer skills and has maintained contacts in workplaces increases their chances for employment and success. Dinah Worman of the Institute of Personnel Development agrees that 'you can teach an old dog new tricks'. She sees older people as multi-skilled and capable of learning new skills. They are known to be more reliable at time-keeping, and better at adjusting to what is put in place corporately. Everyone is different, so age should not figure when matchmaking the person with the role, team or project – in an ideal world.

The Genuine Skills Gap

There is some confusion about the difference between having a skills shortage and having a recruitment problem. Some companies may have difficulty in attracting people to work for them because of their location, pay levels, management culture, activities, unsociable hours or poor transport and shopping facilities rather than because there is a shortage of skills. Peter Robinson, chief economist at Public Policy Research, is sceptical about claims of widespread shortages in the catering industry, which he believes are more likely to be due to low pay, long hours and poor working conditions. The CBI believes that one notable factor of the present skills shortage is that it is not more pronounced than it has been in the past. They demonstrate that with the drop in unemployment there is a pressure on earnings and that this changes as the cycle progresses and unemployment rises again. In the IT sector the need is more for basic clerking, admin and fundamental technology skills than for advanced techie knowledge. Tackling the problem of the millennium bug has involved many more juniors than seniors. The government's attempts to concentrate its efforts on small firms and the unskilled is very sensible. The pay-off from training a novice in marketable skills is higher than refining the existing skills of an old hand.

Small businesses lack the funds and the time for their skilled staff or managers to train more people. Paradoxically, the more successful the business, and the harder people are working to meet delivery times, the more training gaps arise. Caithness Glass had to train more glass blowers quickly to meet a big order and used the local Caithness and Sutherland Enterprise scheme to carry out the training. They managed to do it in two months. Larger businesses can generate savings as a direct result of a programme – RJB mining is saving £1 million per year since their supervisors attended such a programme. Larger organisations have the scope to set up their own separate training units and have the capability to plan for long-term skills needs. A big company without long-term skills planning in place probably does not deserve to survive. Employees need to be alert to possibilities and have their own skills and training programme negotiated, agreed and carried out as part of the job description so that they are able to keep up to date and well able to market themselves should the need arise.

Many firms complain that it is increasingly difficult to find properly qualified staff, from secretaries to engineers. The worst affected businesses are catering, insurance, accountancy and construction. There is a crying need for bricklayers, and carpenters, electricians and plumbers are all in short supply. As the unemployment figures fall, so does the supply of appropriately trained and talented people. Smaller firms suffer most immediately if it is not possible to find the people they need. Regional shortages also come into play. This means that the person who is prepared to move to the part of the country that needs the skills they have to offer, will get employment. The pressure on managers is increasing as organisations expand their businesses, often while cutting back on staff at the same time. Maintaining morale in these circumstances is tough. There is evidence of stress being commonplace and that it spills over into private lives. The pace of change is such that people cannot see the benefits of the things they are doing because they have already moved on to the next things.

Decisions are no longer automatically handed down from above as more attention is being paid to voices throughout the organisation who are trying to get the message across and accepted. Roffey

Park Management Institute conducted a survey, *Management Agenda*, covering 161 senior and middle-ranking managers in the UK, which shows that the organisation is beginning to take back the initiative, to reinstate fast tracks and to look outwards for the next intake of new blood. Graduate training schemes are also re-appearing and may be causing disharmony. Team-working has increased enormously in the nineties, but reward systems have not caught up yet. For example, another person may have done all the legwork but the person who clinches the deal gets both the glory and the rewards. There are more virtual teams evolving, which work across the boundaries of functions and departments. Then there are the relationships with adjacent providers, competitors, customers and external scrutineers such as auditors. These all complete with the traditional employment relationships. People are increasingly nurturing their networks and building their own careers, based on loose-knit teams. You should be rewarded for your contributions to the team and conversely the team should nurture and develop you.

Some organisations are moving the work around rather than their people. At Surrey County Council they have appointed a Director of Workstyle. In Kent they are using a series of tele-centres in towns and villages to help care-managers keep in touch. Job descriptions go out of date so quickly that there has to be a different way of doing things – such as using community or group responsibility.

Valuing the MBA

Business schools have been one of the great success stories of the past fifty years. From their American origins they have spread worldwide and become a massive industry. The global market in executive education is estimated to be worth £7 billion. There are over 100 members of the Association of Business Schools in the UK alone. The traditional MBA took students on a guided tour of the main business functions, with detours through economics and means of analysis. Now the MBA is transforming itself. The corporate MBA, involving companies and business schools, is more corporate orientated and has more limited perspectives.

The schools face increasing competition in the tailored programmes within organisations, and in the phenomenal rise of the
corporate university. They are also suffering from the lowering of
the value of the MBA itself because of the numbers of people who
have this qualification. The whole business is being reinvented.

The corporate university is the foundation of educational
institutions which turn out well-honed employees stamped with
the culture of McDonalds, Disney, Ford and British Aerospace.
These are going to remain in a different league from Harvard,
IMD, INSEAD or London Business School. It is up to the
individual to work out the relevance of their courses for their own
development. Henley Management College works in partnership
with Cable & Wireless on its worldwide Marketing Academy and is
expanding these activities. Ray Wild, the principal, is optimistic
about the message going out to employees that they are working
for a company which 'takes a responsible approach to people'.
Private money and the latest technology are a potent combination,
but the educational capacity and the focus on the individual are
paramount. The new word 'edutainment' is reverberating within
the new short-term climate of employment.

Being Financially Viable

In the destructured workplace it is essential to make management
accounts work for the whole organisation. Managers have the
habit of complaining of information overload if they are given
regular accounts in a densely numerical form, but if they do not
have access to the accounts they complain of being kept in the
dark. So, regular management accounts are an important
mechanism for control, but the decision as to how widely they
should be disseminated is the conundrum. Christopher Pearce,
group finance director of Rentokil and chairman of the Hundred
Group of Finance Directors, asks, 'Is the information circulated on
a need to know basis or more widely because it is a "participative"
company?' He recommends sending it to those who need it so that
they can act on it. Information should be produced only if it is
helping people to improve the results of the company. Most
finance people agree that 'what gets measured, gets done'.

Financial information, properly targeted, is essential to focus managers' attention on their key priorities and let them know if they are succeeding. The question is, what constitutes 'need to know'? Conflict between open and closed cultures is exemplified by the circulation of financial data. The summary of accounts sent throughout the organisation aims to lift the consciousness of the managers beyond their parochial responsibilities. Staff need to know how the organisation is performing in order to support necessary changes.

Many managers simply do not understand what the accounts show, and where there are performance related systems they can fail because they have not read the signs in the figures. What managers really need is not the traditional accounts but an analysis of the processes, products and customers, so that they are aware of their key cost drivers and the contribution to profit of each product line and customer.

Incentives to retain staff
Two increasingly popular methods of structuring remuneration packages are:

1. Flexible benefits, or cafeteria schemes, where employees can choose from a menu of benefits as part of the package. Value is attributed to each of the benefits, for example, company cars, company pensions and health insurance. Employees select the benefits up to an agreed value that best suits their needs, saving the employer National Insurance contributions on the basic salary and, if well structured, accelerating tax allowances.
2. Equity participation by direct share ownership or share options. These schemes can be structured tax efficiently and without giving away a large share of the equity. They can tie employees into the company for years if they want to get the advantage of growth. By taking care of the employees' trust in the firm, a market can be established for the shares and the company can provide the funds (and attract tax relief) for the purchase of its own shares. Shareholders' agreements can be implemented to ensure that, should a shareholder cease to be employed by the company, the shares can be sold back at the

market price or at a predetermined rate.

Modern employers advocate payment on the understanding that encouraging group endeavour and improving organisational performance is their aim. Conversely, the most self-motivated workers are the salespeople who have been rewarded according to performance. The Institute of Personnel and Development (IPD) have recently conducted a survey based on 98 UK employers and found that 25% use formal team pay schemes already in place, while 47% were considering initiating new schemes. Duncan Brown of Towers Perrin confirms that 'More team aspects are coming in as a modifier for pay arrangements.' The key issue is whether team-based pay is more in line with the organisation's objectives than pay based on individual achievement. Volvo is looking at how to cut back on commission while introducing a performance related scheme dependent on the dealership with the objective of encouraging customer loyalty. Introducing a team-based scheme can be complex because it starts with the definition of the team and continues with target setting and agreement on the individual contributions. Team pay is vital for success. Derek Pritchard of Hays Management Consultants states that the true team 'is like a football team. Each member is interdependent on the others and that's the kind of environment where team-based bonuses are applicable.'

High-performance individuals could be demotivated if they feel they are propping up less able staff. Norwich Union stopped using a team element for the sales staff, as Graham Warner explained: 'We did have a team bonus that applied where all the team achieved a certain target, but that didn't work because you could have experienced consultants selling lots of business and some who were newer and sold less.' He highlights the problem where high-achieving executives lose out. Whether the benefits of the team pay for staff outweigh the disadvantages depends on the specifics of the company and its culture. Now that working in teams is the norm, how do you delegate when there are no clear lines of reporting? How do you position yourself in the midst of multi-skilled people? By negotiation. Learning how to get on well with the people working alongside you and getting colleagues to do the things they are least inclined to do is a combination of persuasion, example and negotiation. It is a question of trial and error to start with, but eventually you gain advantage when others remain unaware of what is happening. The basic rules are:

- Prepare
- Discuss
- Propose
- Bargain

The colour agenda set out by Professor Gavin Kennedy writing in *The Negotiating Edge* is both amusing and memorable:

- Red Style: Tough wiseguys use manipulative tactics and aggressive ploys. They can be cornered by an even tougher guy in the group. Typically they blame their victims and they do not believe that sentiment and business mix.
- Blue Style: These people believe in principled negotiation, creating win-win situations, and they use it as an antidote for the red style. They worry about rejection when negotiating and they mitigate their demands early on. They achieve less than they should be able to do.
- Purple Style: This is the key to solving the dilemmas of risk and trust. By blending the red and blue, you create the purple and this fusion expresses the 'reality of exchanges'.

Red uses taking behaviour, Blue uses giving behaviour and Purple is trading behaviour. Awareness is what gives purple behaviour its universal edge. Those who think purple respond to other people's purple behaviour. Purple provides strategies that are open, learnable, certain and 'nice'.

When a company needs capital to grow, there are alternative ways of finding money/value. Raising private equity, floating on the stock market or on AIM, placing shares with private individuals, or a venture capitalist can all be used. Each option has its merits, but the last option – using a venture capitalist – has specific advantages:

- Compared with raising capital by flotation, the backing of a single investor does not involve public disclosure of books and plans to competitors.
- The value of the shares will always depend on the specific circumstances of the business rather than on the ebb and flow of the market as a whole.
- Rapidly growing companies often require several injections of capital. The presence of a strong outside investor tends to make it easier to approach banks for funding.
- Venture capitalists examine the business very closely before investing, which provides the benefit of an independent strategic review.
- Venture capital investors have a clear and uncomplicated objective. It is to make money. Private individuals may well have the added dimension of providing themselves with a job. Even the most experienced private investor cannot match the experience of growing companies which is common amongst the venture capitalists. Partnerships can be exciting and rewarding (and can be disasters) but the link with the venture capitalists does give some protection and much expertise.

Leaving Your Job

Almost everything that is created, developed or built while working for an organisation belongs to it – and not to you. Unless it can be proved that the idea, list, model or whatever was developed by you in your own time, then there is a problem. The burden of proof is on the employee. If you have been headhunted or have decided to change jobs, or even if you have been downsized or asked to leave, there are precautions to be taken:

- Leave as soon as practicable after the decision has been made to go.
- Prior to leaving, discuss your decision only with those who absolutely need to know: this does not include your clients/customers but it does include your immediate boss.
- If asked about the new job, at the exit interview for example, be candid. Avoid the appearance of hiding something.

- Before going, do nothing to disrupt the current employer's business (even if tempted to blitz the computer). Do not disparage the employer to the new company (or to the recruiters), and do not solicit other employees to follow you.
- Do not take with you any documents or computer data you or your colleagues have created during the time you worked there.
- Be careful about paper and electronic trails concerning the process which led to your leaving. Telephone and fax records, e-mail, photocopy charges, credit card charges and the like will be scrutinised, especially if any litigation arises.
- An employment contract with the new employer should only be signed after you have resigned or agreed your leaving conditions.
- Do not work for the new employer until after you have officially left the existing job.
- Have the employer recruiting you undertake to indemnify you regarding judgements, settlements and lawyer's fees incurred in connection with any action during and after the move to the new job.
- Include in a written agreement with the new employer a clause that specifies that you will not use or disclose any trade secrets of former employers. Even if the information exists only in your brain, be careful how you use it in your new job.

From the employer's point of view there are some guidelines too:

- Insist that employees return all company documents and disks before leaving.
- Once the decision has been made, get them off the premises or out of the company as soon as is viable. If they have access to sensitive material consider the implications of their leaving.
- Conduct a thorough exit interview. Their immediate boss should attend the interview. It is helpful to ensure that there is more than one representative of the company present.
- When legally advised, have the employee sign a noncompetition and nonsolicitation statement. This has to be narrowly drawn with respect to geography and length of time (for example, exclusivity of supply of goods or the 'gardening period' for City employees).

- Have the departing employee sign a release document protecting the employer from post-employment lawsuits about discrimination or other alleged mistreatment during the course of employment. Severance pay can be made contingent upon the departing employee signing such a release.
- Pay severance in instalments. This can keep former employees on a tighter rein.
- Confirm the obligations of confidentiality.

Changing jobs can be as nerve-racking as getting fired. These days you never know when your old boss is going to sue you; while the boss has to be wary of tribunals. Most of these situations arise over who owns the information in your head or who did what to whom. As knowledge and intellectual property become more important than physical capital, businesses feel compelled to protect that intellectual capital by taking extraordinary steps. There is a need to safeguard customer lists, marketing plans and business strategies, unlike the days when job mobility was seriously encouraged.

Anyone having access to sensitive, competitive information should be wary of using it for the benefit of the new employer. If and when you change jobs be careful about your dealings with the clients/customers of the former employer. This is the most litigated area. Employees taking client lists and setting up their own company is a typical situation. Your Rolodex may belong to your employer as much as it does to you. The same is true of what is in your head and in your computer. Golden handshakes and golden handcuffs are often used to manipulate the tenure and movement of senior people. The practice of holding on to bonus payments on the basis of due dates is more commonly applied to junior employees.

Coming out of an organisation needs careful preparation to prevent you being lost in the system. Ideas will develop after wide-ranging conversations and you may have the opportunity to explore things you had not even thought of. When coming out of a corporate role, it makes sense to set up your own company into which fees are paid so that tax and expenses can be calculated and covered. By paying yourself a minimal salary to start with, you test the market and keep your National Insurance contributions down. If you split the income with a family member, the household benefits without being penalised by the tax situation. You may decide to do contract work, which will expose you to many different technologies, and you will find it easier to manage your time being outside the permanent office scene. Holidays are difficult to take unless you arrange support systems, and sick pay is not available, so insurance needs to be in place. The essential thing is to keep accounts well from day one – often contractors contract this out to accountants. The more entrepreneurial and risk-taking you are, the more you will enjoy the new life.

Being Self-motivated

The philosopher Kant said: 'It is by their activities and not by enjoyment that man feels he is alive. In idleness he not only feels that life is fleeting but also feels lifeless.' If a job is worth doing it is worth doing well is a strong motivator for some people. Daphne O'Keefe is Vice-President of Sales at TDI Advertising Ltd, an American subsidiary of Westinghouse, whose UK branch has an annual turnover of £80 million. It is one of the world's largest companies and specialises in outdoor advertising such as billboards, buses and London's Underground system. O'Keefe started her career in the Royal Navy, as a radar Wren, then moved into advertising, eventually joining TDI in 1994. She uses her position and income to increase her choices and to be in a position to help others. Money is a highly prized part of selling, and she looks forward to her bonuses and benefits from a high standard of living. She also has a strong support network at work and at home. Where does she find her motivation? It lies partly in achieving goals and targets, getting promotions and corporate recognition, and winning praise, which she shares with her team. She is adamant that having strong values is also fundamental. Energy, passion and a sense of fun help too.

Sir John Browne is the suave and articulate man who runs the day-to-day operations of the merged BP Amoco. Aged fifty, he is a bachelor and lives in Belgravia with his Romanian mother. When he joined the oil company as a university apprentice in 1966, he was continuing a family tradition, since his late father had worked for BP. Sir John came to BP with a first-class degree in physics from St John's College, Cambridge, and a Master's degree in business from Stanford in California. On joining BP as a full-time employee, he was sent to Alaska. Oil exploration and production posts followed before he was made group treasurer in 1984. In 1995 he became Chief Executive. Sir John is liked and respected in the City. He is a non-executive director of Smith Kline Beecham and a member of Daimler-Benz's advisory board. His basic pay rose by 19% in 1997 to £505,000, plus a bonus and benefits package which has taken the amount to £938,000. In addition he was awarded shares worth £815,000. In his spare time he enjoys opera and has a collection of South American art accumulated while working in Colombia.

Companies are starting to make the link between individual aspirations and overall company strategy and are trying to turn the connection to their advantage. Organisations which can select and spend a great deal on advanced technology and can provide the latest in training and product development succeed. All this is good practice and will work well, provided the hearts and minds of the employees are engaged too. London Business School has inaugurated the Leading Edge Project, which is dedicated to aligning business and people-management strategies. John Kick, Human Resources Director for the UK at Hewlett-Packard, says: 'Through my work with the project, I discovered that businesses were very keen for HR to add value . . . so I radically changed the function and turned it into an internal consultancy. Businesses here have now switched from asking us to reduce our costs to asking – we need more value, hire more people and here is the money.' Professor Lynda Gratton, who directs the LBS Forum, reckons that any product or system can be copied but that people are unique.

Nortel, the telecoms company, employs 800 people and currently needs to take on 350 graduates. Maurice Duffy, Resources Director, said: 'It's a flexible free-agent workforce, highly competitive and mobile.' Research shows that people who are highly entrepreneurial, valuing employability above company loyalty and choosing temporary over full-time work, are what is wanted. It is because it is a very competitive market within telecoms that

Nortel had to think innovatively about how to attract and retain the people who would be successful for them. They have begun to use bursaries and scholarships to encourage promising students to consider working for them when they have completed their studies. Work placement and apprenticeships are being introduced and reintroduced to find the young workers. In order to hold on to those who have embraced the company vision, companies have to have a continuous contact system.

Playing in the Marketplace

Glaxo Wellcome recognised that to remain successful in an increasingly competitive marketplace it would have to improve products and reduce the time taken to bring them to the market. This would require teams to work together more closely. Individuals would have to share ideas and learn to trust one another. It took seven years of sustained effort and investment to create the reward mechanisms and to develop the skills for people to work this way. British Telecom discovered that it takes time to transform a group of people traumatised by severe downsizing into one that is capable of embracing the flexibility and trust needed to turn the company into a major telecoms player.

Competitive advantage is gained only when employees trust the company and when their aspirations are matched by the corporate strategic intent. The overall group must work to meet the aspirations of each individual if the business is ultimately to succeed. In modern management theory the position of power has been sidelined. It is there to be shared as widely as possible. The fashion for mega-mergers has exposed the search for external power: by combining the giants they acquire greater bargaining strength in the marketplace. Conversely the need for anti-monopoly regulations and competition policies rest on the belief that corporate power over customers, suppliers and rivals will become too strong unless governments keep an eye on the situation. Where size is power it has to be supported by global distribution and the capacity to spend large amounts on research and development and on other investments. Those who remain smaller bear the brunt of competitive attack.

There is a shortage of people capable of taking charge of these giants. The increased industrial might of the company translates into greater influence, prestige and pay for the executives, and the CEO in particular. Concentrated power has its drawbacks. Often there is a double act at the top to handle the pressures and to spread the load on a complementary basis. Hewlett-Packard, Marks & Spencer, Sony and Chrysler have all established this model. The pooling of personal strengths and experience makes the burden possible to carry successfully. The example of the Chemical/Chase Banking merger involved 56 different integration plans, 3306 major milestones, 13,000 tasks and 3820 interdependencies, which would have collapsed if there had been continuing internal struggles.

Robert Heller in *Management Today* concludes that 'collaborative management breeds excellence. Power, while wonderful for the ego, has no value in itself. The world's biggest drug company will fail unless it is also the best. That demands top management which can hold power wisely – paradoxically, by letting go.'

· 12 ·

Positioning: Staying Ahead

Thunder is good
Thunder is impressive
But it is the lightning that does the work.
                                        Mark Twain

Where Are You?

Headhunters look for busy people. It does not matter whether you
are employed, self-employed or enjoying a portfolio existence so
long as you are being effective. Clients may be looking for someone like you who understands the role they are seeking to fill, so
the headhunter has been engaged. Staying ahead is the ability to
perform and for other people to know about you and what you are
doing. Then you are able to recognise and take opportunities
when they arise. Even if you have no wish to run your own
business, having entrepreneurial flair is an advantage. Big hitters
know how to play hardball, take risks and even gamble on
occasion. What drives you? Some answer that it is a sense of pride
and satisfaction in doing something that is worthwhile and boosts
your ego. Others gain from owning the results of their actions, and
it does not seem to matter whether they are good or bad, but that
the consequences are ongoing. Many organisations like to recruit
self-motivated people.

Think commercially when you are creating a portfolio of
responsibilities. Charles Handy described the combination of
projects and non-executive activities as a new way of managing

working life. Sue Birley, Professor of Entrepreneurship at Imperial College Management School, is convinced that along with self-confidence you need a natural authority, and a talent for recruiting creative people and enabling supporting teams. It is valuable to be able to open doors not only for yourself but for others around you; to act as a sounding board and to learn not to interfere. You need courage to deal with change, either inside a company or as an independent, and it takes time, focus and resilience. You also need to learn to live with uncertainty in the economic climate of the millennium. Martin Leach, publisher of *Human Resources* and *Enterprise*, recommends the use of a support network. His own consists of a mentor, three non-executive directors and fellow members of the Academy of Chief Executives. 'That's like having twelve non-executive directors in your business: they give very positive and honest feedback on how I'm managing and dealing with problems. Mentoring is incredibly valuable. I've just done a five-year plan, aligning personal and business objectives. I try to facilitate good relationships with people in the business, so that everyone has a lot of fun. We get the work done and stick to deadlines but have a lot of laughs on the way.'

The old adage, 'When people need to sell, buy; and when they want to buy, sell', reflects the cycles of activity that affect the economy on a regular basis. Recruitment is a prime indicator of the upturns or the downwaves of the marketplace. Many of you senior executives will lose your jobs in the turmoil that is shaking the world's financial markets. How can you pick up the pieces and transfer your skills and experience elsewhere?

Survival Strategies

A man is in a hot air balloon, lost. He reduces height and asks another man on the ground where he is. 'You are in a balloon, thirty feet above this field,' he shouts. 'You must work in Information Technology,' says the balloonist. 'I do, how did you know?' 'Because everything you told me is technically correct, but no use to anyone.' The man on the ground says: 'Then you must work in business.' 'I do, but how did you know?' asked the balloonist. 'Because you don't know where you are or where you are going, but you expect me to help. You're where you were when you met me, but now it is my fault.' This story, from Martin Waller writing in *The Times* Diary, underlines a predicament: you may be fine in your own little niche, sector, marketplace or whatever, but confronted with an overview of the wider world, how do you navigate?

In their book *Blur*, Christopher Meyer and Stan Davis state that three factors are changing the face of business: speed, intangibles and connectivity. Business transactions and decisions are already being made at lightning speed and this will continue. The Internet theoretically gives consumers anywhere in the world access to information at the click of a mouse. Much of what is traded – knowledge, ideas and expertise – are intangibles. The real-time post-Internet knowledge-based business environment is here to stay. Now that the edges of usual management thinking are being 'blurred', what is the way to deal with it all? The new economy is a reality. The realisation is that old solutions, such as mass production, segmented pricing and standardised jobs, are disappearing. Buyers and sellers are in constantly evolving relationships, and new ways of thinking and doing are emerging. This occurs as people are caught up in the whirlwind of change. Meyer and Davis suggest a strategy for survival:

- Blur the divide between work and life; the line is already indistinct so let them merge. Technology can harmonise home and work schedules. (Taking children to the office occasionally helps to make the family/work scenes blend, but this is rarely possible.)
- Knowledge is king – by sharing it, it increases. The more that is given away, the more will come back.
- Find new ways of doing things and update your skills before they wear out to prevent getting in a rut.
- Prepare and use the web site for yourself as well as for company profiling.
- Find out what your marketplace worth is and do not just wait to be promoted/found.
- Free your mind to consider being self-employed within the

company rather than being an employee.
- Find your individual profile and groove and promote it.
- There is a dual career – inside the company and outside in the marketplace.

Being Competitive

Your income-earning situation is your primary focus and you are trying to position yourself within a competitive marketplace. The RSA study, *Redefining Work* (1998), poses five core questions:

- Can the economy generate a high supply of jobs consistently? There is no fixed quantum of jobs allocated to the UK, so what is the prediction for the twenty-first century?
- Can the intermediate and the voluntary sectors maintain work opportunities, both permanent and temporary?
- Has the UK the capacity in education and training to meet the needs of individuals, businesses and institutions for the more diverse and high-level skills and competencies essential for their success?
- Will the infrastructure, public and private, support people in and out of work, and match the needs of the coming rather than the past world?
- Do people recognise the responsibility of the individual to develop employability, and is the support available sufficient?

Governments have to build redefined models of work and allocate resources accordingly. State pensions, benefits and the like need to be skewed to fit changes: they need to encourage employment as well as control inflation. The key element for the individual is the level of tax. An interesting idea has been suggested by the Institute for Energy and Resources for a tax (they call it Unitax) that would be imposed on energy rather than on labour, income and the traditional targets.

In times of recession, top management starts looking for new ways to make the company leaner and meaner – again. The signals are there. When consultants appear in the workplace and bright young things from the MBA stable start asking questions, what is the best way to react? Look busy, keep your desk tidy, have lots of short meetings with colleagues and be highly visible in the office. Arrive early, start late and keep an eye on the performance appraisals which you have accumulated over your time with that firm. It is not sensible to show alarm by changing the usual way of working, but quiet enthusiasm and a solid contribution to the bottom line are always valued. Watch and imitate the style of visiting consultants and bear in mind that they will regard that style as 'best practice'. Co-operation is not a sign of weakness. Abruptness, rudeness and snide remarks are signs of vulnerability and desperation. Quiet confidence and a smile does work. Sounding curious and keen to learn (but not smarmy) is better than appearing aggressive. Where there are taskforces employed in the review or other processes, it is sensible to get involved. Volunteering displays interest and the right attitude. Being a techie earns brownie points and gives you choices for employment.

If the worst happens and the job you have been doing is no more, keep cool and negotiate. You may be quickly re-employed through your networks and the skills you have to offer. Or you may be among the SOBs (Shoved Out, Better Off) who are eventually happy and no longer looking for the constant corporate environment. In any event, ensure that your leaving package and feedback is acceptable. If you go freelance, you will create opportunities to find out what goes on in other people's businesses. It is an option many people are taking, and when the frightening prospect of working outside salaried work is overcome, you will share the up-and-down experience of those who are doing it already. The Freelance Centre has reported that of 400 British freelancers questioned, 76% said that their quality of life had improved, 45% saw career progression in their activities, and 64% of the under 35s surveyed shared these views. They recommend that you have as many clients as possible so that you do not get too dependent on a few, and that it is worth finding successful and secure projects whenever possible.

Things They Don't Tell You At Business School

- **Entrepreneurial Chairman:** totally uncontrollable, bordering

on the maniacal
- **Complete confidence in the MD:** checking the contract before kicking him out
- **Unique products:** there are no more than ten others in the market
- **Too early to tell:** results so far are grim
- **Working closely with the management:** talking to them once a month
- **Volume sensitive:** massive fixed costs
- **Selective investment strategy:** the fund manager spends most of his time on yachts or planes
- **Superclass:** a global elite with very high incomes
- **Friction-free capitalism:** commerce made easier and cheaper by the Internet
- **Knowbots:** intelligent computers filtering out unwanted e-mail
- **Walton family household:** multi-generational homes
- **Gated communities:** secure housing projects giving protection against crime
- **Lifestyle communities:** housing based on shared interests, such as golf villages
- **Misery Gap:** the difference between pensions and the amount of money needed for a comfortable retirement
- **Contingent workforce:** the majority of workers on short-term contracts
- **Cyber schools:** home or classroom based on-line lessons
- **Personal privatisation:** increased individual responsibility for pensions, health and education costs

Your Style and Appearance

Observe the way people working with you walk around the workplace. There are the busy bees, the amblers, the short, sharp steppers and so on. The busy bees are beloved by management as they appear to be always engaged. They radiate a purposeful attitude to work, and no task is too small or insignificant for their interference. The downside for them is that they are heartily disliked by colleagues and subordinates.

Then there are the slouchers, the absolute opposite of the busy bees. They are looked at by management with a certain fondness because they have a sympathy for someone who has all the cares of the world on their shoulders. The manager is persuaded that anyone who is so miserable must be doing some work and may well be contributing to the corporate cause.

The meanderers are those who are always wandering around and drifting at random through the day. They are not endearing to colleagues or managers, but they are often a good source of office gossip.

The ones to be aware of are those who actively do down anyone in their way, whether their reasons are real or imagined. They think they have the ears of the boss and snivel their way through life. Their victims are the quiet, static hard workers (the drones) who are making no impression at all.

As a survivor it is necessary to be aware of the impression you are making and ensure that you are creating the reactions you want.

Bouncing Back

It is a good idea to sit down and think about how you motivate yourself then draw up a list of guidelines. You can refer to this from time to time to refresh your activities, or to bounce back after a knock. Discover what you need to do as opposed to drifting along. Here are some examples – but do make your own list:

- Being quick to listen and slow to speak
- Being part of a group
- Knowing what is going on
- Finding power and prestige
- Personal fulfilment (work/home)
- The need to learn more
- The need to focus on your own spiritual search
- Creating and meeting expectations
- Living in the present

How is it looking? Are you on track? What are you doing to make your dreams possible? Write your own mission statement.

Corporations have them, so why not create your own? It defines what you want and need from life to give satisfaction and direction to what you are doing. Some examples are 'Be creative and caring'; 'Make a difference'; 'Enjoy stress-free success' – or whatever sums up your personal profile and focus.

Persistence is the most valued and proven attribute for achievement. So do not give up. Provided you know what you are trying to achieve, keep going until you get it. Learning how to make bread may be what you want just as much as being the General in Charge of London, Lord Mayor, Woman of the Year, Captain of Arsenal or winning the Booker Prize.

Some final thoughts:

- Have faith in your abilities and the capacity you have to overcome difficulties
- Think success
- Make decisions
- Be positive

Using Stress

Some kinds of pressure improve performance, but others automatically raise stress levels, such as skipping lunch. A vicious cycle of no lunch break, no recharging of batteries, no change of air and company, leads to people eventually needing to take time off. Lunch breaks and eating healthy food are sensible so that you can be re-energised and perform especially well for the rest of the day. British workers are lunching less and stress levels are rising as a result. A Robinson's (Fruit and Barley) survey in 1998 questioned 500 people in the UK and found that businesses in Greater London feel the effects of stress-related illness most. One in five people admit to taking time off for stress-related illness; 76% of the workforce also admitted to taking out their stress on colleagues and becoming bad-tempered when they are under stress.

Difficulty in concentrating, becoming aggressive or withdrawn and losing the usual sense of honour, not to mention your sense of humour, are clear signals of trouble. Stress busters (such as an engrossing hobby, sport or other distraction) help but won't solve chronic problems like a hopeless marriage, a bullying boss or a blocked career. This kind of stress requires profound solutions. *The Little Book of Calm* (Penguin) has been a bestseller for months (1.4 million sold worldwide), which implies that calmness is what people are looking for in their lives. There are ways of alleviating work-related stress on a day-to-day basis, by reorganising thoughts and patterns. The Australian Paul Wilson has written on the subject and suggests a variety of strategies: putting fun into work, creating a portfolio of calm solutions, and so on.

Dr Rob Briner, the Head of Occupational Psychology at Birkbeck College, University of London, thinks that stress does not exist. He states that it is a confusing term which makes no distinction between the different pressures people experience. The underlying causes of pressure are worth alleviating rather than the outcomes which are described as stress. The secretary who is frustrated by the continuous demands of a chaotic boss is in a different position from the manager who is suffering from depression because he is plagued by late deliveries from a key supplier. A stressed boss means stressed employees, and this unsatisfactory situation will continue unless someone asserts themselves to change things. Everyone's threshold is different. Acceptable levels of pressure are positive and maximise performance, but excessive pressure over long periods is negative and performance suffers. Dr Briner's attitude is that people should talk about what is bothering them and reduce or eradicate the stress by focusing on the problem.

Rapid change, increasingly cut-throat competition and job insecurity have made the workplace a high-pressure scenario. It is time to get away from the idea that working under pressure is macho. Lawyers working through the night on mergers, or people in the finance sector who are only seen to be effective if they are shouting, sweating and bellowing in front of their machines and results boards, will soon display symptoms of stress. Call-centre staff are controlled to such an extent that even their tea breaks are governed by a machine. Managers have targets to meet, and the greater the pressure the less the appeal for the staff, so levels of absenteeism rise and the spiral goes downwards. Having congenial surroundings is of great value, and you may find it is worth earning less to achieve them.

Finding that you are in the wrong job, and acknowledging it, is a tough challenge to meet. Provided the image of the job is good, the rewards are high and there is the excitement of living on a knife edge, you are living under pressure rather than stress. However, it becomes stressful if you are not achieving. Many people who are still there after mergers, demutualisation of building societies, cutbacks in banking branch networks, automation of food processes and so on, feel out of sync with the new culture, and they may have to decide that the emerging role is not for them.

Beating stress at work is not always easy. Should you cut down on alcohol, cigarettes or other addictive habits? Do you need to look at your working conditions, daily routine and the overall design of your job? Stress is aggravated by time, control, self, social, change, physical and lifestyle habits. The old adage of 'Take a deep breath, make a decision, breathe again, carry it out' does help. This is active management of stress. Focusing on what's wanted rather than what needs to be avoided is also a good habit to develop. Here are some key points to bear in mind:

- Find ways of keeping an area of control
- Create personal objectives: ensure that you are clearly positioned for your display of talent and the things you do best so that they can be recognised and used
- Eat well
- Stay in the present
- Manage no more than three things at a time (talking on the phone, reading the screen and gesturing to a colleague passing by . . .)

Developing Relationships

Try applying a management consultancy analysis to your relationships. If you were looking at a business you would be reporting back on performance and profitability, viability and expansion. Would there be encouraging projections from what was showing in your relationships? If you were looking at your nearest and dearest (with yourself) as branded goods through the eye of a marketing specialist, what would you find? Here are some nuggets of gold to add to your survival strategies:

Business Planning
This is probably most useful for young couples, but every partnership can benefit from discussing a joint life plan. Instead of a backward-looking, Where did I go wrong? type of assessment, it is better to agree on objectives in advance. When to have a family or relocate, how to deal with redundancy, short-term project living, ultimate wish lists, travel budgets and so on are worth talking about and including in the plan.

Total Quality Management
In the business world this concept is replacing quality control. With the latter, a product is checked only after it is finished. Now it is considered more effective to make regular checks of systems as well as products and to involve the customer during the production process. Performance measures are important in the process, and for a relationship these might be – 'Do you still love me?' 'When was the last time we played tennis together?' 'How long since we entertained your friends?', et cetera. It is a basic format to nip things in the bud and prevent habits becoming deeply imbedded.

Influencing Skills
Positively influencing and motivating people, rather than just bossing them around, can be a more effective strategy for getting what you want. It is a case of saying 'Wouldn't it be great if . . .?' rather than 'You should . . .' or 'Why haven't we . . .' Partners should feel that they are both participating in decisions.

Learning Organisations
In a learning organisation, staff are encouraged to learn and im-prove constantly, and at the same time to share their experiences and the lessons they have learnt with others. In a relationship, experiences shared may vary from the mundane to the very appealing. Trying things out together can lead to a happy outcome.

Integrity and Feedback

Both in business and in home life, many are dishonest about what they really feel. In the UK the idea that feedback is negative still exists. Make a positive move and give non-aggressive feedback whenever possible. Keep the open and clear lines of communication which you started with, well oiled and used. Surprises only work well when there is an almost telepathic understanding, and then it is not really a surprise at all.

Recognition

There is a major cultural difficulty in the UK about giving encouragement and praise. Everyone reacts well to being appreciated and blossoms with approbation. It is massively demoralising when nobody, especially your loved ones, notices or recognises your good works and kindness.

Renegotiating Contracts

Ways of doing business are totally transferable to private lives. Mutual respect, creating win/win situations, clarity of allocated responsibilities and willingness to renegotiate agreements when there are changes looming, all add up to practical happiness. Contracts can be spoken, written, commercial, psychological or emotional.

Skill Sets

Employees have to keep up with new technology and changes in the marketplace. Resistance to change in a relationship often leads to tension. The advent of children, granny with Alzheimer's, a new teacher, money pressures, neighbours from hell and bosses' demands, are all examples of life changes which need dealing with. Partners have to be frank or else deal with frustration. If there is a stalemate, for example about who does the housework, changing your own behaviour is more likely to have an effect than reinforcing the other's habits by repeating the same performances over and over again.

Setting Aims

Just as businesses agree their mission statements. This is a very simple description of the business goals, making the company's underlying values understandable at a glance. It should be part of your life outside the workplace too, to have your own mission statement. It can be as simple as 'Let's have fun' to a really complex set of ideas and concepts which you and your partner think are important.

The Peter Principle

Employers do not set out to sabotage career paths for their employees but this is exactly what happens when you are promoted beyond your capabilities. This is known as the Peter Principle. When people are promoted to a level of incompetence, they are no longer able to do the things they do best and they are in trouble. The talented classroom teacher who has to become a manager when made head of the school is an oft quoted example. The Peter Principle is operating in the lean and mean companies where those remaining on the payroll are expected to perform even better. This is when quality of work slips, problems are left unsolved, issues are not confronted and conflicts are unresolved, and the level of misery and stress rises for everyone. Once you feel that you cannot meet the expectations of your superiors and have no way of talking about it, you are in danger of being included in the Peter Principle roundabout. The evidence is that you begin to be a clockwatcher, dread each new day and take time off at any opportunity. This is the point when your addictions are embedded. Drinking, eating, indulging in extramarital flings and so on are substitutes for the self-esteem you lack at work.

The further up the ladder you go, the more your problems are multiplied. Good managers are promoted into leadership positions covering strategic decision-making, geographic territory and multiple functions. However, many people are more equipped for the hands-on role than for the overview, and are left undervalued when they do not get promotion. Operating at a distance is another set of skills (very relevant for interactive, virtual and Internet activities), so you must be aware of your potential in this area and decide whether it is for you. Equally common is the predicament facing the person who is good at working to a brief or to requirements set by others, who finds their new role requires them to be in charge and that they are expected to fulfil their reputation for achievement to initiate the requirements on behalf of others. Many people, most volubly women, resent the time and energy spent on office politics rather than focusing on results when they reach head office jobs. If this is your viewpoint, how are you going to deal with it?

Many technical or project managers are excellent at dealing with one thing at a time and become confused with multiple pressures. Job mismatching is always uncomfortable and not always obvious. It can happen to you at recruitment, promotion or more senior stages of work. The whole idea of knowing your strengths and weaknesses, motivation, competencies and delivery skills is so that when decisions are being made about the next step, there are no surprises. As the workplace becomes less and less linear and hierarchical, and more and more project- and team-based this self-analysis needs to be constantly reviewed. Colleagues have to know you well to be able to mention your name at the right times. This is what the headhunters depend on too.

Organisations are beginning to embrace lateral promotion as a meaningful development tool alongside other creative ways such as project secondments and extracurricular activities. Being valued for who you are rather than how you fit the organisational mould would be the ideal way of beating stress. Pick your bosses and colleagues carefully.

Your Lifelong Learning

Business solves problems by discussion plus action. Entrenched attitudes are reviewed and the focus is changed towards improving creativity. Learning is a largely invisible process. People have to want to learn before they are able to. Training and education are the manifestations of the wish to learn and work best when they are sought as opposed to being imposed on the participants. One in five people in the total population lack the numeracy and literacy skills necessary to function effectively. Many employees have these difficulties and need to have courage to remedy the situation. With the right sort of training, staff motivation, productivity and profit can be improved. Workforces can become more flexible, adaptable and competitive. Companies can learn from the activities of their individuals. In the USA, Ford has initiated a programme of team learning and managed to save millions of dollars on the launch of a new car. Many UK companies – for example, Rover, Sainsbury's, Unilever and Tate & Lyle – are now buying into the idea of promoting lifelong learning and have begun to show the business benefits. Other examples include Xpelair of Birmingham, which used Investors in People to develop new benchmarking and communication systems for its 350 employees. Since the scheme was initiated, sales per employee have risen 22%.

Peter Senge, the originator of the idea of 'the Learning Organisation', had the vision of a group of people who achieved their aims by working together in such a way as to enhance their capacities, individually and collectively. Business needs the courage to take a long-term view of people. Such a strategy needs leadership, and will not take root unless it has support from the top. Lifelong learning is more than a fad or a fashion, it is the driver of productive individual and corporate life. It must be grounded in commercial reality. It is not good enough to create innovative education vehicles that are all hype and little substance. There are three dimensions worth mentioning – creating, sustaining and adding value. Motorola University has set an example by starting programmes that teach parenting skills to employees and extending programmes to those who are planning for retirement. The UK needs a well-trained workforce, well founded with vigorous research applied to business and wealth creation, as well as to developing well-educated and highly motivated executives. The core competencies of communications skills, teamwork, innovation and the like have to be fundamental for everyone in and out of work. NatWest uses the 'balanced business scorecard' as a performance management tool. The harder it is to measure a competency or skill or creative thought, the more complex is your contribution.

Believing in Yourself: 'Me Inc.'

If you want flexible hours, work you enjoy and a sympathetic boss, there is one company that can promise it all. Your own. Now more than ever, people are finding it pays to work for themselves. Whether you are working full-time, part-time or are not in paid work at all, think of yourself as a small successful company, with your own business plan and strategy. It is the best career advice you will ever get. Essentially the difference between letting life happen to you and making things happen the way you want them to, is the amount of control you have over your choices. Self-employment, part-time and contract working are already options for millions of workers, and in the next five years their numbers are forecast to increase. Even if you are sitting safely in a job, it is time to adjust your attitudes. The days when you could join a large company and sit tight while you progressed through the ranks are over. Taking responsibility for yourself is the oft repeated theme for success. Sir John Harvey-Jones, ex-Chairman of ICI and well-known business trouble-shooter, always used to say, 'Our destiny is in our own hands, now more than ever before. In my view it is the most liberating and rewarding way of living.'

The economic tables have turned in favour of the 'portfolio worker' – flexible, short-term working is commonplace now that so many companies have small core staffs. It is becoming a sellers' market: companies need you as much as you need them. Me Inc. is scary because it means giving up the income cushion which a regular job provides. That method of earning can be a high price to pay for family needs and personal wishes. Going independent is a way of reducing constraints (provided you have good self-discipline).

The thought processes and skills that are required for Me Inc. are different from those needed in an employee. The ability to bond quickly with new people in a team and complete a project in a set time are comparable key skills, but networking is the lifeline for Me Inc. You will be working independently and you will be called on to integrate quickly into all the cultures which affect your working day, week, life. You need to learn how to make contacts and keep them, and to understand that networking is not just chatting up an important person at a social function. It extends to people you meet wherever you are, which may or may not lead to working possibilities. You will learn from their experiences, knowledge and further contacts.

Your fear factor is based on lack of security and certainty. By organising personal order, fear is diminished. Your success is based on delivering a great service or product, whatever it may be, time after time. Make choices. Find something you like doing, do it well and this will lead to more. Most people need less money than they think, and so by taking the pressure off oneself, the liberation begins. It is all about having a rewarding life in the widest sense. It is about taking pleasure and pride in your work, discovering new things and rewarding yourself spiritually too. Charles Handy writes about 'the philosophy of enough'. Making a list of all the things you can do that other people will pay for is the starting point. Many people start with small projects and gradually increase the volume until their portfolio is a strong feature of their working life. Your reinvented career will have its own rules. You should aim to:

- Learn voraciously and continuously: create opportunities by taking control. Maximise training opportunities, especially where offered by employees. Turn the inevitable job hopping into a personal development programme.
- Concentrate on your networks and on building relationships. Identify and seek out the decision-makers in the areas where your talents will be appreciated.
- Be balanced and set clear priorities for work, home and play.
- Take your working life a step at a time: long-term goals are good but long-term planning is essential.

Germaine Greer asks how the best things in life are free when spending power is the only indicator of personal power. She argues that in Millennial Britain everything has its price: if something cannot be bought or sold it does not exist in the marketplace. Even abstract entities have prices – and she gives the example of her father selling Space for a living. Today it is possible to sell names, stories, genes, organs and anything else that an entrepreneur dreams up and for which there is a buyer. Even health and happiness can be bought in our society. Happiness is not just about spending but is also about paying the top whack for today's market leader. Greer maintains that the sole remaining wizardry is marketing. Nobody wants yesterday's anything, even at half price or less. Developing your image, heightening your profile and making corporate identities, all manipulate the buying public on behalf of the client.

Marketing often makes no difference between true and false, between valuable and worthless, so irrational consumer behaviour is the outcome. The child smashing up his room because he has been bought the wrong trainers is a common example. Greer believes that marketing depends on a galaxy of fictions, of which price is the most inventive. This is evidenced by the huge market in counterfeit designer label goods, which is a fraud perpetuated on a fraud. The biggest myth may be the value of saleability. When what you are selling is yourself, reticence, simplicity and honesty count for as little as truth-telling about any product. The present generation wants instant appeal, with their spending power as the main indicator of personal worth.

Onwards and Upwards

The nineties has seen the fat trimmed away in organisations. Companies that led the restructuring era are now stumbling. Despite industrial upheaval and unprecedented opportunities for growth, BT and Reuters have both considered share buy-backs, a sign of management's inability to identify and implement growth strategies. General Electric has grown by only 4% in its core manu-facturing businesses between 1991 and 1996. Entrepreneurial spirit is necessary for growth. To reignite entrepreneurism, a management philosophy which has worked for Oticon, led by Lars Kolind, is to build on the view that human beings are responsible adults who work through choice rather than coercion. The psychological contract between employers and employees has been weakened by the growth of short-term cultures, and the consequences for the company, the family and the individual are notable. The Institute of Management/UMIST survey, *Quality of Working Life* (1998) covered 5000 UK managers and is an ongoing research study for the next five years. So far it has revealed:

61% have been through restructuring in their work in the last year

66% are insecure in their jobs and have low morale

50% have reduced commitment and loyalty to the employer

82% work more than 40 hours per week regularly

38% work more than 50 hours per week regularly

41% often/always work at the weekend

60% feel that they are kept in the dark about the company strategies

48% say their biggest worry is financial security/employability in the wider market

89% know that they will need to develop new skills (IT and financial management) over the next five years

Each decade has had a unique defining characteristic:

1960s was innovation

After the post-war turbulence and the horrors of the war in Vietnam, people in the workplace were keen to try out whatever ideas they had. It was the era when the Prime Minister, Harold Wilson wanted the 'white heat of technology' to be part of the country's economy and prosperity. There was a belief that automation and technology would lead to a twenty-hour week.

1970s was industrial strife and conflict

It was the battle for power between employer and employee that led to the three-day week and misery for the whole population for a long period.

1980s was enterprise

This was a time of privatisations, mergers and acquisitions, process engineering, strategic alliances and so on. The buoyant free market culture epitomises the decade.

1990s is recession followed by anxiety

After the fallout of severe recession, the impact on the workplace has been the break-up of the psychological contract between employer and employee. UK employee job satisfaction has dropped from 70% in 1985 to 48% in 1995. This is having a serious effect on all concerned.

2000s will depend on personal responsibility
Work is about you. As Studs Terkel put it in his book *Working*,
'Work is about a search for daily meaning as well as daily bread,
for recognition as well as cash, for astonishment as well as torpor,
in short, for a sort of life rather than a Monday through Friday sort
of dying.' For every single-minded achiever born knowing that
they are going to be another Richard Branson, there are hundreds
of ordinary mortals who find out what they want to do the hard
way. Often this involves doing something else for a while,
including jobs you find boring, undermining, difficult or worse.
So, if you are waking up with Monday morning blues you must
take charge and do something about it. Optimism helps, and
awareness of opportunities advances you, but action is the way to
make things happen.

Making any move can be a revitalising experience. Matching
your personality to the personality of the role requires discernment, concentration and understanding of what the job or project
is all about. For example, have you decided whether you are an
extrovert and like having people around, or whether you work
better on your own? Are you a self-starter? Do you like intellectual
or more practical tasks? Then take another look at the work
situation and see what it requires. By challenging yourself with
goals and rewarding yourself with achievement you will be able to
move on:

• People who are encouraged to set themselves specific goals are
  not only more committed to those goals but actually achieve
  them.
• People who achieve their goals set higher ones next time, and
  those who fail to meet them set lower goals.
• Continual success increases the desirability of achievement.

The more positive your attitude, the more happy you will be.
Seeing the glass as half-full and not half-empty is a start. The more
alert and aware you are, the more your antennae will pick up
opportunities and you will recognise how to react and what to do

to forward the proposition. Just as the man in the balloon had the overview of the landscape below, so the more you listen and evaluate your experiences the wider will be your understanding and your expectations. Take the fear out of change and move on from one challenge to another.

Many people wait for something to happen, for the headhunter to call, or for someone else to take responsibility for them. On the other hand, it may be your basic instinct is to act and not just react. As well as enabling you to choose your responses to particular circumstances, this empowers you to create those circumstances and make choices. The people who end up with the good jobs, run successful businesses or manage project after project are those who look for the solutions to the problems rather than getting fixated on the problems themselves. They are like terrier dogs – they never give up.

In order to manage the world around you, from Grandma to Godzilla, you must manage your world within. You know how to become clearer about your motivations, how to listen and hear what others are really saying, and about being stuck in doing the same old things over and over again. Now is the time for release. It is about putting creativity into your own life. It is about deepening the understanding of who you are, what you have to offer and where you can be effective. It is not just about the salary cheque, the clear desk, seeking advantage, managing your assets, or fulfilling your responsibilities. 'Play is learning without being taught', according to a noticeboard in Battersea Park. It is about enjoying your whole life. It is about making work work for you.

The real act of discovery consists not in finding new lands, but in seeing with new eyes.

Marcel Proust

Index

productivity 34
professionalism in UK boardrooms 178-179
profiling companies 29-33
progress reporting 73-74
Proust, Marcel 257
psychometric testing 87-90, 160
Public Policy Research 223
public sector recruitment process 148-150
public speaking 183-185
public-private sector crossover 152-153

quality improvement, focus on 23
Quality of Working Life (Institute of
  Management/UMIST) 216, 254
quality revolution 194

radicalism, professional 33
rat race mode 207
recognition 59, 248
recruitment
  agencies 69
  and choice 12
  deterrents to 223
Recruitment and Employment Services, The
  Federation of (FRES) 83
Redefining Work (RSA Report, 1998) 9, 249
referees, legal implications 90-91
references 90-92
regulatory squeeze 213-214
relationships; *see also* employee-employer
  investment in 126
  nurturing 246-249
  recognising linkages 199
Release —1.0 (Dyson, E.) 114
remuneration packages 143, 227-229
renogiating contracts 248
repatriation difficulties 134; *see also* expatriate
replication of information 98
Research in Employment and Technology in
  Europe, Centre for (CREATE) 101
researcher briefing 73
resistance to change 195-198
resource utilisation 203-206
résumé *see* curricula vitarum
retention of talent, necessity for 169-170
retirement 217-219
revitalisation by moving 256
reward systems, inadequacy of 225
rewards, leaders and staff 142-143
rhetorical technique, guidelines 183-184
Richards-Stewart, Jennifer (Actua Soccer) 143
risk
  containment 171
  and freedom 210
  and reward 170
  and women 41
  and the Y generation 17
The Road Ahead 202
Robertson, Ian (Howgate Sable) 72
Roffey Park Management Institute 34

satisfaction 28
Scardino, Marjorie (Pearson Group) 143
Scheibel, Professor Arnold (University of
  California) 201-202

Schein, Edgar 193
Scientific Management, Principles of (Taylor, F.W.)
  192
search and selection
  consultancies 69-70
  process 73-76
  success in 75-76
  system 71-73
secondment
  International Secondments (DTI) 132-133
  and opportunity 177
  pre-retirement 218
security
  of data as technology grows 107
  financial in retirement 54
  job and CEOs 171
segmentalised corporations 189
selection
  schemes 34-35
  techniques 88
self-
  appraisal, being the best 92
  awareness 21, 182
  belief 251-254
  confidence 59-60, 182
  definition see egonomics
  employment 38
  evaluation and energy 26
  motivation 21, 233-235
  service and intranets 104
  visualisation 24-25
Senge, Peter 251
shareholder value added (SVA) 52-53
Shell International, managing global executives
  136
SHL (testing) 89
short-term solutions 203-206
sifting applicants 87
Sign of the Times (IoD Report, 1998) 178
The Silent Generation (Born 1925-45) 12-13
skill sets 248
skilled incompetence 11
skills shortages 223-225
small business
  and employment 208
  and interim management 205
Small Business Management 163
Smith, Adam 49, 192
Socratic model for management 48
software
  as machinery 95
  testing 117-118
specialisation, new age 129
specification for search 73
stakeholder pensions 54
state pension age, irrelevancy of 217
stocktaking see career checks
Storey, Professor David (Warwick University)
  208-209
strategic eccentricity 160
strategy co-ordination 53
stress, positive aspects 244-246
style and appearance 242-243
success and people management 146
succession planning 140